AFRICA
The Roots of Revolt

AFRICA
The Roots of Revolt

by
JACK WODDIS

THE CITADEL PRESS
NEW YORK

ACKNOWLEDGEMENTS

For help in writing this book I have to thank many people who are too numerous to mention here. Without their advice, information and suggestions the going would have been far more difficult, and the end result so much the poorer. Finally, I would like to convey my warmest thanks to my wife, Margaret, who, by typing the manuscript, assisting in the proof reading, checking the figures and in countless other ways—not least of which was her continued patience and encouragement over two difficult years—helped to make this book possible.

J. W.

CONTENTS

LIST OF TABLES

TABLES

ABBREVIATED REFERENCES

ABBREVIATED REFERENCES

African Revolution: Special issue of *The Economist*, 1958.

Apthorpe Report: *Present Interrelations in Central African Rural and Urban Life* (Eleventh Conference of the Rhodes-Livingstone Institute for Social Research), ed. by R. J. Apthorpe, 1958.

Batten: *Problems of African Development*, by T. R. Batten, 1947–55.

Buell: *The Native Problem in Africa*, by Raymond L. Buell, 1928.

CCTA: *The Human Factor of Productivity in Africa*, Inter-African Labour Institute, Commission for Technical Co-operation in Africa South of the Sahara, 1956.

Carpenter Report: *Report of the Committee on African Wages*, 1954.

de Castro: *The Geography of Hunger*, by Dr. Josue de Castro, 1952.

Davidson: *The African Awakening*, by Basil Davidson, 1955.

EARC: *East Africa Royal Commission 1953–1955 Report*, Cmd. 9475, 1955.

ECSA: *Economic Survey of Africa Since 1950*, U.N., 1959.

Hailey: *An African Survey*, by Lord Hailey, 1938.

Hailey (Revised): *An African Survey Revised, 1956*, by Lord Hailey, 1957.

Hinden: *Plan for Africa*, by Dr. Rita Hinden, 1941.

Hodgkin: *Nationalism in Colonial Africa*, by Thomas Hodgkin, 1956.

Keiskammahoek Survey: *Keiskammahoek Rural Survey*, vol. ii, *The Economy of a Reserve*, by Professors D. Hobart Houghton and Edith M. Walton, 1952.

Leys: *European Politics in Southern Rhodesia*, by Colin Leys, 1959.

Noon: *Labour Problems of Africa*, by John A. Noon, 1944.

Northcott: *The African Labour Efficiency Survey*, ed. by C. H. Northcott, 1949.

NSG: *Special Study on Economic Conditions in Non-Self-Governing Territories*, U.N., 1958.

Pim Report: *Report of the Commission Appointed to Enquire into the Financial and Economic Position of Northern Rhodesia*, col. No. 145, 1938.

Plewman Report: *Report of the Urban Affairs Commission*, 1958.

Roper: *Labour Problems in West Africa*, by J. I. Roper, 1958.
Schapera: *Migrant Labour and Tribal Life*, by I. Schapera, 1947.
Unesco: *Social Implication of Industrialisation and Urbanisation in Africa South of the Sahara*, prepared by the Africa Institute for Unesco, 1956.

INTRODUCTION

INTRODUCTION

THIS book originated in a discussion I had early in 1955 with Abdoulaye Diallo, at that time one of Africa's outstanding trade-union leaders, today the Guinea Republic's Resident Minister at Accra and Secretary-General of the Conference of African Peoples.

In the course of our talk he emphasised that their working and living conditions were no longer regarded by the African people as the key question in Africa.

"What is important today, what is the significant new thing in Africa," emphasised Diallo, "is not our conditions but what we are doing to change them."

Five years later this remark has even more force, for today there are already some twenty independent African states, and in all African territories the movement of the people for independence and democracy and to end colonialism is fast gathering pace and breadth.

What has brought about this great change? Why is Africa now standing up? And why are the walls of colonialism beginning to tumble down before its mighty roar for freedom?

It was to answer these questions, and influenced by the remarks of Diallo, that the idea first arose of writing a book which would show what the African people are doing to wipe out their misery and oppression. In the course of doing this, however, it soon became obvious to me that the very conditions from which the African people were so anxious to liberate themselves had to be described and explained; that the roots of the great revolt now embracing the whole African continent could only be understood by examining what imperialism had done to the African people over the past sixty years, and what were the economic and social changes which had influenced the people's upsurge.

Thus one book became two—the first, presented here, to examine the roots of revolt in Africa; the second, which is in preparation, to explain the problems facing the African people's national movements, both in the pre-independence stage of their struggle and in the effort to build up their new, independent countries.

In this year of 1960—Africa's year of destiny—millions of people throughout the world are more aware than ever of the evils which colonialism has imposed on the African people. In particular, people have rightly been incensed by the practices of apartheid and racial discrimination which are so widespread wherever European settlers hold sway in Africa. It should never be forgotten that racial discrimination has an aim far more important than the discrimination itself—the aim of economic exploitation.

The root and fruit of racial discrimination is profit.

Racial discrimination serves the interests of those who live by profit because it helps to maintain a system of exceptionally cheap labour which is the basis of exceptionally high rates of profit.

Behind the refusal to allow an African to enter the same train compartment, the same hotel, the same lift, or the same restaurant as a European, lies the whole system of colonialism, which robs an African of his land and his produce, compels him to live in disease and poverty, denies him education and technical training, refuses him access to skilled jobs, pays him starvation wages, herds him into slums or impoverished Reserves, refuses him social security, and fences him off from every form of democratic expression, including the franchise and full trade-union rights, by which he may seek to eliminate his appalling social and economic conditions. It is therefore to these forms of discrimination, if they may be termed such, that this present volume devotes most attention.

In following the customary practice of concentrating on "Africa South of the Sahara", I am in no way subscribing to the view that there are two Africas with no interests in common. Africa is a single continent, and the cause of the Algerian people concerns the people of Ghana or Kenya, just as the cause of the African people in the Union of South Africa is supported by the people of Tunisia and Morocco. The Sahara is no longer accepted by the African people as a dividing line. On the contrary, as Nkrumah has said, "*Today, the Sahara is a bridge uniting us.*"

Nevertheless, the customary designation of "Africa South of the Sahara" has laid its impress on all the available books, studies and reports, so that in studying African problems one is largely driven by necessary considerations of time and labour to follow in the wake of previous studies and to make the same arbitrary division. It is for these reasons of convenience, therefore, and not in support of any political theory about "Arab Africa" and "Black Africa", that this has been done in the present volume.

Most studies on Africa written during the twentieth century have been written by Europeans. This is not so much a striking testimony to the great interest displayed in African affairs by students in the West—though the interest undoubtedly exists— but rather an exposure of the stifling of African culture and education which has accompanied imperialism wherever it has gone on safari. The sad consequence is that the overwhelming majority of these studies—one might say almost all of them— are written from a Western standpoint. Many, it is true, would probably claim that their purpose was to make a detached, objective, scientific study of African questions. And within that frame of reference the fruits of such scholarship are by no means without considerable value. At the same time, the authors of these studies, usually in perfectly good faith, have overlooked the extent to which their "impartial" examinations have entirely neglected the views of the African people themselves, as expressed by African political and trade-union organisations and by African leaders. Happily, this tendency is now less evident.

In this present volume every effort has been made to utilise, where possible, the opinions, demands and ideas of the African people themselves, of their trade unions and political organisations, of their spokesmen and national leaders, of their writers and thinkers. It is their attitude, their indictment and their policy and programme which constitute the only realistic starting-point of all studies on Africa today. And it is in support of their powerful declarations on behalf of more than two hundred million Africans that this book has been written.

JACK WODDIS.

London
June 1960.

AFRICA
The Roots of Revolt

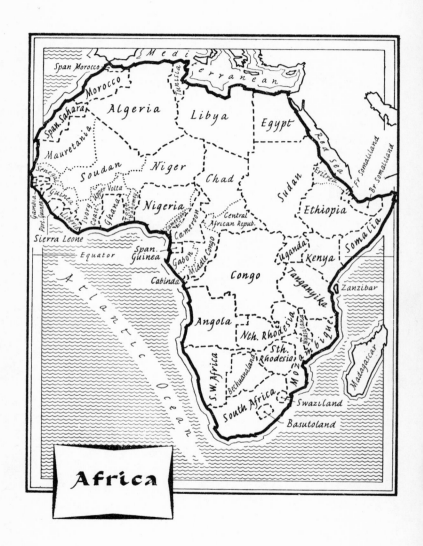

Africa

CHAPTER ONE

"RESTORE OUR LAND!"

THE history of Africa's relations with the West has been a history of robbery—robbery of African manpower, its mineral and agricultural resources, and its land. Even though direct slavery no longer exists, labour, resources and land remain the three dynamic issues over which the struggle for the future of Africa is being fought out. The form of this struggle, it is true, is a political fight for national independence; but the abolition of foreign control of labour, resources and land is the substance for which this independence is being sought.

Despite important changes that have taken place in Africa in the last twenty years, the main characteristic of its economy remains its colonial character, its basis in cash crops and mineral extraction for the profit of foreign monopolies.

Land and its ownership is therefore a touchstone for the African national movement. It was, in fact, in protest against the seizure of land, that the African National Congress was formed in South Africa in 1912.

When in 1932 Jomo Kenyatta, at that time general secretary of the Kikuyu Central Association, said, "What Africans want now is not commissions but the restitution of their land", he was speaking not only for Kenya but for Africans throughout the continent. For the downright expropriation or robbery of African land—"alienation" is the polite word used in official quarters— is a root cause of African impoverishment today.

Both during and since the great scramble for Africa by the Western imperialist powers at the end of the nineteenth century, land-grabbing has been a central aim. By direct seizure, conquest, pressure on chiefs, trickery, swindling, the repudiation of pledges and promises, by every means open to them, the representatives of the European powers took land. And, despite Hailey's allegation that "the period of alienation has for all practical purposes come to an end",[1] the practice has steadily continued during these past twenty years—and even takes place today.

In the Union of South Africa, 89 per cent of the land was taken from Africans or reserved to Europeans. In Southern Rhodesia it was 49 per cent, and the same in Swaziland. Even though in other territories the percentage was less—9 per cent in the Belgian Congo, 7 per cent in Kenya, 5 per cent in Nyasaland, Ghana and South West Africa, and 3 per cent in Northern Rhodesia[2]—it still meant that the acreage per head of the Europeans was far greater than per head of the Africans.

More important still, the land left to the Africans was the poorest, while that taken by the Europeans was the best. Speaking of Northern Rhodesia, Hinden has pointed out that despite the size of the country "land has become a very scarce and precious commodity for the Africans"[3]. Although the mere acreage figures might not bear out the above contention, says Hinden, she stresses that "crude statistics have little meaning", for the Africans are confined to the "poor soils", with poor irrigation facilities which compel them to crowd into the few areas which have water supplies. On top of this, there is "a wide distribution of the tsetse fly, which effectively rules out cattle-raising over five-eighths of the country, and infects human beings themselves with the deadly sleeping sickness. . . ." These enormous handicaps have proved, says Hinden, "nothing short of catastrophic" to successful agriculture.

And the same can be said of other African territories. The Africans have been not only robbed, and terribly robbed, of land, but their *best* land has been taken by Europeans, and they themselves have often been confined to the worst scrub-land, waterless, semi-desert, or malarial, and infested swamp-lands—land which, even with enormous reserves of capital and the utmost use of modern machinery and technique, would require a prodigious effort to make habitable and fertile.

In Kenya, for instance, some 4,000 white farmers have been given the monopoly of 16,500 square miles of the White Highlands, which are estimated to contain no less than thirty per cent of all the good land in Kenya. As Mr. Stonehouse, M.P., has

[1] Hailey, Lord: *An African Survey Revised, 1956*, p. 689, London, 1957.
[2] Figures taken from map-chart in Hailey (Revised), op. cit., p. 68f.
[3] Hinden, Dr. Rita: *Plan for Africa*, pp. 69–70, London, 1941.

pointed out,[1] even if one were to add all the European commercial people and Civil Servants in Kenya to those Europeans actually engaged in farming, it would mean that a mere one per cent of the total population of Kenya—60,000 out of about six million—possesses thirty per cent of the best land.

In Southern Rhodesia, as well, "most of the Native Area", says Ken Brown,[2] a former Land Development Officer in Southern Rhodesia, "is poor soil, usually the poorer types of granite-sand known technically as Class III land; while the European Area contains nearly all the areas of fertile soil in the Colony." He adds that in many parts of the country it is embarrassing for a European to drive through a European Area into a "Native Area":

"The change in soil-type coincides almost exactly with the boundary-line and is startlingly obvious."[3]

Even the "Native Purchase Areas", supposedly suitable regions of Southern Rhodesia for developing an African "middle class of farmers", are often situated, says Brown,[4] "in areas of poor granite-sand or even poorer fine-grained sandstone soils. Others . . . are in hot, malaria-infested areas, where great illness and suffering are caused among the people settling there (especially as there are no hospitals or clinics within easy reach). Others . . . are cursed with country so broken and rocky that agriculture is impossible over most of the area."

Describing this policy of taking the best land from the Africans in Southern Rhodesia and giving it to the Europeans, Leys[5] says that the result of the recommendations of the Reserves Commission was to reduce the Reserves up to 1920 by over six million acres. Moreover, he emphasises, for lands taken out of the existing Reserves and given to the Europeans there were substituted for the Africans *"lands in low-lying areas away from the line of rail, a policy which reflected the desire not to put into Reserves any land which might yield profits—especially mineral wealth—to European settlement."*

Could there be more evident robbery?

Understandable, therefore, is the intense feeling in Africa on

[1] Stonehouse, John: *Prohibited Immigrant*, p. 132, London, 1960.
[2] Brown, Ken: *Land in Southern Rhodesia*, p. 5, Africa Bureau, London, 1959.
[3] ibid., p. 6.
[4] ibid., p. 23.
[5] Leys, Colin: *European Politics in Southern Rhodesia*, pp. 9–10, London, 1959.

the land question, which is a dominant point of policy in all the programmes of the African national movements. Talking of this great resentment felt by Africans towards the European powers who have robbed them of their land, Hailey says:[1]

"This feeling is general and is by no means confined to those communities whose land has been taken for this purpose. . . . Whatever other reasons may exist for the estimate made by Africans of the character of a Government, the fact that a considerable area of Native lands has passed permanently into the hands of non-Natives will always tend to colour any judgment that is formed of it."

This is especially true of Kenya where the question of land is the central issue. The great grab for the land in Kenya began at the beginning of the twentieth century, at the dawn of the imperialist epoch. In 1901 there were only thirteen European settlers—but already by the end of 1904 some 220,000 acres of land had been taken by them. Seizures followed fast. Syndicates, speculators and aristocrats—all took their slice. The East African Syndicate took 320,000 acres; the Uplands of East Africa Syndicate Limited, 350,000 acres; Grogan Forest Concessions, 200,000 acres. Lord Delamere, who was later to become a leader of the white settlers, obtained 100,000 acres. Between 1905 and 1914 nearly 4,400,000 acres were taken from the Africans in Kenya. And so it went on, until "about half the land in Kenya that is worth cultivating", according to Dr. Norman Leys, was in the hands of Europeans.

In 1939, under an Order in Council, the famous Kenya Highlands, a rich, fertile plateau below Mount Kenya, totalling some sixteen thousand seven hundred square miles, was reserved for European occupation only. These White Highlands, among the richest lands in all Africa, were thus handed over to two thousand European settlers and their families, leaving some four million Africans to manage on inferior land.

Completely understandable, therefore, is both the bitter hostility which Africans feel towards those who have robbed them of their land, as well as their desperate attempts to cling to whatever land they can. Throughout the Report of the East

[1] Hailey (Revised): op. cit., p. 686.

African Royal Commission[1] one comes across this feeling, which even the dry, dessicated officialese cannot entirely conceal.

"Those who occupy land fear that they may lose it or be deprived of it without proper compensation and with no opportunity to purchase other land in its place. Those who have no land fear that they will never be able to acquire it."[2]

The Royal Commission was compelled to admit that:

". . . conceptions of 'Crown land' and of 'Public land' which relegate the customary right holders to the legal position of occupiers at the will of the state have often, and particularly in so far as the state's powers have been exercised for the purpose of disposing of land to non-Africans, or for what the African regards as purposes of non-African profit, *given the African a sense of insecurity in his land holding, notwithstanding the statements of policy and the complicated administrative machinery designed to reassure him.*"[3] [Own italics—J. W.]

But why should the African be "reassured" by "statements of policy and the complicated administrative machinery"? On the contrary, his whole experience tells him that he has everything to fear from such reassurances. Every fresh step to rob him of his land has been accompanied by official protestations that it was all being done in his own interests. When the Reserves were set up he was told it was to "protect African lands from further encroachment by Europeans". When lands were taken from Africans and set aside as "Crown lands", again the African was informed that it was a measure to stop the "uncontrolled" taking over of land by Europeans; henceforth the Government would control the take-over. Africans have remarked that each measure for their "protection" has always meant the further taking of their land.

Joshua Nkomo, president of the banned Southern Rhodesia

[1] *East African Royal Commission 1953–5 Report*: Cmd. 9475, H.M.S.O., London, 1955.
[2] ibid., p. 51.
[3] ibid., p. 349.

African National Congress, has drawn attention, for example, to the Southern Rhodesian Land Apportionment Acts of 1931 and 1941, "ostensibly passed for the protection of what land had been left under African control" but used "for the purpose of dispersing and impoverishing the African population and retaining political and economic power in the hands of the settlers."[1]

In his speech to the General Assembly of the Church of Scotland, May 25, 1959, the Very Rev. Dr. George MacLeod stated that under the Land Apportionment Act the Africans were left with 63,000 square miles, while the Europeans got 75,000 square miles. (There are 2,290,000 Africans in Southern Rhodesia, compared with 178,000 Europeans.) Dr. MacLeod added that "so far, 80,000 Africans have been moved to conform with the Act, and another 90,000 were to be moved before the apportionment was complete."[2]

The 1951 Land Husbandry Act has had a comparable disastrous effect on the African people. Under this Act, arable land is cut down to a maximum of eight acres per family—and this of the poorest soils. Up to the time of the Act every African had the right to reside in the Reserve and cultivate land there with the permission of the chief. Now, through the Land Husbandry Act, this right has been taken away. "The Government", says Brown,[3] "anticipates fewer right-holders with larger holdings, and this, together with the natural population increase, will gradually force more and more Africans out of the Reserves and into the urban areas or European farms to seek a livelihood." Brown estimates that "over half a million indigenous Africans will have virtually no rights of residence (and certainly no security of tenure) in the land of their birth!"

The Southern Rhodesian African National Congress claims that already "over a million have been declared landless".[4] And Sir Edgar Whitehead, the Prime Minister of Southern Rhodesia, is reported to have said[5] that out of some two and a half million

[1] Nkomo, Joshua: "The Crucible of Privilege: Southern Rhodesia", *Africa South*, July-September 1959, 3, No. 4, p. 59.
[2] *East Africa and Rhodesia*, May 28, 1959, p. 1131.
[3] Brown, Ken: op. cit., p. 20.
[4] Southern Rhodesia Freedom Day statement, issued in London, for September 12, 1959, by the London Office of the Southern Rhodesian African National Congress.
[5] Speech in Bulawayo, November 1958. Quoted in above-mentioned Southern Rhodesia Freedom Day Statement.

Africans only 307,000 would be able to get land holdings in African areas.

Impoverishment of the Peasantry, an Aim

It is not intended here to go into any detail concerning the seizures of African land. Much has already been written on this score and even defenders of imperialism cannot deny what took place, even though they might try to justify it. It is, however, important to examine why this land-robbery occurred, why it is maintained and even extended, and what have been its consequences for the African people.

It is, of course, true that a basic reason for this act of robbery was a simple one of primitive accumulation—to take land because of the minerals it contained and the crops that could be grown on it. But this is only part of the answer, for an examination of European land utilisation in Southern Rhodesia, Northern Rhodesia and Kenya, for example, shows that *only a very small proportion of the land reserved for Europeans has, in fact, been used by them.*

What is the reason for this apparent mystery? Why is it that the Pim Report[1] on Northern Rhodesia, in 1938, could discover that:

". . . large areas from which natives were evacuated are practically empty of inhabitants. . . . For example, one-third of Ndola district and two-fifths of Mkushi are practically uninhabited as well as large areas in other districts such as Broken Hill. Of the 23,000,000 acres left available as Crown land in the railway belt 2,000,000 acres only have been alienated, including 76,000 acres alienated for mining purposes. The area under European cultivation is approximately 70,000 acres, and the number of producers 260."

In the Abercorn district, where 5,500,000 acres of land were set aside for European settlement, the Pim Commission found only 100,000 acres actually alienated, and of that *only 500 acres under European cultivation.*

Even today only five per cent of the 4,500,000 acres of land

[1] Report of the Commission appointed to enquire into the Financial and Economic Position of Northern Rhodesia, Col. No. 145, 1938. (Pim Report.)

owned by Europeans in Northern Rhodesia is actually cultivated. And it is the same story in Southern Rhodesia; in 1957 only 1,100,000 acres of the 48,000,000 acres occupied by the white settlers were under cultivation.[1] (The actual total area reserved for Europeans is about 52,000,000 acres, but of this about 4,000,000 are set aside as game reserves.) Kenya, again, reveals the same phenomenon: only six per cent of the 16,700 square miles of the White Highlands is cultivated by the settlers.

The reason for this, and for the wholesale taking of land in so much of Africa, was two-fold: to prevent the African peasant from becoming a competitor to the European farmer or plantation owner; and to impoverish the African peasantry to such an extent that the majority of adult males would be compelled to work for the Europeans, in the mines or on the farms. *Thus not only the enrichment of the Europeans but the deliberate impoverishment of the Africans became a cornerstone of official policy.*

The Europeans went to extraordinary lengths to prevent African competition in agriculture. The steps taken seem even more extraordinary when one bears in mind the official accounts of African "backwardness" and "inefficiency" as farmers. In fact, as many commentators have revealed, it is the European settlers who have been proved such inefficient farmers. Even with the best lands in their possession they have had to be constantly subsidised and aided by governments, and "protected" against African competition by the introduction of various restrictions or limitations on African agriculture, and by the introduction of various discriminatory measures in favour of the European farmer.

If railways were already built, the Europeans took good care to ensure that the lands they possessed included those portions adjoining the rail routes; and in the same way, new lines were built with European interests in mind. It was the same with access to main roads and markets. The European farmer was given all the advantages.

---

[1] K. Brown states: "There is a surfeit of land in the European area; and many European farmers can and do make a handsome living off their thousands of acres by improving and developing only a few of them." (*Land in Southern Rhodesia*, p. 24.) He comments that in most Reserves "men with six or eight acres of sand soil can see with their own eyes across their own Reserve boundary-line thousands of acres of European farmland, mostly undeveloped and often virtually unused".

The Pim Commission pointed out that the Northern Rhodesian Reserves Commission had laid it down that the native Reserves were "to be situated in country *away from the railway line*", even though they realised that this "might be considered as conflicting with the principle of equal economic opportunities for Europeans and natives." The "equal opportunities", of course, were never seriously intended as anything more than window-dressing.

As with transport facilities, so with prices; it was the European settler who was favoured. Under the 1935 Maize Control Ordinance for Northern Rhodesia, European growers received 7s. 9d. a bag of maize in 1936, the African farmer from 5s. to 6s.[1] This same Maize Control Ordinance also restricted the African share of the home maize market to one-quarter, leaving the other three-quarters in the hands of the few hundred European farms.

A recent publication of the Rhodesian Institute of African Affairs[2] states of Southern Rhodesia that while the European producer received 40s. per bag of maize for the 1957 harvest, the African producer got only 27s.

Yet, despite the advantages provided for Europeans, Hinden was able to write of Northern Rhodesia in 1941: "European agriculture has, it is generally agreed, been a failure."[3] And this although "all the legal provisions for its success were carefully secured by the Europeans for their prosperity."[4]

The same applies to Southern Rhodesia. "No great examination is needed", says Brown,[5] "to see that European agriculture in Southern Rhodesia must be among the most inefficient in the world."

A similar tale could be told of Kenya. S. and K. Aaronovitch[6] have shown, in considerable detail, the failures of European farming in Kenya between the two world wars, despite considerable government assistance. Here, too, "the dominant thought of the settlers has been to avoid competition from the Africans."[7]

Thus, as regards coffee-growing in Kenya, S. and K. Aaronovitch have explained[8] how Africans were restricted in

[1] Pim Report, p. 228.
[2] *The Progress of Africans in Southern Rhodesia*, pp. 22-3, Rhodesian Institute of African Affairs, Bulawayo, 1959.
[3] Hinden: op. cit., p. 45.   [4] ibid., p. 48.   [5] Brown, Ken: op. cit., p. 24.
[6] Aaronovitch, S. and K.: *Crisis in Kenya*, chapter 6, London, 1947.
[7] ibid., p. 83.   [8] ibid., p. 86.

growing coffee, partly by the high cost of the licence, partly by the limitation in acreage,[1] and, after this was removed in 1939, by the restriction of African coffee-growing to certain areas, especially for the valuable arabica coffee. The fear of the Europeans, they point out, was that "increased production by Africans would not only threaten their markets, but would diminish the flow of labour from the Reserves."

This question of the flow of labour brings us right to the heart of a fundamental aspect of European land policies in Africa. *To put it in a nutshell, a major aim of European land policy in Africa is to ensure cheap labour for European mines and farms.*

When gold and diamonds were discovered in South Africa at the end of the nineteenth century, and railways began to open up the whole continent, European capital began to flow, in an ever-increasing stream, particularly into South Africa, and European settlement followed in its wake. Lenin has explained that the reason for the big export of capital to such areas as Africa is that "in these backward countries profits are usually high, for capital is scarce, the price of land is relatively low, wages are low, raw materials are cheap."[2] Nowhere is this more true than in Africa, where the price of land was nominal. But to make these high profits, European companies and farmers needed the cheap African labour. This labour, however, was not so easy to obtain. Africans have never forgotten the terrible centuries of slave labour which wrought such incalculable damage to African economic, social and cultural development. They were naturally reluctant to work for Europeans, especially in view of the wages and conditions which they realised it entailed.

Moreover, Africans could exist without offering themselves for European employment. In Bechuanaland, for example, Schapera has explained:

"Before the coming of the Europeans, all the Native inhabitants of the Territory were *economically self-sufficient*. . . . In the main, each Bantu household produced its own food by raising crops and breeding livestock; it also built its own huts, and made most of its own clothing and domestic utensils. . . .

[1] Similar restrictions were imposed on Africans wishing to grow sisal or pyrethrum.
[2] Lenin, V. I.: *Imperialism, the Highest Stage of Capitalism.* In *The Essentials of Lenin*, vol. 1, p. 688, Lawrence & Wishart, London, 1947.

Certain utensils and other goods were made and bartered by specialist craftsmen, who supplemented in this way their income from farming. . . . *Since the coming of the Europeans this old self-sufficiency has broken down. . . ."*[1]   [Own italics—J. W.]

The breaking down of this self-sufficiency, the destruction of African subsistence agriculture, became a central aim of imperialist policy, pursued since the beginning of the twentieth century to this very day—for a stable African peasantry, able to exist independent of European farms and mines, is the last thing imperialism will allow. As Ezekiel Mphahlele has so succinctly put it:[2]

"If a stable peasantry *were* to be consciously established, how many would come to work for 3s. 6d. a day in the mines?"

But to secure African labour for European enterprises was to prove no easy task. A triple attack was launched, the three prongs consisting of land control, forced labour and taxation.

"When, in the early stages of African economic development, large numbers of wage earners were first required, notably to exploit the new mineral discoveries, employers were faced with a problem of great labour scarcity. . . . Pressure amounting to compulsion was applied to obtain labour *which the offer of wages alone could not attract in sufficient numbers.* In different areas and at different times there was a resort to such various means as *slavery, direct statutory compulsion, pressure through the imposition of personal tax, the curtailment of native lands, assistance given by administrative officials to the efforts of private recruiters, and the use of chiefs to recruit their people as labourers.*"[3] [Own italics—J. W.]

In the following chapters some examination is made of the role of the taxation system in African territories as a means of driving Africans out to seek wage labour; consideration is given, too, to the use of varying degrees of legal compulsion and pressure to

[1] Schapera, I.: *Migrant Labour and Tribal Life*, pp. 6–7, O.U.P., 1947.
[2] Mphahlele, E.: "The Dilemma of the African Elite", *The Twentieth Century*, April 1959, p. 319.
[3] "Interracial Wage Structure in Africa", *International Labour Review*, July 1958, pp. 38–9.

bring about the same result. Both of these measures, however, were related to the land and agricultural policies pursued by the governments in most of the territories. These policies consisted in robbing the African peoples of their best land—and in some cases of most of their land—and preventing, by various measures of discrimination and restriction, the emergence of a flourishing African rural economy. The old subsistence agriculture was broken not only through land seizures and forced labour but by the introduction of the cash poll tax system which compelled Africans to obtain cash. Any attempt on the part of Africans to escape the net, to obtain the cash by turning from subsistence agriculture to the development of cash crops, and so avoiding wage labour for Europeans, was largely balked by the government policy of favouring European settlers and discriminating against and restricting Africans. Only in West Africa, where large-scale European settlement had not taken place, and in Uganda, were the African people able, to some extent, to escape this fate.

Hailey has written:[1]

". . . the land still provides for the great majority of Africans the sole means of subsistence. If for any reason this fails the peasant, his only alternative is to join the ranks of migrant labour, at the cost of a journey which may often run to hundreds of miles."

This statement, however, is misleading. It is not a question of the land "failing the peasant"; it is deliberate imperialist policy to impoverish the peasantry so as to have a steady supply of cheap, migrant labour for the European farms, mines and other enterprises.

The seizure of African land and the destruction of traditional African agriculture has been accompanied by a decline or even a large-scale elimination of village crafts and industries which find themselves unable to compete with imported foreign goods. In many parts of Africa imported textiles have resulted in "a complete disappearance of domestic weaving".[2] Other crafts, it is

---

[1] Hailey (Revised): op. cit., p. 685.
[2] *Special Study on Economic Conditions in Non-Self-Governing Territories*, U.N., 1958, p. 118 (NSG).

said, "have suffered similar decline".[1] In Nigeria, according to Forde and Scott,[2] "traditional guilds of smiths have decayed, leaving their members impoverished and threatened with social degradation." Similarly, in French Africa "deterioration of African craftsmanship is very rapid . . . certain objects, such as household utensils, produced by African craftsmen have disappeared, calabashes being replaced by basins, wooden bowls by plates."[3] Labouret[4] states that the collapse of African handicrafts has been so sweeping in some areas that special vocational schools have had to be established in order to preserve these crafts.

The process which has gone ahead in Africa has been summed up in these words:

"Not the expansion of home trade, but the involvement of the indigenous peasantry in world-trade operations has been the turning point. The indigenous communities have been brought into contact with world trade centres and their economies have become linked to the sensitive commodity markets of the distant world. *In less than half a century the closed system of family economy has broken into pieces under the pressure of circumstances.*"[5] [Own italics—J. W.]

"Today, from Some People the Land is Taken"

The seizure of African land, as has already been noted, did not occur solely at the time of the scramble for Africa at the end of the nineteenth century. Throughout the twentieth century, and continuing until the present day, the colonial governments in the various African territories have, by legal enactment or other drastic measures, carried forward their policy of slicing away the land from the African people. Even when land-hungry African peasants squat on land classified as "Crown land" but which has not yet been set aside for European settlement, they are brutally turned off.

[1] ibid.
[2] Forde, D., and Scott, R.: *The Native Economies of Nigeria*, pp. 30 et seq., London, 1954.
[3] France: *Assemblée de l'Union Française, No. 280* (21 juillet, 1953).
[4] Labouret, H.: *Paysans d'Afrique Occidentale*, p. 288, Paris, 1941.
[5] NSG, op. cit., p. 117.

Such was the case at Olenguruone in Kenya, towards the end
of 1949, when, in the half-light of an early dawn, a squad of
armed police, commanded by European officers, descended on
the 11,800 men, women and children of Olenguruone, and
threw them out of their huts, which they then burned to the
ground. Crops and foodstocks were destroyed, and livestock
numbering 1,600 head of cattle and nearly 9,000 goats were
confiscated.

After the State of Emergency was declared in Kenya in 1952,
thousands of African peasants were treated in similar fashion;
even those living on land legally belonging to them were driven
off as "Mau Mau suspects" to concentration camps, their huts
burned or bull-dozed to the ground, their livestock seized and
their land taken. Leaders of the Kenya Africa Union, in particular,
suffered in this way.

On October 31, 1951, the African Cooks, Washermen and
House Servants' Association in Tanganyika sent a petition to the
United Nations Trusteeship Council in which, among other
poignant complaints, they asked:

"Why we Africans, our lands are been sold?

"Why we are driven from our original lands since our forefathers, and we are placed on hills, and the rich people take
our lands?

"Why the graves of our forefathers are dug out?"

That this complaint did not refer to the distant past but was
specifically related to present-day experience is shown by the
complaint sent to the United Nations by the Wameru people in
August 1951, against the forcible eviction of 3,000 Africans from
their land in Meru Land in the Arusha District of Northern
Tanganyika. The 3,000 evicted persons are from the Wameru
people who live on the slopes of the Meru Mountain. In 1905,
much of their land was taken from them by the German imperialists, Tanganyika being one of the areas cut away by the Germans
during the "scramble for Africa". In 1923, after the Germans had
been forced to surrender Tanganyika during the First World
War, the British Government offered the former German-held
lands for sale. The Wameru people applied to buy back their
own land; and by 1939 they had completed payment and were
once more in possession of their land.

This possession, however, was to last little more than one decade. In June 1946 the Government of Tanganyika set up the Arusha-Moshi Land Commission, under the chairmanship of Judge Mark Wilson, to work out proposals for redistributing the land in the Moshi and Arusha Districts of Northern Tanganyika. There was a reason for this, revealed in the words of the Commission itself: "Land in the Arusha and Moshi Districts is literally more precious than gold."[1]

With a verdict such as that it was inevitable that the Wameru people would once again fall victims to the usurpation of their land at the hands of the imperialists. By the terms of reference given to it, the Commission was charged with making "comprehensive plans and recommendations for the redistribution of such lands, and to advise Government as to the availability or otherwise of land in the areas in question for further non-Native settlement." There is no doubt that it was not alone the richness of the lands in question which whetted the appetites of the imperialists, but equally their concern to impoverish the African peasants and drive them out to work as cheap labour on the large European sisal estates and other plantations and farms.

The Commission carried out the drastic work for which it had been set up. Its verdict was for the Wameru people to give up their lands. On December 10, 1950, the forcible eviction began. Police arrived in Singisi, the heart of Meru Land, set fire to houses and cut down trees. On July 2, 1951, families living in Leganga were forcibly ejected, and ten days later the same fate befell families living in Daluti. On November 17 over two hundred police and mercenaries arrived in Engare-Nanyuki; they set fire to the people's homes, burned their crops and drove away their cattle. With cynical unconcern for the fate of the Wameru people, the government offered them, as an alternative, land in the Kingori and Ongatongoshu area, which was already their own tribal land, not used because its arid and tsetse-ridden nature made it unsuitable for cultivation or grazing.

[1] This land, it should be remembered, was the area of Tanganyika which agents of Lord Delamere tried to annex to Kenya in the 1920s because of their hostility to the Africans' growing of coffee in the Arusha and Moshi districts. Failure to achieve this aim resulted in the settlers demanding the curtailment of African coffee-growing—a request which was acceded to by the Tanganyika Government. (For further details see Raymond L. Buell: *The Native Problem in Africa*, vol. i., pp. 493–4, New York, 1928.)

In Central Africa, too, the eviction of Africans from the land continues. In 1957 some 45,000 Africans in Southern Rhodesia were turned off land earmarked for European use yet lying idle. This is apart from a further 20,000 turned off their land in the Zambesi valley to give way to the lake rising behind the Kariba hydro-electric scheme. Another 30,000 have been driven off their land by this scheme on the other side of the frontier, in Northern Rhodesia.

Even in the Union of South Africa, despite the fact that close on ninety per cent of the land has been taken from the African people, land seizures are still taking place. A recent account by Govan Mbeki in *New Age*[1] gives a vivid description of the fate of many African peasants in the Ciskei and the Transkei.

> "In the Transkei today from some people the land is taken away; from others it is their stock. . . . With fiendish thoroughness the Nationalist Government is carrying out the process of dispossession and is compelling more and more people to look on the [European] farms as the only means of making a livelihood. Recently an order has been issued in the Transkei that people who have arable allotments but have no stock are to forfeit such allotments. On the other hand those who own stock and have no arable allotment are to be denied the privilege to graze such stock on the communal pasturage."

As recently as April 23, 1959, *The Times* reported that 3,000 Africans were refusing "to heed a South African Government warning to leave the farms they have occupied since 1896 in the Middleburg district, now declared an all-white area."[2]

"Not Merely Stagnation, but Deterioration"

Throughout Africa one can witness the inevitable and tragic consequences of this European policy of land-robbery and the strangulation of African agriculture. In every African territory sixty years of imperialist exploitation have been sufficient to plunge the majority of African peasants into the most abysmal depths of poverty and misery.

[1] *New Age*: January 29, 1959, p. 5.
[2] The forcible moving of Africans from their land in Windhoek, in South West Africa, in December 1959, led to twelve Africans being killed and forty injured.

The herding of Africans into the poorest land has meant a terrible land shortage which figures alone do not adequately convey. Overstocking and overpopulation have been the unavoidable result, coupled with the most intensive exploitation of the soil. The old, traditional African farming method of shifting cultivation, which allowed land to return to grass for considerable periods (a few years at a time) and so regain its fertility, is no longer possible. Instead, in a desperate attempt to provide sufficient food, the peasant is driven to keep his land continually under crop. This exhausts the land—and so the crop yield diminishes, and the crisis, for man and soil, deepens.

Hinden describes the process in these words:[1]

"The land, throughout most of Africa, is held communally. Private rights to any particular strip of territory are very uncommon. Agriculture follows the 'shifting' system. Trees are felled and bush burnt to fertilise the soil; crops are grown on the cleared space, and after a short period of cultivation the 'farm' is abandoned and the cultivator moves on to his next clearing. Village sites move together with the shift of cultivation, and this system can be continued indefinitely if the population is sparse enough. All that is necessary is to allow an adequate period of time to elapse for the regeneration of the trees and bush, and then the trees may once again be lopped, the bush burnt, and cultivation recommenced. But, as soon as the population becomes too dense for its area, the forests will not be given time to regenerate, and the fertility of the soil will ebb."

And this is precisely what has happened in so much of Africa. The population has become "too dense for its area" largely because government policy has crowded it into insufficient reserves.

Brown[2] has shown how this process has gone ahead in Southern Rhodesia. It is often argued, he says, that if Africans were given more land, they would only ruin it.

"This is a fallacy," replies Brown. "The fact is indisputable

[1] Hinden: op. cit., p. 66.
[2] Brown, Ken: op. cit., p. 17.

that when, before the advent of the Europeans, Africans had abundant land, *the erosion they caused was negligible* and the *soil maintained its fertility and structure."*   [Own italics—J. W.]

It is, he asserts, *"the coming of the Europeans which has changed this and caused most of the soil erosion and soil exhaustion in the Reserves."* Among the reasons he gives for this deterioration are the limitation of land for Africans, and the agricultural policy pursued by the Native Agriculture Department. While many authorities tend to put the main blame for the spread of erosion and the exhaustion of the soil on to the shifting system of agriculture practised by Africans, Brown argues that, on the contrary, "from a conservation point of view, and particularly on sandveld soils, the system was almost perfect."

But the Native Agriculture Department has done its best to switch the Africans in the Reserves from shifting cultivation (which left the land fallow for several years so as to restore its fertility) over to continuous cultivation. From a conservation point of view, stresses Brown, "this system of continuous cultivation is basically wrong for the Native Areas." Such advice, he says, would never be given in the European farming areas, but in the Reserves the land development officers "can advise nothing else because of the shortage of land".

The contention that it is the agricultural methods of the Africans, and their refusal to accept "modern" Western methods, which are the prime cause of the decay of the African agrarian economy does not stand up to any serious examination. In fact, many recent studies have stressed the suitability of African methods for African conditions, *given an ample supply of land.* And these same studies have also warned of the indiscriminate use of Western methods which, though of value in European conditions, can do immense harm in the very different conditions of Africa.

In the Belgian Congo and Uganda, for example, it has been proved that the European system of clean weeding "may be actually detrimental under tropical conditions as it destroys the structure of the soil and exposes organic matter to rapid oxidation. In general, methods of intensive farming applied in Europe have frequently had disastrous results."[1] In Nigeria, too, it has been

[1] NSG, op. cit., p. 133.

found that Western innovations "are often inappropriate to the environment of tropical Africa."[1] In French West Africa, early peasant resistance to oxen-ploughing (launched by the French authorities) was found to be justified by later events, and led to the construction of lighter ploughs and an appreciation of the danger of too deep ploughing under African conditions.[2]

Many recent studies of traditional African agricultural methods have shown that they embody a "great volume of empirical knowledge".[3] This knowledge, it is said, comprises a large number of basic crops and numerous varieties, each with its distinct qualities, its specific requirements, its preferred seasons, and different uses made of it.

"The African cultivator is a great expert in the plants and ecology of his region. He knows equally numerous methods of the preparation and conservation of soil, each corresponding, on the one hand, to certain ecological formations and, on the other, to certain combinations of crops and their successions. This is all the more important since African agriculture is more complex than European agriculture."[4]

In fact, so complex is African agriculture that it has been said that it takes almost a lifetime to learn it, and "no modern combination of agricultural research station and agricultural school has so far come near devising any better system of agriculture. . . ."[4]

No one would want to claim that traditional African agriculture has said the last word on the matter. But much expert opinion is coming round to the view that what is required technically speaking—and this is quite apart from the question of land-ownership and distribution—is "a synthesis of modern technology and the empirical knowledge of the peasant."[4] As Wilson has said,[5] "The traditional African farmer has a profound

---

[1] *The Economic Development of Nigeria*: p. 193 et seq., International Bank for Reconstruction and Development.

[2] NSG, op. cit., pp. 133–4

[3] ibid., p. 134. (See also P. de Schlippe: *Shifting Cultivation in Africa*, London, 1956.)

[4] NSG, p. 134.

[5] Wilson, F.: *Peasant Farming in Tropical Africa*, p. 19. Albert Howard Memorial Lecture, 1954, London, 1955.

understanding of his environment and it is essential that this should not be lost under the influence of Western education."

How unsound European advice, combined with acute land shortage for Africans, has led to the increasing destruction of the soil in Kenya has been described by S. and K. Aaronovitch:[1]

"To make up for the poor yields, steep slopes and hillsides are cultivated, only to result in more soil wash and gullying, which spreads the damage to the areas below.

"Shortage of land means less pasturage for stock, and over-grazing adds its quota to the damage. The herbage is given no chance to grow; it dries out, leaving the soil unprotected to the action of the rain and the resultant soil wash. . . . These consequences of land shortage are serious enough. They have been made even more serious by the pressure on the part of the Agricultural Department to grow cash crops,[2] such as maize and wattle bark. The African was encouraged to plant his maize in plots by itself and keep it clean-weeded in order to obtain higher yields. By this method of planting and without a strict rotational cropping system, the soil soon lost its stability and began to erode. It has now been realised that the African's own methods were far more sound. He would interplant maize and beans with sweet potatoes, the latter having a heavy-growing, spreading vine. As the grain crops were taken off the land so the sweet potato vine would spread, giving much better protection to the soil."

Thus overcrowding and land shortage, combined often with incorrect advice from European officials, have resulted in the decline of soil fertility, erosion, and, for the African peasant, ruination. By 1946, Col. C. E. Ponsonby was telling the House of Commons: "*Already eighteen districts in Kenya itself are receiving famine relief.*"[3] Negley Farson noted:[4] "*All but a minute proportion now spend some six months of every year in a state of semi-starvation.*"

[1] Aaronovitch, S. and K.: op. cit., p. 46.
[2] The compulsory growing of certain cash crops, coupled with restrictions on the growing of other crops, is a common practice in European possessions in Africa. In both cases the African peasant is compelled by the Europeans to do what the *latter* desire and to sell at prices *they* decide.
[3] *Hansard*, July 9, 1946.
[4] Farson, Negley: *Last Chance in Africa*, London, 1946.

Several years later the East Africa Royal Commission reported:[1]

"Throughout our enquiry we were impressed by the recurring evidence that particular areas were now carrying so large a population that agricultural production in them was being retarded, that the natural resources themselves were being destroyed, that families were unable to find access to new land, and that land which should have been lying fallow was being encroached upon."

The Commission Report adds:[2]

"One of the most vivid impressions which we have formed as a result of our enquiry is the fundamental poverty which prevails in the East African territories."

No less disastrous has been the effect of governmental land policies in Northern Rhodesia. Throughout this territory one can see eroded soil, destroyed villages and appalling poverty.

Even twenty years ago the Pim Commission described as follows the conditions in the largest Reserve in the Fort Jameson district, with an area of 500,000 acres and a population of 54,000 Africans:[3]

"In a thickly inhabited portion of some forty-one square miles the density of the population is 119 per square mile. Cultivation without the necessary long periods of fallow is destroying the surface vegetation and bush. Sheet erosion exists to a considerable extent and gully erosion is beginning. . . . An adjacent area of thirty-three square miles is in a similar condition and has a population density of 156 per square mile."

Other Reserves are described in similar vein. They have, as Hinden rightly says, "become centres not merely of stagnation, but of deterioration."[4]

[1] EARC, op. cit., p. 37.
[2] ibid., p. 40.
[3] Pim Report, op. cit., p. 60.
[4] Hinden: op. cit., p. 75.

"It is difficult [writes Hall[1]] for any one who has not been through the country to realise how far the destruction has proceeded in some areas; one sees nothing but gaunt hillsides, mottled with red, yellow and purple where they are bared down to the deep subsoil or the rock, and spare vegetation in the bottoms, gnawed and broken down by the starving animals wandering through it."

Similar scenes are to be seen today in Southern Rhodesia, where erosion and loss of fertility by the soil is widespread. The report of the Natural Resources Board for 1954, making a plea for "plain speaking", declared that "it is no exaggeration to say that at the moment we are heading for disaster. We have on the one hand a rapid increase taking place in the African population and on the other a rapid deterioration of the very land on which these people depend for their existence."

The very devastation of the countryside throughout so much of Africa—which is itself a natural consequence of a government policy of creating a land shortage and overcrowding for Africans—begins a viciously descending spiral which can only be broken by breaking the colonial system itself. Faced with impoverishment, and driven by the poll tax, the African peasant is forced to leave his rural economy and become a migrant labourer. As a result whole villages are largely denuded of their able-bodied males. In Northern Rhodesia, for example, by 1941, 110,000 able-bodied men, *including eighty per cent of the men between fifteen and thirty-five, had been taken off agricultural work.*[2]

A recent traveller in Northern Rhodesia says:[3]

."I went into many villages in Northern Rhodesia hundreds of miles away from the Copper Belt where only old men and women were living. All the able-bodied men . . . were off to the mine. . . ."

Thus food production has been left mainly in the hands of women, children and elderly men. But traditional African

[1] Hall, Sir A. Daniel: *The Improvement of Native Agriculture*, p. 59. (Heath Clark Lectures, London, 1936)
[2] Barnes, Leonard: *Soviet Light on the Colonies*, p. 163, London, 1944.
[3] *Times Educational Supplement*, March 6, 1959, p. 388.

agriculture involves much heavy work, including the climbing of trees to lop off branches for burning to make ash for seed-beds, the construction of fences to keep out animals, and so on. Women, old men and children are unable to cope with this work. The decline becomes a catastrophe. Famine sets in. And so the agrarian crisis deepens and deepens.

Noon, for example, says:[1]

"The villages of Nyasaland are threatened with the collapse of their entire economic structure by the absence of as high as seventy per cent of the adult males."

He adds that "the successive stages of this cycle are the departure of men for the south, then the deterioration of local agriculture, which in another turn of the wheel forces a greater number of males to leave the protectorate."[2]

The 1938 Colonial Office Report on Nyasaland gave 113,500 or 27·7 per cent of all adult males as being engaged outside the colony. By 1954 the figure had risen to 160,000—so the further decline in agriculture can well be imagined.

"Whole territories," says Davidson,[3] "such as Nyasaland and Ruanda-Urundi, have become little more than reservoirs of migrant labour; and their consequent impoverishment is visible for all to see. Nothing in all Africa is sadder to the heart and eye than the great Native Reserves of the Transvaal and the Cape Province."

And this is the pattern throughout most of imperialist-held Africa. How near to the edge of catastrophe African agriculture has been forced by the land robberies and the devastating blows of the migrant-labour system which, like a giant grab, constantly dips, scoops and denudes whole villages of their manpower, is strikingly indicated by a United Nations Report in 1953,[4] which says:

[1] Noon, John A.: *Labour Problems of Africa*, p. 39, University of Pennsylvania, 1944.
[2] ibid., p. 113.
[3] Davidson, Basil: *The African Awakening*, p. 103, London, 1955.
[4] *Aspects of Economic Development in Africa*, March 20, 1953, p. 67. U.N. Document E/2377.

". . . where migrant labour has been drawn from the indigenous agricultural economies in high proportions, this has often had a deleterious effect on output and on farming practices, giving rise to a *vicious circle in which the outflow of labour reduces productivity, and falling productivity increases still further the pressure on workers to seek wage employment.*"

It adds that "*eventually a stage may be reached at which the system of migrant labour, based on the labourer's retaining his place in a subsistence agricultural community, may break down.*"   [Own italics—J. W.]

"Land Does Not Beget"

Probably no better illustration of what this has meant for the African people can be given than Keiskammahoek, considerable detail for which has been provided by the remarkable Keiskammahoek Rural Survey.[1] Keiskammahoek District, a native Reserve in the Ciskei area of the Union of South Africa, consists of 220 square miles, and at the time of the 1946 census had a population of 18,391, of whom 17,243 were Africans.

There is a Xhosa proverb: "Men and beast beget, but land does not beget." This saying vividly epitomises the economic plight of all native Reserves. Overpopulation, overstocking, denudation of the vegetation, soil erosion and poverty—such are the general characteristics which have developed. And in Keiskammahoek one can see the reasons.

Keiskammahoek is a farming area, but, says the survey, "the land is unable to support its present population. There is no effective alternative employment in the neighbourhood. Although Keiskammahoek is far removed from the major industrial centres of the Union, economic necessity drives large numbers of people, both men and women, out to earn a livelihood in such places as Cape Town, Johannesburg, Port Elizabeth and East London."[2] (Cape Town is 845 miles away by rail, Johannesburg 642.)

[1] Between 1947 and 1951 a comprehensive survey of the district was carried out under the auspices of the National Council for Social Research, and directed by Professor Lindsay Robb. The findings were subsequently published as the Keiskammahoek Rural Survey. Vol. II of this survey, entitled *The Economy of a Reserve*, and from which many quotations in this chapter were taken, was prepared by Professors D. Hobart Houghton and Edith M. Walton, and published in 1952.

[2] ibid., pp. 3–4.

"The majority of people go out to work for a period of a year or so at a time, then they return home for as long as their savings will permit, and when these are exhausted they go out to work again. Some, however, emigrate to the cities, make their permanent homes there, and do not return to the Reserves."[1]

Keiskammahoek has fifteen villages—but no essential services, no water, no lighting, no sanitation. Its main economic character is that it is a group of peasant farmers attempting to subsist upon the produce of their stock and primitive agriculture. But they cannot produce enough food to support themselves and so have to purchase considerable quantities which are imported into the district. This is paid for, says the survey, *"principally by the export of the large number of workers."*[2] In fact, so dependent are the villagers on the earnings of the emigrant workers that it would be more accurate, says the survey, to say that the economy of the district rests *"firstly upon the fact that it is a reservoir of labour for the mines and industries of the Union, and secondly upon the subsistence farming of those who remain behind."*[3]

This development has wrought havoc on the population balance of the Reserve. The survey, in fact, reports that even in 1936 there was a most disproportionate absence of men of working age. Within ten years, it noted, there was a marked increase in the emigration of young women workers. As a result *"the trend is leading towards a district population comprised mainly of aged and young."*[4] Already, at the time of the survey, the people of sixty-five years and older, and children under fifteen, comprised more than half the population; and, at the rate at which trends were developing, these two categories of old and young *"would constitute sixty per cent of the total population in another generation."*[5]

And yet, under the present system, there is no possibility of halting this trend, for "the export of labour balances about half the import trade of the district."[6]

The dilemma is inescapable:

". . . if men and women leave the district to work, they cannot devote the labour necessary to increasing the long-term

---

[1] ibid., p. 4.   [2] ibid., pp. 4–5.   [3] ibid., pp. 4–5.
[4] ibid., p. 34.   [5] ibid., p. 34.   [6] ibid., p. 66.

productivity of their land; if they remain at home to improve production, they forgo the income from more remunerative employment in the cities.''[1]

But there is really no choice of staying *or* emigrating. The acute poverty of the Reserve *compels* emigration. *Nearly seventy-five per cent of the population had an average income of under 2s. per week; more than half of these received between 1s. and nothing at all. Only four per cent of the population had incomes of more than 5s. a week.*[2]

Emigration in its turn, however, gives the screw a further twist and deepens the crisis still further. Emigration, in fact, as the survey points out, is "at one and the same time both the result and the cause of the poverty of the Reserve"—though basically, as we have seen, the very policy which led to the creation of Reserves was directed towards the creation of an impoverished peasantry. The poverty of the Reserve, which gives rise to emigration and hence to increased poverty in the Reserve, is itself the product of imperialism, which robbed the African people of their land and dealt a death blow to their agrarian economy.

So drastic has been the decay of African agriculture that without emigration the African people could no longer survive. This, in fact, is the pass to which the present system has reduced them.

"*The people of this district are . . . seen to be dependent upon the earnings of emigrants for their very existence, and it is poverty which forces them out to work.*

"*But this very exodus is itself a potent cause of the perpetuation of the poverty at home, for the absence of so many in the prime of life inhibits economic progress and certainly accounts in no small measure for the low agricultural productivity of the district.* In many cases land is not ploughed for the simple reason that there is no one to do the ploughing."[3]   [Own italics—J. W.]

How great the exodus has been is partly revealed by the results of the 1946 census. These showed 64·4 per cent, or nearly two-thirds, of the population as being of pre-working age (under eighteen) or retirement age (sixty years and over). The survey

[1] ibid., p. 82.   [2] ibid., p. 101.   [3] ibid., pp. 112–13.

estimates no less than 53·9 per cent of males of working age as being away from the district at the time of the census.

It is difficult for those who have no knowledge of life in a Reserve to appreciate what a tremendous burden is left for the women to share as a result of the emigration of their menfolk.

Before they can even start to clean, wash or cook, the women have to go, usually long distances, to fetch water in buckets from the rivers; wood has to be collected and carried in bundles from the forests; and then mealies have to be stamped and ground before they can be cooked. On top of this, the women have to walk miles to the trading stations to bring back, in their baskets, the small quantities of food necessities which their meagre finances enable them to purchase in one shopping expedition. Their poorly constructed huts require constant attention. The thatch on the roof usually requires renovating once or twice a year; the mud walls need constant re-plastering, especially in the wet season; and the mud floors require smearing twice or even four times a week, and complete resetting two or three times a year.[1]

An actual timing of the tasks of 355 women and girls at Keiskammahoek showed that an average of a quarter of a fifty-six-hour week was spent on the wastefully uneconomic tasks of fetching water and wood and stamping and grinding mealies. When all the other time-consuming but imperative tasks of the able-bodied women are taken into account, it becomes only too obvious how disastrous is the absence of the able-bodied men for any improvement in agriculture.

Despite the enormous labour which the women have to expend on all these jobs, they still manage to put in six- to eight-hour days in the fields—though not very often. Babies are left in the care of young girls. Water is fetched in small cans and wood in little bundles by girls under fourteen making two or three times as many journeys as adults would normally do. And, in addition, neighbours help one another with weeding, ploughing, and harvesting.

But the struggle is in vain. The odds are too great. And the African agricultural economy sinks lower and lower. Under existing conditions the land in the Reserve is entirely incapable of supporting its population.

[1] ibid., pp. 140–1.

"Today, even an exceptionally good harvest produces food enough for only half the nutritional requirements of the people living at home; in a drought year scarcely one-twentieth of requirements are produced. Few families can get through the winter on their stored harvests. On the average, the value of home-grown crops together with the produce from livestock consumed by each person in the locations amounts to scarcely £1 per annum when the harvests are poor . . . in the locations alone, such is the poverty of the people that even in years of drought and poor harvest an average of only £4 *per capita* can be spent on food purchases."[1]

Again and again the survey returns to the point that it is the poverty of the district, the sheer economic need to exist, that leads to labour migration.

"Under conditions of such manifest poverty in the vast majority of the families it is obviously imperative for at least one member of the family to engage in remunerative employment outside the district with a view *to meeting the family's barest subsistence requirements*."[2]   [Own italics—J. W.]

Yet even this is only a partial solution—and that for only some of the families. Wages in the cities to which emigrant workers go are low, but expenses for food, clothing, rent and transport are high. It is only by dint of great self-sacrifice, including usually going without a midday meal, that migrant workers are able to save anything for the families left behind. The average amount of remittances sent or money brought home by migrant workers is £20 per year per family. But this average figure conceals the terrible plight of so many.

'. . . *some families receive nothing. Some have no cash incomes whatsoever from any source. One third of the families have a total cash income from all sources of less than £13 a year, which falls far short of the average expenditure on food alone. Total annual expenditure on food, as well as on anything else, may be as low as £3 for an entire family*."[3]   [Own italics—J. W.]

---

[1] ibid., pp. 177–8.   [2] ibid., p. 179.   [3] ibid., p. 180.

Only the remarkable generosity and solidarity of the African people, their natural tendency to aid and succour one another, saves such families from death. It is an African tradition that "so long as there is food available, no member of the community should be allowed to starve". It is this which saves many families from complete starvation and removes from the shoulders of the authorities the responsibility of the thousands of deaths from famine each year which would otherwise occur.

The fate of the African people of Keiskammahoek is the fate of the African peasantry throughout the Union. It is not an exceptional district.

"Cursory analysis of economic conditions in the remaining twenty-five districts in the Ciskei, Pondoland, Themuland and the Transkei suggests that the picture which has emerged from this economic survey of Keiskammahoek, a picture of overpopulation, overstocking, poverty, mass emigration, inefficient farming and destruction of the pasture and the soil is, with only minor modifications, true of a vast area of 14,000 square miles inhabited by over a million persons."[1]

This is an area larger than Holland, and the people affected, including those away working in the cities and mines, number about one and a half million, or a sixth of the entire African population in the Union.

Commercialisation of Land

But not only in the Union of South Africa do such conditions exist. The destruction of African agriculture in the Union is paralleled by the disaster which has overtaken the African peasants in Northern and Southern Rhodesia, in Nyasaland, Kenya, Tanganyika, Bechuanaland, Swaziland, the Belgian Congo, the Portuguese territories and also in parts of British and French West Africa.

A previously mentioned U.N. report[2] states that in the majority of the African territories "meat is a rare luxury, and except in certain pastoral tribes, milk is not consumed even by children".

---

[1] ibid., pp. 190—1
[2] NSG, op. cit., p. 91.

In some areas, "only five to six hundred children out of every thousand born alive reach the age of five years".[1]

And the root causes of the disaster are the robbery of African land, the driving of the African people into restricted areas of poor land, and the forcible break-up, with the aid of compulsory labour and the poll-tax, of the traditional African subsistence economy.

Although in West Africa, for example in Ghana and Nigeria, and to an extent in Uganda in East Africa, a class of independent farmers has emerged, linked with trading and commerce, yet in most of Africa the pattern has been not only the destruction of subsistence agriculture but its replacement by utter ruin and starvation. Even in Nigeria, as the Report of the Nigerian Livestock Commission revealed in 1951, fifty-one per cent of the children in the northern provinces die before they are six, and a third of all children admitted to hospital are suffering from malnutrition; in the eastern provinces seventy per cent of the children admitted to hospital suffer from malnutrition. In Nigeria as a whole "over 20,000,000 people are living on an agricultural subsistence of a very low order, and malnutrition and disease are widespread".[2] An investigation into the diet of peasants in the northern territories of the Gold Coast in 1945–6 revealed a terrible picture of starvation; food consumption was the equivalent of only five to six hundred calories per person a day, while the norm for a man engaged in physical labour was from three to five thousand calories.[3]

In countries such as Ghana, Nigeria, Uganda (and to a lesser extent in other territories) individual holdings and the growing of cash crops on a large scale by African farmers have resulted in a certain difference in the land pattern from that described in previous pages. All the more significant, therefore, is the fact that, despite the emergence in these territories of a stratum of relatively rich African farmers, employing African labour, and thus becoming an important sector of a growing African capitalist class, for the *majority* of African peasants it is the familiar story of poverty.

[1] ibid., p. 94.
[2] House of Commons Select Committee on Estimates, Fifth Report, 1947–8 Session.
[3] *West Africa*, April 6, 1946.

This development has considerable relevance for all African territories, since so profound has become the agrarian crisis, as revealed, for example, earlier in the Pim Report (Northern Rhodesia) and more recently by the East Africa Royal Commission, and by the Keiskammahoek Survey and the Tomlinson Commission Report (Union of South Africa), that the imperialist authorities, aware that they stand on the brink of a complete agrarian breakdown throughout East and Central Africa, have recently sought to shore up the crumbling rural economy and to establish an ally for themselves in the African countryside by encouraging, on a limited scale, the growth of an African farming class. These farmers, hope the authorities, will become a richer, more satisfied and contented section, and thus more likely to co-operate with the white settlers.

For a number of years now Africans have been under pressure from colonial governments to abandon their traditional system of communal land tenure and to adopt instead individual title to land, either freehold or leasehold. In this way African land, like European land, would become a commodity to be bought or sold on the market, or rented out. The East Africa Royal Commission Report goes to considerable lengths to argue in favour of such a change, emphasising, in the customary fashion of official reports, that it would be in the interests of Africans to make this change. Coupled with this imperialist proposal to go over to the commercialisation of land is the renewed pressure to abandon subsistence farming in favour of the growing of certain cash crops under conditions, however, which will prevent real competition with Europeans, and at prices determined by European settlers or by European monopolies controlling the international market.

Although by the end of the nineteenth century classes were in process of formation in parts of Africa and forms of feudal land ownership were coming into being, over most of the continent the land was still held in common and was valued for its *use*. *Ownership* of the land in the commonly accepted sense of the term in Europe, carrying with it freehold rights and the power to sell land, did not exist.

"Land", says Batten, "was considered by most Africans in much the same way as Europeans think of sunshine and air— equally plentiful, equally necessary, and equally to be shared by all members of the community according to their needs. Land had no price and was not for sale."[1]

Batten[2] points out that although an individual, under this traditional form of tenure, "may have the *use* of a particular farm, his rights in it, and what he can do with it, are limited by other rights over the same land held by the members of his family, clan or tribe." There were, of course, many variations of custom within this generalisation.

The situation was sometimes modified, says Batten, by conquest or by the development of strong central governments ruling over large areas, as among the Chagga and the Baganda in East Africa, the Basuto in South Africa, and, in West Africa, in the emirates of Northern Nigeria, and the kingdoms of Dahomey, Ashanti and Benin. In these cases the central authority was strong enough to take over from smaller groups their traditional function of allocating land.

At the same time, in areas of dense population, where trade was developed and land less plentiful, other modifications were already taking place, even before the advent of European imperialism. Among the Kikuyu in Kenya, for instance, a man could pledge his land to his creditors—but he parted only with the *use* of it; and once his debt was paid, he could take his land back. Also, persons from other tribes were allowed to hold land after donating gifts to the clan authorities; yet even here, the gifts were not recognised as the payment of an actual price for the land, but merely as a thank-offering for being admitted into the community. "Membership of the community, not payment of price, was the condition of land-holding."[3]

Over most of Africa customary forms of land tenure, varying in the details of their application, continue to this very day, although conquest by Western imperialism has introduced important modifications into them. A key factor in the development of traditional land tenure in Africa was the fact that there was a plentiful supply of land, and that production was for subsistence. Owing to usurpation by Europeans, land is no longer so plentiful for the African people; and the general consequence of European land policies has been the break-down of subsistence agriculture. Moreover, colonial governments have

---

[1] Batten, T. R.: *Problems of African Development*, part I, p. 25, London, 1947–54.
[2] ibid., p. 24.   [3] ibid., p. 26.

directly introduced new forms of tenure by law, as for example
the institution of the *mailo* system under the Buganda Agreement,
as well as the system of leasing Crown lands to Africans, as is
done in Northern and Southern Rhodesia.

In Kano in Northern Nigeria, land was even being sold before
the arrival of Europeans; and since then, with the introduction
of money and the spread of cash crops, the tendency to sell or
lease land has become more marked, though it is still on a limited
scale.

"Even in the Ibo country of south-eastern Nigeria where the
ease with which land passes temporarily from hand to hand
on pledge or lease has been noted as remarkable, 'yet the sale
of land is strongly forbidden by native law and custom'.[1] Yet
sales do occur elsewhere. Thus in the Kiambu district of Kenya,
Kikuyu Native Councils have laid down rules and conditions
governing the selling of holdings, and sales and transfers of
land are common in some parts of Southern Nigeria and the
Gold Coast, especially in the towns. The areas in which land
can be transferred by cash sales are at present extremely small,
but their significance must not therefore be underestimated.
The tendency exists, and changing conditions will strengthen
it as African economic development proceeds."[2]

But will the commercialisation of African land, the introduction of rent and the buying and selling of land, bring to the
African peasant any more security than he enjoys at present?

Batten rightly doubts whether the development of individual
tenure "does in fact promote that security which is urged as one
of its chief advantages".[3] He points out that under customary
tenure neither drought nor trade depression affect the landholder's security as a landholder. "He may go hungry, and he
may have to reduce the quantity of the produce he gives to his
chief, but he has no *money* rent to pay as a condition for remaining
in possession." To those who might interpolate that a system of
freehold tenure would give equal security, Batten points out that
a system of landholding which enabled invididuals to raise credit

---

[1] Green: *Land Tenure in an Ibo Village*, p. 36, London, 1941.
[2] Batten: op. cit., p. 34.
[3] ibid., p. 35.

on land could lead to debt and the polarisation of classes on the land.

> *"Freehold tenure in Africa . . . would appear to provide a probable though not certain security of tenure for some at the expense of greatly increased insecurity for others."*[1]   [Own italics—J. W.]

Batten's doubts appear to be confirmed by developments in Basutoland. Here the introduction of profit farming in place of the traditional land tenure has resulted in the formation of a class of landless or semi-landless rural families along with a "simultaneous concentration of the land in the hands of the more privileged or the more enterprising".[2] Among the 160,500 households on holdings of under eighty acres, surveyed in 1950, almost seven per cent were landless, and a third of the total were subsisting on holdings of less than four acres. Some 90,000 households had from four to fifteen acres each, and 6,740 households had fifteen to eighty acres. Over the eighty-acre limit, a number of chiefs were in possession of one to two hundred acres.[3] It is estimated that "even more extensive are the indirect holdings of the capitalist farmers".[4]

The tendencies noted in Basutoland have also been observed in Ghana, Nigeria and other parts of West Africa, as well as in Uganda. They are also appearing in Kenya, Tanganyika and in Central Africa.

Thus Batten's warning appears to be well founded. The commercialisation of land, the creation of individual holdings, *under present-day conditions in Africa*, in which African economic development is held back by European control of land, natural resources and labour, and where the African producer, whether buying or selling, finds himself in a market dominated by powerful European monopolies, can provide no lasting solution to the lot of the African peasant. At best it can lead to the emergence of a stratified rural population, with a small comparatively rich section at the top, and a growing army of poor, landless or semi-landless proletarians at the bottom.

It is this which explains African reluctance to support the

---

[1] ibid., p. 37.   [2] NSG, op. cit., p. 120.   [3] ibid., p. 120.
[4] ibid., p. 121.

current British Colonial Office campaign for changes in traditional land tenure.

In Kenya, where the "land consolidation" scheme is leading to the establishment of larger smallholdings in the possession of a fewer number of Africans, the New Kenya Group, led by the former Minister of Agriculture for Kenya, Mr. Michael Blundell, has proposed Africans being given the right to *purchase* land on the White Highlands. Obviously, few Africans will be able to afford such a purchase. Moreover, the Kenya Government, in advocating a somewhat similar measure, has openly stated that its aim is to "provide machinery allowing leases between races in all areas".[1] This will mean allowing Europeans to purchase land in the African Reserves. It is understandable, therefore, as *The Times* has commented, that "The African elected members while demanding the opening of the White Highlands, are prepared to fight tooth-and-nail for their own land to remain in tribal control."[2]

The example of Kenya illustrates that for the *majority* of Africans all the new proposals for altering the land tenure system can lead to no improvement in their miserable conditions. As has happened so often in the past, each government measure to "assist" or "protect" them leads to more loss of land.

At the most, it will be a small section of richer African peasants, together with the European farmers, who will benefit from these changes. And it cannot be emphasised too often that this is precisely the intention of these land tenure reforms and, indeed, of all the official proposals for "land reform" in Africa. As Batten has rightly commented:[3]

"The quantity of labour offering itself at low wage rates is likely to fall sharply if colonial governments succeed in making the rural areas prosperous centres of agricultural production. It must be remembered that *rural poverty has been the greatest of all forces which help to make an ample supply of migrant labour available.*" [Own italics—J. W.]

The big European mining companies and the European

[1] *The Times*, June 8, 1959.
[2] ibid.
[3] Batten: op. cit., p. 134.

farmers and plantation owners who employ this cheap migrant labour are certainly mindful of this fact, and will therefore not find it in their interest to end this "rural poverty".

Even in West Africa, where there already exists a pattern of individual farmers—small, middle and rich—the pressure for full commercialisation of land is being exerted.

"West African land law frequently puts obstacles in the way of an African pledging as security his land and buildings. Such legislation, originally designed to protect the African from exploitation and to preserve local custom and tradition, has now outlived its usefulness; the safeguards have become shackles. . . . This question is one which merits the early attention of West African Governments, for the introduction of land registries and the replacement of the present multifarious, intricate and uncertain laws by something like a uniform system of land tenure would be a boon to the business community."[1]

But what may turn out to be "a boon to the business community" and apparently of benefit, too, to the Bank of West Africa Limited, is not necessarily in the interests of the African peasant. As long as Western monopolies and European settlers monopolise the land of Africa and dominate its markets, the majority of peasants will continue to live in abject poverty, and no changes in land tenure systems will, of themselves, save the peasants from their plight.

In fact, proposals for encouraging the development of an African farming class too often turn out to be mere devices for robbing the bulk of Africans of their land. This, for instance, is what has happened in Southern Rhodesia.

"The Native Land Husbandry Act is ostensibly intended to produce a middle-class of small African farmers, holding land in freehold instead of communally. But so far, *its main result has been to force thousands of Africans off the land*—providing a useful float of labour for European enterprise."[2]

[Own italics—J. W.]

[1] Mr. Sylvester Gates, C.B.E., chairman of the Bank of West Africa Ltd.: *The Times*, June 3, 1959.
[2] Nkomo, Joshua, op. cit., p. 58.

Cash Crops

Coupled with proposals for individual title to land is the concentration on cash crops. The cultivation of cash crops, on which government officials put so much stress as a means of strengthening the economy of the African territories, is pursued so relentlessly and with such a ruthless disregard for anything but the utmost and quickest possible profits, both for the European plantations as well as for the big European trading companies which buy up the crops from the African peasant-farmers, that the fundamental agrarian crisis is only aggravated.

TABLE I

COMPOSITION OF THE VALUE OF DOMESTIC EXPORTS OF CERTAIN
NON-SELF-GOVERNING TERRITORIES, 1950–54, AVERAGE

Territory	Two Main Agricultural Products	As % of total value of exports
Gambia	Ground nuts and oil, oil palm products	97
French West Africa	Ground nuts and oil, coffee	60
Gold Coast*	Cocoa	68
Zanzibar	Cloves and products, coco-nut products	96
Bechuanaland	Cattle, hides and skins	76
Uganda	Cotton, coffee	89
Basutoland	Wool, mohair	74
Nyasaland	Tobacco, tea	74

* Including British Togoland.
(Source: NSG, 1958, op. cit., p. 91.)

Monoculture, a typical symbol of colonialism, is nowhere more marked than in Africa. Whole territories are given up entirely to one or two crops—cocoa in Ghana, cotton in Uganda and Sudan, coffee in Kenya, palm oil in Nigeria, sisal in Tanganyika, and tobacco in Southern Rhodesia. No matter whether such production is conducted in the form of large European plantations as in Kenya or Tanganyika, or is based on individual African holdings as in Ghana or Uganda, the soil becomes overexploited and deterioration rapidly sets in.

Crop rotation, to maintain the fertility of the soil, was "often used by Africans before the coming of Europeans" says Batten,[1] but "the effect of cash-cropping has been that in many areas traditional rotations have been abandoned for the continuous

[1] Batten: op. cit., pp. 56–7.

planting of one type of crop, and the effect on the soil has naturally been bad."

Another danger introduced by cash crops is plant disease, which Batten says is "greater now than it was in earlier times". Many of the present cash crops, such as cocoa, coffee, sugar, cotton, citrus, wheat, maize, were not indigenous to Africa. Grown under African conditions, without the necessary scientific preparation or fully taking into account the different climate, these crops have become more liable to disease. The import of diseased seeds and plants are another cause of the spread of plant disease in Africa itself. The cotton boll-worm, for example, is said to have been brought into Africa from America.

The growth of cash crops, whether by European plantations or African farmers, has resulted in the wholesale destruction of valuable forest land. Coming on top of the considerable cutting down of trees by European timber farms, by mining companies to clear land and make pit props, and to provide firewood for both domestic and industrial purposes, the result has been little short of disastrous. Around Broken Hill in Northern Rhodesia, says Batten,[1] "every tree in an area of thirty square miles was thus destroyed."

In the drive for cash cropping, some thousand square miles on the northern and eastern borders of the high forest of the southern province of Nigeria are said to be cleared every year. Similar devastation is to be met with in other parts of Africa. So much forest has been cleared to make way for cocoa farms in Ghana that in one area, where it has been cleared right through to the savanna forest, the dry wind from the Sahara now blows through the gap, producing conditions dangerous for the cocoa crop itself.

Moreover, with so much land, manpower and resources given over to cash crops, mainly for export, the production of food for domestic requirements becomes neglected and famine and undernourishment spreads.

Dependence on one, or a few, cash crops leaves these territories dangerously exposed to all the vicissitudes of price changes for their products on the international market, and makes for economic instability.

The slump of the 1930s, with its accompanying catastrophic drop in agricultural prices on the world market, produced a

[1] ibid., p. 75.

deep crisis for African farmers, even in the relatively more prosperous areas of western Africa where the growing of cash crops by African farmers was well developed. Indebtedness—the dreaded Asian symbol of peasant poverty—made its appearance. A study in one village in the rich cocoa-producing region of Ghana (then the Gold Coast) made between 1932 and 1935 revealed that among the 1,200 people of this village, who had an average family income of under £22 a year, private debt had already reached a total of £4,486 on which the average rate of interest charged was thirty-seven per cent. Hancock[1] points out that at the then current cocoa prices the mortgaged farmers had no hope at all of clearing their mortgages and recovering their farms.

"The best they could hope for was that their creditors would let them stay on their land as 'caretakers' under a share-cropping arrangement."

How dangerous price fluctuations are to the African farmer was also noted by Dr. Richards in her study on Northern Rhodesia,[2] where she found African farmers on three-acre Government plots outside Luanshya "who were caught in the slump of 1933 and were threatened with eviction if they did not find the rent".

But even with favourable market prices, it is not the poor African farmer who benefits from the growth of cash crops. Batten gives the interesting illustration relevant for Uganda, of the history of a cotton shirt, passing through its various stages from raw cotton to a cotton shirt bought by Africans.[3]

"First, there is the labour of planting, hoeing and picking, with seed and tools as the necessary equipment. To this must be added the labour of transport to a buying centre and, perhaps, some capital in the form of sacks or baskets, or possibly a bicycle. At the buying station a price is paid—*perhaps a penny in the case of enough cotton to make the shirt*. . . .

---

[1] Hancock, W. K.: *Survey of British Commonwealth Affairs*, book II, part 2, p. 280, O.U.P., 1942.
[2] Richards, Dr. Audrey: *Land, Labour and Diet in Northern Rhodesia*, p. 275, London, 1939.
[3] Batten: op. cit., pp. 109–10.

Up to this stage only African labour and capital have been involved. The price is low, but little skill and hardly any capital have been used.

"The raw cotton is now ginned and baled. Here the labour is not great. It is made easy by the use of capital in the form of expensive machines and by some highly skilled labour which keeps them in good order. The reward for this service is again only a very small sum, but the great quantities of cotton the machines can quickly deal with enrich the owners of the capital and give the highly skilled men in their employ a much higher reward than the farmer enjoys. *Africans do not share much in the wealth produced at this stage:* most of the ginneries are owned by Asians or by Europeans: some Africans help to supply skilled or semi-skilled labour and are rewarded accordingly, but *the majority work as porters and at other jobs requiring little skill.*

"The cotton is now sold at a higher price to the spinners and the price is further raised to pay for the labour and capital involved in *transporting the cotton by road, rail and sea to some cotton-manufacturing country.* There the spinner and the weaver both apply further labour and capital, and the price steadily rises as the cotton takes on a more useful form. More labour and capital are employed by the wholesale and retail merchants who guide the manufactured cloth back to the African consumer. Only at the last stage, and not always then, does the African re-enter the picture, if he owns capital in the form of a sewing machine, uses African labour, and takes his reward by selling imported cloth at a higher price in the form of shirts. *But most of the labour and capital applied to turning raw cotton into shirts is non-African, and hence most of the reward*—the difference in price between a few ounces of raw cotton and the manufactured shirt—*cannot add to the total wealth owned by Africans.*"

[Own italics—J. W.]

While what Batten says here regarding the addition of more capital and more labour at each stage in the process is largely true, this is not the whole explanation. The reason why the African farmer is paid one penny for the raw cotton which he later purchases back, in the form of a shirt, for a number of shillings, is because the market at both ends—when he sells and when he buys—is dominated by the big European monopolies. It is big European companies which force the price of the raw materials produced by the African down to the barest minimum, just as it is big European companies which compel the farmer, now a purchaser, to pay through the nose for the goods he requires. This "scissors spread" between the low prices paid to Africans for agricultural raw materials and the high prices they have to pay for imported manufactured goods is a common phenomenon in all colonial countries. It is, in fact, the source of the super-profits which European capitalists make from colonial exploitation. Obviously the Western monopolies have no intention of "killing the goose that lays the golden eggs", and therefore all the official emphasis on cash crops is simply a further means of favouring the interests of the big companies which enrich themselves at Africa's expense.

In his competition with European farmers or plantation owners, the African farmer finds all the cards stacked against him. Batten is forced to admit that the European plantocracy in Africa "can bring to bear on colonial governments a weight of influence out of all proportion to their numbers, and that there is a possibility that this influence may be used to advance their own interests at the expense of those of Africans".[1] The "possibility", as Batten calls it, is, in fact, usual practice.

In this way the European farmers and their families receive privileges in education, health, social services, and public utilities as compared with Africans. Further, they receive, in addition to such social benefits, economic advantages which favour them at the expense of African farmers—tax concessions, favoured prices, access to rail routes, financial credits. And, in addition, the colonial governments favour the Europeans in the matter of the workers who are employed on their plantations: plantations are the last form of enterprise in the African colonies in which Africans are allowed to form trade unions (and, even then, they function with still greater difficulty and harassment than most); and wage minima for farms and plantations are generally much below other wage minima, and in many cases do not exist at all.

In short, European farms and plantations in Africa are given every possibility by the colonial system to flourish at the expense

[1] ibid., p. 143.

of both African workers and peasants. Significantly Batten remarks:[1]

> "Some people may doubt whether plantations could be successful in tropical Africa if they had to withstand free competition from peasant farmers while contributing their full share of taxation to the central government."

But as long as the European plantocracy retains the political power in its hands, and remains, with the mineowner, the virtual ruler of so much of the African continent, the African peasant will never be given the opportunity to engage in "free competition" with his European rival.

While in East and Central Africa, the home of the big European capitalist farm and plantation, the official talk is all of "aiding the individual African farmer", in West Africa, the traditional home of the "sturdy peasant", the striking new development is the growth of plantations, mainly European-owned.

There is no contradiction here. In East and Central Africa, the white settlers, who largely dominate the political and economic life of the territories, and who occupy a commanding position in agriculture, are seeking, very late in the day, to establish a small stratum of individual farmers who, they hope, will become their political allies and supporters in the face of the growing mass discontent of the mass of impoverished peasantry. Hence the gestures towards aiding African farmers, gestures which, as we have already seen, are largely illusory.

In West Africa, on the other hand, where the territories are rapidly winning their political independence, the traditional method of imperialist exploitation has been through the large European trading companies to whom, via countless middlemen, the African producers have had to sell their crops. Political independence will increase the power of these African capitalist farmers, who will certainly demand higher prices for their products. To offset this, and partly also to act as a means of pressure, the European monopolies are now passing over to plantation development in this part of Africa.

Thus in Ghana, acting on the advice of *European* advisers, the government is apparently going to develop the large-scale

[1] ibid., p. 144.

production of rubber. "The main hope of the government", states a correspondent in *West Africa*,[1] "is clearly placed on attracting foreign capital to establish and manage rubber plantations: approaches have already been made to the U.S. Government."

Similarly in Nigeria, plantation development has made considerable progress in the past few years. Since 1952 nearly forty new estates covering 125,000 acres have been developed, and it is estimated that by 1962 the 1952 plantation acreage in Nigeria (excluding the Cameroons, where there have been for some time considerable plantations) will have increased some six hundred per cent![2] Oil palms and rubber are the two commodities being most affected, the great Dunlop plantation of 20,000 acres in Eastern Nigeria being described by *West Africa* as "one of the most exciting economic developments Nigeria has seen". There is no doubt that the Dunlop company is more excited by the prospects than the people of Nigeria. It has been estimated that in Africa to put a man to work in a plantation costs about £500, whereas to put a man to work in a modern factory needs an investment of £2,000. It is understandable, therefore, that for some Western companies the plantation is the more attractive proposition for investment.

It is in the face of such giant plantation firms, favoured in every way, as we have seen, by colonial legislation and practice, that the African farmer strives to develop. The main beneficiary of the cash-crop concentration is the big European monopoly, both in the form of planter and as trader, along with the auxiliary transport, shipping, docks, banking, insurance, and so on.

"Land to the Tiller"

The land and agricultural policies for Africa pursued or proposed by the ·imperialist governments are not intended to assist African agriculture; their starting-point and fundamental purpose is the maintenance of colonialism and the safeguarding of imperialist interests, including a constant supply of cheap African labour.

[1] *West Africa*, April 18, 1959, p. 367.
[2] *West Africa*, May 30, 1959, p. 505.

Quite contrary are the policies advocated by the African national movements in the different territories. These policies start from the standpoint of the interests of the African people, not the imperialists; and their implementation would end the misery of the African countryside, and lay the basis for a prosperous agriculture.

"The land shall be shared among those who work it."

So runs the demand of *The Freedom Charter*, adopted by the Congress of the People at Kliptown, near Johannesburg, on June 25 and 26, 1955. It continues:

"Restriction of land ownership on a racial basis shall be ended, and all the land redivided amongst those who work it, to banish famine and land hunger;

"The State shall help the peasant with implements, seed, tractors and dams to save the soil and assist the tillers;

"Freedom of movement shall be guaranteed to all who work on the land;

"All shall have the right to occupy land wherever they choose;

"People shall not be robbed of their cattle, and forced labour and farm prisons shall be abolished."

Though adopted as a programme for the Union of South Africa, there is much in these demands that echoes the voice of Africans in almost all territories. In Asia, where feudal landlordism has been predominant for so many years, "land to the tiller" has been the slogan which has captured the hearts of millions of land-hungry peasants. In China this slogan has been put into practice; the feudal landlords were dispossessed, and their land was confiscated and distributed to the landless or land-poor peasants. All this made possible a joint effort by the peasants to abolish their age-long poverty. In a few short years the results have been phenomenal. Huge areas have been irrigated; famines have been completely eliminated; record harvests are reaped; and knowledge and electric light have come to the village.

In Africa, though feudal landlords exist in some areas, it is the European imperialist—the big plantation owner and farmer, and the trader—whose dominance is the main obstacle to a prosperous African agriculture. This is recognised by the African independence movements and finds expression in all their programmes, which, in one way or another; give voice to the idea that "to banish famine and land hunger" the land should be restored to the people of Africa and "redivided amongst those who work it".

No responsible African independence organisation, or trade union, no national or working-class leader, argues today in favour of a return to the village life of the past. Tendencies there may be to idealise what has gone, but these carry no decisive weight in the national movements for independence. What was positive in the ancient traditions—the communal feeling and activity, the knowledge of the special characteristics of African soils, climate and plant life, the forms of quasi-democratic consultation, the folk arts and crafts—these will certainly be carried forward and developed when the African continent has won its freedom.

But traditional African village life contained, too, the seeds of decay. It was based on a backward form of economy which, while it could sustain the people, gave no possibilities for development. Moreover, on the basis of this form of economy existed a social order and a culture which perpetuated ancient superstitions and shibboleths, and maintained the people in ignorance and obscurantism.

In contemplating the fate of African subsistence agriculture it is not out of place to recall the writings of Marx on India. Marx saw clearly how the impact of imperialism had destroyed the former primitive communal land ownership and subsistence agriculture, yet he shed no tears for the passing of this backward form of economy:

"Sickening as it must be to human feeling to witness those myriads of industrious, patriarchal and inoffensive social organisations disorganised and dissolved into their units, thrown into a sea of woes, and their individual members losing at the same time their ancient form of civilisation and their hereditary means of subsistence, we must not forget that these idyllic village communities, inoffensive though they may appear, had always been the solid foundation of Oriental despotism, that they restrained the human mind within the smallest possible compass, making it the unresisting tool of superstition, enslaving it beneath traditional rules, depriving it of all grandeur and historical energies."[1]

Africa's path of development has, of course, been very different from that of India, or indeed, from that of Asia as a whole, whose special features (the climate, the conditions of the soil, the existence of great desert stretches, making artificial irrigation "the first conditions of cultivation", to use Engels' term, thus necessitating the formation of strong central governments in charge of irrigation and public works, along with the usual preoccupations of war and plunder) have been analysed by Marx and Engels in their various writings, in which they speak of an "Asiatic economy".

But, despite the differences, Africa and Asia share certain things in common. Both fell under the heel of Western imperialism. In both continents the existing communal village life and subsistence agriculture were destroyed and the people impoverished as a result. In both, to borrow the words of Marx, "England has broken down the whole framework of . . . society, without any symptoms of reconstruction yet appearing. *This loss of the old world, with no gain of a new one,* imparts a particular kind of melancholy to the present misery"[2] of the people. [Own italics— J. W.]

In bringing about the destruction of the old order in Africa the imperialists have, just as in India, done nothing to "emancipate or materially mend the social condition of the mass of the people".[3] On the contrary, they have plunged the African peasant down to the utmost depths of poverty and disaster, producing as a result that peculiarly African phenomenon, the *continually migrating peasant-worker,* confronted with the "loss of his old world", yet "with no gain of a new one". It was not without reason that a report on the effects of migrant labour in Nyasaland, in 1953, correctly forecast that:

"the Nyasaland-born natives will have acquired a mistrust

[1] Marx, Karl: "The British Rule in India", *New York Daily Tribune,* June 25, 1853. In *Marx and Engels On Colonialism,* p. 36, Lawrence & Wishart, London, 1960.
[2] ibid., p. 33.
[3] Marx, Karl: "The Future Results of British Rule in India," *New York Daily Tribune,* August 8, 1853. In above volume *On Colonialism,* p. 80.

and loathing for administration by the white people which
has made a wilderness and called it peace."[1]

But a "wilderness called peace" exists not only in Nyasaland.
Similar wildernesses are to be found throughout the African
continent. Sixty years of imperialist exploitation have been
sufficient to wreak this terrible damage. Real peace, and the
transformation of these wildernesses into the flourishing fields
and farms which a free people, aided by modern technique and
State aid, could create, demands, as a first step, the elimination
of colonial rule and the return of the land to the African people.

[1] Cmd. 5949, para. 95.

CHAPTER TWO

"WE REJECT THE POLL-TAX SYSTEM"

THERE are very few authorities on Africa nowadays who would contest the view that the poll-tax system imposed on the African people by their European rulers has played a major part in breaking up the traditional subsistence agriculture and village life, and in driving Africans out to seek labour in European-owned mines and farms and other enterprises.

It is important, however, to appreciate that the introduction of the system of taxing Africans *irrespective of their income*—for under poll tax every African male over eighteen (sometimes sixteen) is taxable—was a deliberate measure intended quite openly to create an African wage-labour force for the European masters. It was never looked upon mainly as a source of revenue, as is the usual case with taxation systems, but as a means of forcing the African into a money economy—which means, in the prevailing conditions of Africa, working for wages. Taxation of Africans was generally introduced towards the end of the nineteenth or beginning of the twentieth centuries, especially after the discovery of diamonds and gold in the Union of South Africa, and the discovery of minerals in other territories.

"It was difficult initially to persuade Africans to leave their villages and to come to industrial centres to work for the white man. Whatever processes it is alleged were used to stimulate the movement—*various forms of cash taxation, like poll tax and hut tax*—it has increased steadily since the discovery of diamonds and the opening up of the fields in the latter part of the nineteenth century, and each new industry has attracted from all directions a flood of migrant labourers."[1] [Own italics—J. W.]

[1] Niddrie, David: "The Road to Work: Human Problems in British Central Africa," *Rhodes-Livingstone Journal*, **15**, No. 15, 1954.

The same general point is made by Schapera[1] in his study on Bechuanaland. He describes how after the discovery of diamonds in the Union from 1870, and then later of gold on the Witwatersrand in 1884, the demand for labour arose. To cope with this demand various measures were taken to persuade, cajole or compel labour to leave the rural areas in favour of working in the mines, until *in 1899, the Administration for the first time imposed a hut tax, and thus forced upon the people the necessity of finding a regular sum of money each year.* [Own italics—J. W.]

It is true, of course, that there had been some degree of wage labour prior to this—as domestic servants to traders or missionaries or on railway and building jobs—but, generally speaking, it was only after the imposition of cash taxes that wage labour really began to be an important factor in the African economy.

Schapera[2] has described the process in these words:

"The people have been drawn into an elaborate system of exchange economy, through which they are linked up with and even dependent upon the markets of the world. New commodities of many kinds have been introduced, many of which can be obtained only from the traders and other external sources of supply. . . . *Money has also become established as the principal medium of exchange, and the imposition of taxes, both by the Administration and by the tribal authorities, has made its acquisition a universal necessity.*" [Own italics—J. W.]

Orde Browne,[3] in writing of the various forms of pressure utilised originally to create wage labour in Africa, refers to "heavy taxation" which was "imposed so as to provide a stimulus".

In Kenya, the same process went ahead.

"When Europeans began to build the railway inland from Mombasa to Uganda, they were unable to induce Africans . . . to undertake the manual work involved. . . . *When taxes were imposed on the African, first the hut tax and then the poll tax, work for money became a necessity on his part. In other words, his first*

---

[1] Schapera, op. cit., p. 7.
[2] ibid., p. 8.
[3] Browne, Orde G. St. J. *The African Labourer*, p. 29, London, 1933.

acquaintance with money in association with work was with it as an
imposition."[1]   [Own italics—J. W.]

That the poll-tax system was, in fact, devised with the precise
aim of driving African peasants out to work is clearly shown by
statements of the European settlers in Kenya. One Governor,
Sir Percy Girouard, is reported to have said:

> "We consider that taxation is the only possible method of
> compelling the native to leave his Reserve for the purpose of
> seeking work. Only in this way can the cost of living be
> increased for the native, and . . . it is on this that the supply
> of labour and the price of labour depends. To raise the rate of
> wages would not increase but would diminish the supply of
> labour. A rise in the rate of wages would enable the hut or
> poll tax of a family, sub-tribe, or tribe to be earned by fewer
> external workers. . . ."[2]

Buell[3] states that a "large number of witnesses before the
Labour Commission of 1913 believed that native taxes should
be raised to increase the labour supply". He adds that in 1922 one
farmers' association passed a resolution urging that taxes should
be collected during the coffee season "so as to induce natives to
go out and work". Another farmers' association "urged the
government to increase the poll tax to relieve the acute labour
shortage, and to remit this tax if the native worked a certain
period of time for a European".

Writing a despatch to the British Foreign Office in 1896
concerning conditions in Nyasaland,[4] Sir Harry Johnston,
famous "Empire Builder" in this part of Africa, emphasised:

> "Given abundance of cheap Native labour, the financial
> security of the Protectorate is established. . . . All that needs
> to be done is for the Administration to act as friends of both
> sides, and introduce the Native labourer to the European

---

[1] *African Labour Efficiency Survey*, p. 58, London, 1949. Ed. by C. H. Northcott.
[2] *East Africa Standard*, February 8, 1913. Quoted by Norman Leys: *Kenya*,
p. 186, London, 1925.
[3] Buell, Raymond Leslie: *The Native Problem in Africa*, vol. i, p. 331, London,
1928.
[4] *Trade and General Conditions Report*, 1895–6.

capitalist. A gentle insistence that the Native should contribute his fair share to the revenue of the country by paying his tax is all that is necessary on our part to ensure his taking a share in life's labour which no human being should avoid."

An obvious African retort to this nauseating hyprocrisy is that since the European coupon clippers do not take "a share in life's labour which no human being should avoid" they have lost all claim to be regarded as human beings.

It is not without significance that, generally speaking, it was at the beginning of the twentieth century—that is, at the dawn of the imperialist epoch, when the export of European capital to Africa (and to other colonial regions) was stepped up and the exploitation of African labour became an important factor in the profit-making activities of the big European companies—that taxation of Africans on a capitation basis began to be introduced. Poll tax was introduced in Southern Rhodesia in 1904, and hut and poll tax in Northern Rhodesia in 1905. Hut tax was first introduced in Kenya in 1901, and taxation of Africans in Tanganyika was introduced by the German authorities in 1897. (Since 1922, when Tanganyika became a British mandate, and later a Trust Territory, the Africans have paid a hut tax, together with a poll tax for every African male over sixteen who does not own a hut.)

In French possessions in Africa the system of *prestation* was introduced. This was an obligation on Africans to pay a form of labour tax by performing labour for a specific period. Performance of work was redeemable by a cash payment—but since the acquisition of cash usually meant going to work, the usual double squeeze operated, and labour was thus extracted from the African in one way if not the other.

In the Belgian Congo a labour tax, "in practice unlimited in duration" according to Hailey, was imposed on Africans. In 1910 it was replaced by a capitation tax on adult males.

Portuguese African territories were subjected to similar taxation pressures associated with the obligation to perform labour. The usual pattern is a personal tax on all adult males over sixteen and under sixty. The tax payments may be discharged by work for government and municipal departments and, in Angola, for private employers. Hailey points out that in the

Portuguese territories "a certain number of observers have asserted that the application of the tax laws is utilised by officers of the Administration for securing the labour required by the European cocoa, coffee, or sisal plantations or enterprises such as the diamond mines".[1] On the grounds of delay in payment of taxes, Africans are pressured into discharging their debts by performing labour.

"Firstly to Pay Taxes, Secondly to Live"

From its commencement taxation of Africans, as an economic prod to drive them out to seek wage employment, has never been regarded by the Administration as a single, self-sufficient method of securing labour. It has always been linked with the land-restriction policies examined in the previous chapter, with the deliberate destruction of the old self-sufficient African subsistence agriculture, and with various forms of compulsion and labour recruitment, associated with the whole system of migrant labour, which are examined in more detail in later chapters.

Taxation of Africans could not have had such a decisive effect on compelling them to engage in wage labour if other avenues were open to them to obtain cash. But this is precisely what the imperialists were determined to prevent; and thus, as we have seen above, the Africans were robbed of the best lands, millions of acres of good farming land were deliberately left idle so that African farmers could not enrich themselves, Africans were overcrowded into Reserves, robbed openly of their cattle, often denied the right of growing certain cash crops, or restricted by quota systems, discriminated against in comparison with the European farmer as regards transport or the selling-price of his crops, and in countless other ways so hampered and harassed and stifled that to earn cash meant, in reality, to work for the Europeans.

Schapera has explained the dilemma of the Africans in these words:

"They could increase the output of their traditional forms of production, and so provide a surplus for export; they could

[1] Hailey (Revised): op. cit., pp. 675–6.

produce new crops and other commodities specially for the market; or they could work for cash wages. *The first two methods have up to the present proved inadequate. Wage-labour has consequently become an indispensable source of income for the people generally.*"[1]

He adds significantly that in Bechuanaland the income derived by Africans from agriculture and animal husbandry "*is not enough, and has to be supplemented by working at some paid occupation ...*"
[Own italics—J. W.]

De Briey,[2] writing of a study undertaken at the request of the Bechuanaland Administration, states that during the years 1938–42 the population spent an average of £709,955 each year, but their income was only £242,500, leaving an annual deficit of £467,500. Expenditure, points out de Briey, was "an irreducible minimum", because, apart from expenses on food, it consisted of direct and indirect taxes. To make up the deficit by the sale of livestock was denied to most, since "only three out of four families can earn a regular income from their livestock", and only one family in every fourteen possesses any animals. And so, compelled to pay taxes, the African "*has no alternative to enrolling himself as a wage-earner in order to balance the family budget by means of his wages*".

The same compulsion was to be seen at work in Northern Rhodesia, where, at the time that Buell made his voyages in the 1920s, "the absence of railways and feeder roads" made it "impossible for the natives to produce crops for export. . . . Inasmuch as they are unable to sell products of their toil, *most of them must, in order to pay this tax, seek work from European employers.*"[3]
[Own italics—J. W.]

Hancock[4] makes the same point, mentioning the five northern districts of Nyasaland where the total sum collected in taxation in one year amounted to £18,379. But wages earned locally amounted to only £13,000, and the sale of crops to a mere £1,000. "How could the natives," asks Hancock, "secure the extra £4,379 which the government took from them in taxation? *Only by*

[1] Schapera: op. cit., p. 122.
[2] Briey, P. de: "Industrialisation and Social Problems in Africa," *International Labour Review*, May 1951, **lxiii**, No. 5, p. 479.
[3] Buell: op. cit., p. 240.
[4] Hancock, op. cit., p. 115.

selling their labour outside the Protectorate." [Own italics—J. W.] In addition to the point stressed by Hancock, however, it is worth noting in his example that as much as £17,379, in fact, had to be earned by wage labour to pay off the taxation, clearly demonstrating what a decisive role has been played by the poll-tax system in forcing Africans to take up wage employment.

Segal's pointed remarks on the Union of South Africa[1] are also of relevance here:

> "Since it is, of course, impossible that their shrivelled farms should support so many millions, the Africans survive by exporting their able-bodied males to the white farms and urban areas, subsidising their crops with the cash wage of migratory labour. And should diligence and luck make it somehow unnecessary for many of the men to desert the Reserves, the poll tax levied on all African males between the ages of eighteen and sixty-five was increased by a minimum of seventy-five per cent last year to £1 15s. 0d. a year. Thus, what land hunger cannot accomplish, is achieved by the government itself."

Thus, from its very inception, taxation was closely linked with the official policy of ruining African agriculture. These were two arms of the same attack. Impoverish the African with one arm—and demand cash taxes with the other. There was, for the majority of Africans, only one way to obtain cash under these circumstances—work for the European. Or, as Muga Gicaru has explained in his moving description of the life of the squatters in Kenya,[2] "go on working for the white man in order *firstly to pay taxes* and secondly to live."   [Own italics—J. W.]

Taxation and Labour Migration

Broadly speaking, the process described in the above pages can be paralleled in every African territory. Taxation and the ruin of African agriculture led to the creation of African wage labour. And since the opportunities for wage labour did not lie

---

[1] Segal, Ronald M.: "The Creeping Tragedy of South Africa," *New Statesman*, February 28, 1959, p. 295.
[2] Gicaru, Muga: *Land of Sunshine*, p. 19, Lawrence & Wishart, London, 1958.

within the reserves themselves, and often not even within the particular territory, labour for Africans meant migration. Consequently, taxation of Africans was not only associated with the drive to obtain supplies of African labour but was also linked with labour migration and the subsequent forms of labour recruitment.

Schapera points out that "since the earliest days of recruiting, one of the methods by which labour agents have induced Natives to enter into contracts of employment has been to give them an advance on their wages."[1] This has been particularly true as regards advances to pay taxes, and in fact the whole system of migrant labour and labour recruitment has frequently been directly connected with taxation and its collection.

Schapera points out that:

"District Officers themselves have at times actively encouraged recruitment.[2] This has usually taken the form of instituting a special drive against tax defaulters, the men being warned that they will be prosecuted unless they pay their arrears immediately, *if necessary by taking an advance from a labour agent.* Technically this may not have constituted coercion but the Natives concerned would almost certainly have interpreted it as an instruction to seek work on the mines or elsewhere unless they were able to pay."[3]   [Own italics—J. W.]

Nor does the Administration hesitate to put pressure on the chiefs to compel men to migrate in order to earn their taxation money. Schapera says:

"The chiefs were paid a percentage commission on the amount of tax collected from their subjects, but were also continuously harassed by the Administration if their tax returns fell below expectation. Labour migration was a convenient means of enabling people to pay their tax, and conse-

[1] Schapera: op. cit., p. 108.
[2] The present writer was assured by M. W. Kanyama Chiume, a former member of the Nyasaland Legislative Council, that the same thing happens in Nyasaland, even young teenage boys being persuaded in this way to migrate for work in the mines.
[3] Schapera: op. cit., p. 151.

quently the chiefs almost everywhere began urging and even forcing poor men out to work."[1]

Thus the pressure exerted on the chiefs by the Administration was simply transferred by the chiefs into pressure to force men out to work—and this, indeed, was exactly what was intended.[2] *It was not revenue which was the main aim of the poll-tax system, but labour.* And to obtain this labour, says Schapera, the chief would sometimes call in the labour recruiting agent from Zeerust, "and the men concerned would be taken away by lorry, even if they objected". He adds that when he discussed this matter in 1932, when men were similarly sent to work in the mines against their will, he was told that "many men, who would not have otherwise thought of going out to work, were in effect forced to by the fear that, if they were unable to find money for their tax, they too would be sent away to the mines".[3] Either way, whether they agreed to be recruited or not, the mines would get them.

How serious is this threat to tax defaulters is revealed by Hailey.[4] Dealing with Tanganyika in the period up to 1951, he says that the number of tax defaulters who discharged their liability by work reached as high as 59,000 a year.[5]

And always the end result is the same. Go out to work for the white man to earn your tax, or go to prison for failure to pay tax and be forcibly sent, as convict labour or tax defaulter, to work for the white man. Either way, the European wins, the African loses; either way, the African has to work, and the European master gets his labour.

Poll Tax is a Labour Tax

In describing the causes of labour migration, Schapera says[6]

[1] ibid., p. 152.

[2] A striking example of how the tax system is used to force men to work was revealed by the Report of the Commission Appointed to Enquire into the Disturbances which occurred in the Port of Tanga, in August 1939. (Dar-es-Salaam, 1940.) The report revealed that the strike-breakers used by the Tanganyika Landing and Shipping Company were "tax labourers" from the Maweni "labour camp". *The company paid off the tax arrears of these men, and then took them on as labourers!*

[3] Schapera: op. cit., p. 153.

[4] Hailey (Revised), op. cit.

[5] Officially this practice has since been abolished.

[6] Schapera: op. cit., p. 121.

that "certainly the most important" cause of all "is economic necessity". An enquiry he made among men who had recently returned from the Union of South Africa revealed the following: Of 297 replies only six said that they had originally left home for miscellaneous reasons such as love of adventure, attractions of town life, dislike of herding cattle, and so on. All the remainder said they had gone for the specific aim of earning money, and the particular purposes for which money was required provided this striking picture:

To pay taxes	119
To pay taxes, buy clothes, etc. ..	83
Because of poverty	39
To purchase clothing	29
To buy cattle, clothing, etc. ..	16
To give to one's parents	5
	291

This analysis helps to demolish the argument so often put forward that labour migration arises because of the need to obtain the bride price, or a simple adventurous desire to "go to town". Over two-thirds (202) of those in Schapera's sample mentioned taxation as a key cause of their departure; and altogether about eighty per cent (241) were apparently *compelled to migrate by sheer poverty or the necessity of finding money to pay taxes.*

These figures, though not decisive—for the sample is small, and relates to only part of one territory, Bechuanaland—do, as Schapera says, "point to an obvious conclusion", that the majority of men are driven abroad by economic needs. One can go farther than Schapera here, and state that of these needs taxation is a key one.

Now this is extremely important; for a number of authorities, including Schapera himself, in defiance of his own figures, though compelled to admit that taxation of Africans on a capitation basis played a key role in the formation of African labour, claim that it is no longer of importance.

Schapera constantly contradicts himself on this matter. He

rightly says[1] that: "One series of special wants is represented by taxation. Unlike many other wants, taxes and levies cannot be postponed; unless they are paid annually by a certain date, prosecution may follow. Hence, if a man has no other means of raising the money, he will go out to work." Schapera himself demonstrates very ably that, generally speaking, "a man has no other means of raising the money"—and yet he attempts to play down the role of taxation, arguing in the face of his own figures that "a more common incentive . . . is the desire to purchase clothes or some other goods". On what does he base this assertion? Not on the analysis of the 297 replies he received to his questions; these clearly show that taxation played a role in influencing the emigration of two-thirds of the workers questioned—and of these taxation alone was given as the reason by over a half. Schapera argues that since not every man recruited to the mines accepts an advance for the payment of taxes "this can only mean that he has discharged his fiscal obligation". Did it never occur to Schapera at what a cost this African worker discharged his obligation? That it was precisely the sacrifice entailed in doing this which left him in such a desperate plight that he had to go out to work to provide for his other necessities?

But Schapera, in fact, exposes his own argument. The very figures he gives[2] for the number who do *not* take advances for taxes show that out of 292 cases examined no less than 205 took advances of £2 10s. 6d. each to pay taxes, tribal levy and war levy, a further 39 took £1 2s. 6d. for war levy, and only 48—about sixteen per cent—took no advances at all for taxes or levies.

In an appendix, Schapera provides for the year 1932 a month-by-month analysis of the goods consigned by rail to Africans in the Kgatla Reserve. That is to say, a list of the goods sent back by migrant workers. Taking one of these months' imports as an example, that of November, we find the following revealing catalogue:

"2 bags mealie meal; 1 pcl bag; 1 bag malt; 1 bag Kafir corn; 1 bag mealie meal; 1 bag mealie meal; 1 bag Kafir corn; 1 bag mealie meal; 1 bag salt; 1 bag plough shares; 1 bag blankets; 1 parcel twine; 1 case clothes, 1 empty drum;

[1] ibid., p. 141.   [2] ibid., op, cit., p.110.

1 package chains; 1 bag Kafir corn; 1 pcl clothing; 1 pcl clothing; 1 parcel chains; 1 bag sugar; 1 bag clothing; 2 sewing machines; 1 bag clothing and blankets, 1 bag pots and pans; 1 bed, etc., 1 chair; 1 pcl thatching twine; 1 plough; 1 bag mealie meal, 1 bag mealies; 1 bale buckets; 1 pcl groceries; 1 saw, 1 bag dishes; 1 pcl grain bags; 4 chairs, 1 bag blankets; 6 bags mealies; 1 bag Kafir corn; 2 gates (chief); 3 empty drums; 1 case blankets, 1 case soap; 1 empty drum; 1 bag mealie meal, 1 bag Kafir corn; 2 plough wheels; 1 door; 1 plough."

What a picture this tells of the plight of these migrant workers! One of the main items they send back is *food, and the cheapest possible food at that.* And for the rest of these pitiable articles, in which clothes and blankets predominate, is it not clear that economic necessity, not the search for luxuries, has driven these men out to work?

That being the case, how can it be argued that taxation, which in 1958 was increased to £2 in Bechuanaland, is not a major factor? Taxes of £2 have to be taken alongside the average earnings in the South African mines of about £1 a week. The African cannot pay-as-he-earns. He must pay his taxes in a lump sum. In Britain, where average industrial earnings are about £12 a week, that would mean paying out £24 cash down. But even that is not a real equivalent, for the African worker is always on the verge of absolute poverty. Every penny, quite literally, is a real sacrifice for him. To find the cash for his taxes means therefore either obtaining it by some immense sacrifice—which then compels him to seek work to make up for his loss; or to accept a wage advance from a labour recruiter, in order to pay off the tax. In either case, the end result is the same; *the African is driven out to work through the taxation system.*

Hailey, in trying to play down the role of taxation today, argues that "broadly speaking the direct Native tax has ceased to present the number of unpleasant problems which half a century ago were so obvious to observers of African affairs".[1] Dealing specifically with the Union of South Africa, he claims:

"Though the taxation of Africans was designed in the first instance mainly with the object of increasing the supply of

[1] Hailey (Revised), op. cit., p. 681.

labour, especially in the mines, this object is now no longer
of importance. It is significant that the rate of tax has not been
increased in the thirty years that have since elapsed"

—that is, from the time of the 1925 Native Taxation and
Development Act.

Unfortunately for Hailey, a large part of his argument has
been unkindly demolished for him by the recent action of the
Government of the Union of South Africa. As from January 1,
1959, the poll tax payable by African men was increased from
£1 to £1 15s.[1] In commenting on this increase, a leader of
the African National Congress, Moses Kotane, asserts:

> "Like the pass laws and permit regulations *the taxation of
> Africans is imposed essentially for labour compulsion purposes.*"[2]

Kotane's whole analysis is of considerable importance, since it
expresses the clear-cut view of an African leader himself on this
question, and it is striking to see how contrary it is to the view of
such a European authority on African affairs as Hailey.

In explaining African opposition to the poll-tax system, Kotane
states that "the majority of those who are forced to pay taxes are
too poor to do so" and that they are "already overtaxed". In
this respect, he points out that, in addition to the compulsory
poll tax, Africans have to pay such taxes as the hospital tax,
2s. 6d.; local tax, 10s.; education tax, 2s. a month; services levy,
3s. a week; pass fees, 2s. a month—apart from fines and compound
fees. And this in face of an average wage of £12 a month in the
towns, and only £2 2s. 10d. a month on the farms. Citing the
fact that a hundred and fifty to two hundred thousand Africans
in the Union are imprisoned annually for their failure to pay the
former tax of £1, Kotane states:

> "It is obvious that the new taxes will be a tremendous
> hardship and cruelty for the already suffering African
> people."

---

[1] Significantly, it has also been increased considerably in recent years in a
number of other African territories.
[2] Kotane, Moses: "The Poll Tax Increase", *Fighting Talk*, September 1958,
xii, No. 6, p. 5.

Summing up his estimate of the role of the poll-tax system, Kotane asserts, in opposition to the views of Hailey and others:

".... *the poll tax, unlike taxes paid by non-Africans, is a labour tax imposed as a form of pressure to compel Africans to leave their areas to go to work for Europeans. It was never intended for amenities and social services. . . . Africans are still driven by the tax out of the Reserves to the farms and to the towns, and off the farms into the towns.*"

It is with justice, therefore, that Moses Kotane, speaking in effect for all Africans,[1] declares:

"*We reject the poll-tax system.*"

---

[1] Statistics, facts and arguments are not the only forms of proof. The reaction of people is often a far more important means of judging the economic and social effect of an aspect of government policy. And in this respect it is surely not without significance that some of the most important mass movements in Africa in the last sixty years have been associated with protests against taxes (the Bai Bureh War in Sierra Leone in 1898; Bambata's rebellion in Natal in 1906; Kenya in the 1920s, Nigeria in the 1930s, and Northern Rhodesia in the 1940s are cases in point). In 1955 demonstrations and riots against taxes took place in Sierra Leone—the leader of the demonstrators, Peter Kamara, protesting to the District Commissioner: "*The tax is too much—we cannot earn it.*" And as recently as January 1960 serious riots took place in Bukadi, Uganda, against tax assessments: a number of chiefs (who are responsible for helping to assess and collect taxes) were killed by the angry people, while over 1500 demonstrators were arrested, and some killed by police fire.

CHAPTER THREE

"NOW WE MUST STEAL HIS LIMBS"

COMPULSION to work for Europeans has been the lot of the African for over four hundred years. From the enormous and shameful slave traffic of the sixteenth to nineteenth centuries down to the present day, African labour for Europeans has been associated with force and compulsion.

Modern capitalism, said Marx, dates from the sixteenth century. And an essential element in its growth was slavery and the slave trade.

> "The discovery of gold and silver in America, the extirpation, enslavement and entombment in mines of the aboriginal population, the beginning of the conquest and looting of the East Indies, *the turning of Africa into a warren for the commercial hunting of black-skins*, signalised the rosy dawn of the era of capitalist production."[1]   [Own italics—J. W.]

Stigmatising the above "idyllic proceedings" as "the chief momenta of primitive accumulation", Marx drew attention to the special place allotted to slavery in the growth of British capitalism. *"Liverpool waxed fat on the slave-trade. This was its method of primitive accumulation."*[2] [Own italics—J. W.] Great as was the slave traffic carried on in the seventeenth and eighteenth centuries by the Dutch, French, Spanish and Portuguese, it was nothing compared with the slave trade of Britain. "Nearly four times as many African slaves were transported in British bottoms as in all the ships of all other nations combined", wrote Redding.[3] This monstrous slave trade and the resultant slavery itself were pivots in the emergence and growth of capitalist industry.

[1] Marx, Karl: *Capital*, vol. i, p. 751, Lawrence & Wishart, 1954 edition.
[2] ibid., p. 759.   [3] Redding, J. S.: *They Came in Chains*, p. 17, New York, 1950.

"Without slavery," explained Marx,[1] "you have no cotton; without cotton you have no modern industry. It is slavery that has given the colonies their value; it is the colonies that have created world trade, and it is world trade that is the precondition of large-scale industry."

But while English "gentlemen" built up their huge fortunes from the blood and bones of African slaves, for Africa it was a catastrophe. DuBois has written:

"Whole regions were depopulated, whole tribes disappeared. It was the rape of a continent seldom if ever paralleled in ancient or modern history."[2]

On the estimate that for every slave imported into the western hemisphere about five were killed in Africa or died on the high seas, DuBois asserts that slavery meant to Africa the frightful loss of some *sixty million souls*. Marx spoke simple truth when he declared that capitalism came into the world "dripping from head to foot, from every pore, with blood and dirt."[3]

Any consideration of African labour today, of its birth, growth, conditions and struggles, must always take account of this terrible background. Not only will the memory of this disaster never be erased from the minds of the African people, but its very basis, *forced* labour, is still a widespread practice of the European exploiters who have battened on the African soil and people for so long. It was not until towards the end of the nineteenth century that the European powers reluctantly abandoned direct slave labour, only to substitute for it new, slightly less open forms of compulsion, forms which combined economic pressure with "legal" obligations. In previous chapters we have examined how the imperialists used the economic compulsions of land hunger, poverty and the poll tax, to drive Africans out to work. But economic compulsion alone has never satisfied the European employer, especially in view of the open unwillingness of Africans to take up European employment. And if the African would not willingly work for Europeans, *then he had to be made to*.

---

[1] Marx, Karl: *The Poverty of Philosophy*, Lawrence & Wishart, London, 1956, p. 124.
[2] DuBois, W. E. B.: *Black Folk: Then and Now*, p. 142, New York, 1939.
[3] Marx, Karl: *Capital*, vol. i, p. 760.

"We have stolen his land. Now we must steal his limbs. . . .
Compulsory labour is the corollary of our occupation of the country."[1]

Such was the demand of Colonel Grogan, notorious leader of
the white settlers in Kenya. Acting on this principle, the European
authorities throughout Africa hastened to comply with the wishes
of white settlers and European companies, and introduced various
forms of compulsory labour to back up the economic compulsion
of land shortage and the poll tax. Admitting that "one cannot
entirely neglect the part which it [compulsion] has played in the
past history of African development", Hailey[2] says that: "Its
use by some of the Administrations in order to secure manpower
for public purposes has been defended on the ground that it is an
adaptation of the indigenous usage by which communal labour
is used for making village roads or the like." This claim of the
Administrations will not stand up to any serious examination.
Hailey himself agrees that "the analogy is not convincing". Yet
his reason for saying this—"this traditional use of labour seldom
took the peasant far from his home"—is only part of the answer,
and a very small part at that. Noon[3] has correctly pointed out
that, although a certain amount of obligatory communal labour
was traditional in African society, one must not lose sight of the
fact that "forced labour in Native society was well safeguarded
by customary usages and that, therefore, it never attained the
degree of exploitation characteristic of the early years of European
domination of the continent."

Bad as were the conditions under which forced labour was
exacted by Europeans from Africans, even this is not the basic
difference between traditional communal labour and forced
labour. The former, at least in its origins, was a communal effort
for communal interests. The latter, however, was a brutal form
of colonial exploitation, in which Africans were forced by non-
African rulers to perform labour not in the interests of the community but in the interests of the profit-seeking Europeans. It
was, in fact, little removed from direct slavery; and consequently
has always been most detested by Africans both as a form of

---

[1] Grogan, Colonel Ewart S., in *From Cape to Cairo* by Ewart S. Grogan and
Arthur H. Sharp, London, 1902.
[2] Hailey (Revised): op. cit., p. 1362.
[3] Noon: op. cit., pp. 6-7.

robbery and as a monstrous humiliation and indignity. It is not without significance that a major cause of the big protest movement in Kenya in 1923 was opposition to the system of forced labour then being operated.

General hostility to the forced-labour systems in Africa became so widespread in the 1920s that in 1930 all the major powers with colonial possessions in Africa, with the exception of Portugal, felt obliged to ratify the Geneva Convention on Forced Labour. This convention, however, although it acted as a form of moral pressure on the powers concerned, was so riddled with exceptions that the basis for utilising various forms of compulsion to secure labour still remained. Hailey has admitted that "the exceptions are important: compulsory military service, convict labour, civic obligations, work in any emergency whether in war or peace, and minor communal services. . . ."[1]

The emergencies mentioned by Hailey are important, for it is the common rule in British possessions to grant colonial governors exceptional powers over persons and property during times of declared emergencies; and such declarations are made not in circumstances which would be regarded in any country as a national emergency but on each and every occasion when the African people show any degree of challenge to their miserable conditions of life. Thus even a strike becomes a pretext to declare a state of emergency; and by this device, assisted by his powers to direct labour in such circumstances, the governor always has a ready means of obtaining unwilling strike-breakers or compelling strikers to return to work.

Although, as Noon says,[2] the 1930 Forced Labour Convention meant that from then on labour could "no longer be impressed for purposes of private employment", in practice this has not been true. During the Second World War, for example, forced labour was used in a number of private enterprises in Kenya, Tanganyika, Nigeria, Sierra Leone, Belgian Congo and French African territories by the simple device of classifying these enterprises as "essential industries". It is instructive, as Noon has remarked,[3] to note the alacrity with which European employers

---

[1] Hailey (Revised): op. cit., p. 1365.
[2] Noon: op. cit., p. 7.
[3] ibid., p. 8.

and colonial officials in Africa "return to forced-labour measures at the slightest provocation".

Habits do, indeed, die hard, and in one form or another compulsion to work is still exercised by the Administrations in most African territories. In Southern Rhodesia, for example, unemployed Africans can be conscripted for up to ninety days' labour for agricultural purposes. In Northern Rhodesia and Nyasaland, says Hailey, Native Authority Ordinances allow the use of compulsion in an emergency. In Tanganyika, under the Native Authority Ordinance, legal provision exists for exacting compulsory labour for "essential public works and services". For the years 1951–2 Hailey provides the following figures:[1]

> 4,102 men requisitioned for porterage duties
> (10,656 man-days worked)
> 10,461 men requisitioned for minor public works
> (95,203 man-days)
> 4,578 for work undertaken for Native Authorities
> (104,513 man-days)

This is a total of some 19,000 men forced to perform some 210,000 man-days' work.

In Uganda compulsory labour is allowed under the Native Authority Ordinance for up to thirty days; those unwilling to perform this work may commute their labour by paying cash. In Nigeria and the Cameroons there still remains compulsion for porterage; and in Sierra Leone, under the 1932 Forded Labour Ordinance, compulsory labour may be used for construction and maintenance of public highways and government buildings, the movement of government stores, and the transport of private persons in cases of "urgent necessity".

As far as French possessions in Africa are concerned, officially speaking, compulsory labour is now prohibited by an Act of April 11, 1946, and by the Labour Code of December 15, 1952. Hailey points out, however, that "despite the comprehensive terms of these laws, reports from French West Africa and the Cameroons continue to imply the existence of various types of labour which contain some element of compulsion".[2] This is

---

[1] Hailey (Revised): op. cit., p. 1367.
[2] ibid., p. 1369.

confirmed by the actions of the workers themselves in these territories and the constant demands of their trade unions that the Labour Code, for the enactment of which they fought so long and so bitterly, should be fully applied in practice and not just left as a paper document. Among the forms in which forced labour is still exacted in these territories one can mention the use of tax defaulters and the *prestation* system. (See also previous chapter.)

In the Belgian Congo, despite official claims to have followed an enlightened labour policy for the past two decades, a number of decrees laying down various forms of forced labour are still on the statute book;[1] while in Ruanda-Urundi amending legislation of 1949 provides for the use of tax defaulters on building roads, on porterage and for the construction of State works. It is widely believed—and Hailey gives credence to this allegation—that unpaid forced labour was used in Liberia in the reconstruction of roads in the recent period.

"Little Better than Slavery Itself"

But it is not only that there are specific cases in which African workers are subjected to forced labour. The whole labour system in Africa is based on thinly disguised forms of compulsion. As Marx has reminded us, the colonial system is itself "brute force,"[2] and Africa is no exception.

True, the African workers have organised and, by dint of bitter struggle, have won certain working-class rights, mainly in the teeth of bitter opposition from the big European monopolies. But these rights are still limited, under constant attack, and tell only part of the picture of present-day labour in Africa. One does not need the tragic hell of the prison-camp at Hola, where men were beaten to death *for refusal to carry out forced labour*, to demonstrate that labour in Africa is linked with compulsion.

The use of force to compel African prisoners at Hola to work was no isolated incident. In fact, throughout the emergency period in Kenya, forced labour was used on a really mass scale. At one time it was estimated that as many as 70,000 prisoners

[1] ibid., p. 1371.
[2] Marx, Karl: *Capital*, vol. i, p. 751.

in Kenya were engaged on forced labour. Some reports place it even higher. Apart from work on clearing the bush and soil conservation, these prisoners were compelled to work in quarries, on building new roads, stone-breaking and constructing the new Embakasi airport.[1] Not only were women also compelled to perform much of this labour,[2] but a former rehabilitation officer of the Kenya Government[3] reported that juveniles, in shackles, had been made to perform work. She added that, according to information from an American missionary, the duty officer at Kamili prison had stated that he had seen *a child of only eight years, in shackles, working in the quarry.*

The use of prison labour is a common practice in British colonies in Africa, but in times of emergency, when the Governor has absolute powers over the use of African manpower, forced labour is used on a really large scale.

Kenya is no exception here. The crisis in Central Africa and the resultant declarations of emergency in the three territories was followed by extensive use of forced labour. Especially was this so in Nyasaland, but it was practised on a considerable scale in Northern Rhodesia, too.[4] Furthermore, legislation enacted in Nyasaland and Northern Rhodesia since the emergency makes it possible for forced-labour practices to continue.

From time to time the veil is lifted and there, in all its nakedness, stands the barbarous system of forced labour. Workers from French African territories who have no money to pay for their fare to centres of employment are "sold" by lorry drivers to "labour collectors", who in turn pass them on to employers, such as cocoa farmers, at a considerable profit.[5] In 1959 the Nigerian *West African Pilot* alleged that "slave labour" was still being used

[1] See Circular of Kenya Public Relations Officer, August 15, 1953; *The Times*, September 30, 1953; *The Observer*, March 28, 1954; *Kenya Weekly News*, May 7, 1954; *The Times*, May 15, 1954; "Survey of Forced Labour Camps", by Jack Ensoll, *Kenya Weekly News*, February 4, 1955; Patrick Monkhouse, *Manchester Guardian*, September 2 and 9, 1955; Rotary talk given by Mr. Johnson, reported in *East African Standard*, June 17, 1955.
[2] See question put by Mrs. Barbara Castle, M.P., to the Secretary of State for the Colonies, *Hansard*, December 14, 1955.
[3] Fletcher, Eileen: *Peace News*, May 4, 1956.
[4] *The Times*, April 9, 1959.
[5] *Report of the Committee of Enquiry into the Working and Living Conditions of Workers in the Mining Industry*, Accra, 1953.

by some private companies, and editorially asserted that a traffic in slave girls was going on, the girls being sold from Eastern Nigeria to other regions of West Africa.

It is significant that since the United Nations was formed and the Trusteeship Council established, the British authorities have ceased to publish information on forced labour in British colonies. Despite this conspiracy of silence, which prevents the compilation of any reliable statistics, any impartial examination of the laws and practices prevailing in Africa will quickly reveal how many are the forms under which forced labour can be practised, and how massive is the interference with the freedom of the African worker to sell his labour in the market. Compulsory unpaid work for porterage, making roads, and for "public works"; restrictions on the workers' freedom of movement; the obligation to carry travel permits, denial of the right to leave freely the place of work (for example, in mines and plantations) or one's place of habitation (compounds), confinement to specific zones, locations, or Reserves; the collective hiring of workers by recruiting agencies; the labour-contract system, accompanied by penal sanctions for "breach of contract"; the arbitrary prolongation of labour contracts for debts to the employer through fines or purchases in the employer's shop; labour conscription for "military purposes"; forced labour to discharge tax debts; the large-scale use of unpaid prison labour; and the compulsory growing of certain crops—such is the huge area of compulsion within which African labour is forced to work. And yet some commentators talk of a mythical African worker who is "free to sell his labour in the market".

When the African worker himself speaks it is not to extol the "freedom" he is alleged to enjoy in the disposal of his own labour, but, on the contrary, to expose his slavery; and in this respect, it is significant how often the very word *slavery* is used by African organisations.

"This Association strongly objects to the Labour Utilisation Board and calls for its dissolution. This Board, a government creation, *is more of a slave market* than a centralisation of man-power. Africans are recruited from all over the Territory *by means which are far from being voluntary. These unfortunate Africans are transported as far from their homes as 800 miles in such a way that would make one's blood run cold. Cattle are better treated than these prospective labourers.*"

So runs a petition from the Chagga Cultural Association of Tanganyika to the United Nations Trusteeship Council (October 5, 1951).

"We have been given over to the callousness of our employers and the greed of unrestrained competition so that a small number of very rich men have been able to *lay a yoke little better than slavery itself upon the masses of poor Africans*"

complains the Tanganyika Government Employees' Association in a petition to the Trusteeship Council on October 1, 1951.

Such complaints are echoed all over the African continent. Strongly indicative of the feelings of the African people towards their work for Europeans is the habit which grew up among squatters in Kenya of giving to the word "to work" the meaning "to slave for the white man". Of a man working for himself in his own garden people will say *e mugunda*—"he is in his garden". And they will ask: *Wathii mugunda kana wira?*—"Are you going to your garden *or to slave?*"[1]

While it is, in the main, economic compulsion—agrarian poverty combined with the poll-tax system—which drives the African out to work in European enterprises, compulsory labour remains an important factor. It is deliberately retained by the colonialist powers to coerce those Africans who show a reluctance to respond to the economic spur; and in this connection the use of convict labour and the labour of tax defaulters is of significance.

To one degree or another, forced labour is practised by all the colonial powers in Africa; but in two areas in particular, the Portuguese territories and the Union of South Africa, it is practised on such a scale and plays such a key role in the labour policy of the governments concerned that it will, perhaps, be instructive to look into the matter a little further.

379,000 Slaves

Of Portuguese Africa (Angola, Mozambique, Sao Tomé, and Principe), Hailey merely says, in his most polite and restrained

[1] Gicaru, Muga: op. cit., p. 58.

language, that the United Nations *ad hoc* Committee on Forced Labour "expressed in 1953 the belief that, though forced labour was in principle forbidden, there were certain restrictions and exceptions in the legislation which permit the exaction of forced or compulsory labour."[1]

How considerable and all-embracing are these "restrictions" and "exceptions" has been admirably described by Davidson,[2] whose study of Angola establishes beyond all doubt the extent to which forced labour is the basis of the whole economy in this territory where "there are now more slaves . . . than there were fifty years ago".[3] In fact, as Davidson says, forced labour in Angola is practised on such a considerable scale that it can be described as "the flywheel of the country's whole economy".[4] The system, as explained by Davidson, is that every African male in Angola, "or in practice those above the 'apparent age' of about ten years old",[5] is obliged to show that he has worked for six months in the year previous to the enquiry, or is working at the time of the enquiry. If he is not so working, then he is sent for forced labour. Those employers who want forced labour simply indent for it, as they would indent for materials, from the Government-General. Forced workers, called *contradados*, or contract workers ("really slaves", rightly says Davidson), are requested accordingly from the local administrators, who in turn press their local chiefs to conscript the number of men required. A correspondent of the *New York Herald Tribune*, describing this system, wrote: "If the required number is not forthcoming, police are sent to round them up."[6]

Examining the files of the Native Affairs Department at Luanda, the capital of Angola, Davidson found that these were listed "379,000 *contradados*, or forced workers who are really slaves".[7] Some idea of the treatment meted out to these slaves can be obtained from the experience Davidson narrates of his meeting with Senhor Monteiro, general manager of the Cassequel sugar plantations:[8]

"I asked him what happened when a forced worker refused to work.

[1] Hailey (Revised): op. cit., p. 1375.
[2] Davidson: op. cit., pp. 190–232.
[3] ibid., p. 196.   [4] ibid., p. 197.   [5] ibid., p. 198.   [6] February 15, 1948.
[7] Davidson: op. cit., p. 196.   [8] ibid., pp. 216–7.

"He looked at me in some surprise.

" 'Oh, but they will work. They do.'

" 'Still, supposing they won't?'

" 'Then we send them to the police station.'

"Put them in prison: yes, and flog them. Witness after witness (although not Senhor Monteiro) told me this—some nonchalantly, taking the thing for obvious and natural, some with bitter loathing, some with painful memories.

"This flogging is usually by a hide whip, a *chicote*. But there is also the *palmatória*. A European in whom I have every confidence . . . has described for me a *palmatória* which he saw in use not long ago.

" 'It was a sort of mallet carved from one piece of hard wood, with a handle some ten or twelve inches long, the head being a disk some three inches across and an inch and a half thick. On each side of this disk five tapering holes were bored. These were in the pattern of the dots on the five of dice. The way this implement of torture was employed is this. The victim holds one hand out palm up. The operator brings the *palmatória* with a sharp forceful blow on the outstretched palm. Under the force of the blow the flesh is sucked up into these tapering holes. The lessening diameter of the holes pinches the enclosed flesh and produces intense pain. The victim then presents the palm of the other hand and the operator hits it. So the hands are struck alternately with a regular beat for the ordered number of blows.

" 'The Africans give *palmatória* a name of their own which might be translated "the pain". A tough individual may take four or five blows in silence, but after that one cannot restrain his cry of anguish. . . .' This informant thought death would follow 150 blows; others tell me not."

Davidson's findings in Angola are paralleled, and essentially confirmed, by an investigation carried out on the other side of Africa, in the Portuguese territory of Mozambique. This enquiry was conducted by Professor Marvin Harris, an American anthropologist at the University of Columbia.[1]

[1] Harris, Marvin: *Portugal's African "Wards"*, an African Today pamphlet published by the American Committee on Africa, New York, 1958.

The essence of the forced-labour system in Portuguese East Africa, explains Prof. Harris, is that *all African males are presumed by law to be "idle" unless they can prove to the contrary. Those unable to supply proof of their employment are subject to conscription for six months on public works, unless they "volunteer" to work for private contractors.* This is what is known as the *shibalo* system, a system under which any African, on the simple decision of a district administrator, can be compelled to undertake forced labour. These *shibalos* are paid the minimum legal wage for the region in which they work, ranging from 15s. to 35s. per month; at least, that is the theory, though in practice, as Davidson has convincingly demonstrated for Angola, it is a lucky African who, at the end of his term of compulsory labour, receives the full wages he has earned.

"The government and private employment together", writes Harris, "probably employ 100,000 *shibalos* under contract during a given year. The significance of the laws against idleness, however, is by no means restricted to the actual capture and impressment of *shibalos*. Of far greater importance are the effects produced upon the labour force by the threat rather than the fact of conscription for forced labour . . . [which] is to force not merely 100,000 workers but the overwhelming majority of Mozambique African males to participate in the European economy on terms which are deeply injurious to Native welfare, but highly lucrative for the Europeans, especially in the neighbouring territories."

Explaining in another study[1] the unavoidable compulsion either to submit to forced labour or to take up employment in South Africa, Harris writes that the African male in Mozambique "*had to choose between working for Europeans in Mozambique or working for Europeans in the Transvaal. No third choice existed. Those who remained at home were subject to forced labour and did so usually only as a calculated risk.*" [Own italics—J. W.]

South Africa and Southern Rhodesia are the main beneficiaries of this compulsory labour-migration, Harris estimating a grand total of 400,000 of these migrant workers being employed in

[1] Harris, Marvin: "Labour Emigration Among the Mozambique Thonga", *Africa*, January 1959, **xxix**, No. 1, p. 60.

these two territories. This figure, which, he says, should be regarded "very conservatively", should be taken alongside the 1950 figures of the total active male population between the ages of eighteen and fifty-five in Southern Mozambique—600,000.

This means that some two-thirds of all the mature, able-bodied men of Southern Mozambique are employed in foreign territories. If one adds to this total the number of *shibalos* and domestics employed in the cities, then, says Harris, "*a staggering percentage, perhaps as high as seventy-five per cent, of Southern Mozambique's adult male population*" turns out to be engaged in some form of wage labour involving their protracted absence from their village.

A further form of forced labour exercised in Portuguese East Africa is the compulsion on African peasants to produce crops according to the instructions of the colonial administration.

> "In this modern serfdom", writes Harris, "the role of the medieval lord is exercised by twelve private Portuguese companies, each of which has received monopolistic concessions over the cotton production of vast areas. . . . *Indigenas* within the concession areas of each company are assigned cotton acreage by the administrative authorities."

They have no choice in the matter, says Harris, and must plant, cultivate, and harvest cotton wherever they are told, and the raw cotton must be sold to the concession company of their area at prices fixed by the Government far below those available on the international market. Any hope of escaping from this serfdom to take up wage labour is denied, for within the concession areas all recruiting of wage labour by foreign or domestic employers is prohibited.

It is not difficult to imagine the plight of these wretched peasants under this system. The acreages assigned for planting are usually such as to make it impossible for the peasants to grow at the same time their own food crops. Food production has accordingly dropped catastrophically to famine levels. For their compulsory toil, these conscripted peasants receive next to nothing. In 1956, for example, the half-million African cotton-producers employed under this scheme received less than £5 per annum each to maintain their entire families. But even this is not the worst, for, according to the Bishop of Beira, the peasant in bad years *receives nothing.*

Bastille—Buchenwald . . . Bethal

The scale and conditions of forced labour in the Union of South Africa are little different from those of Portuguese East Africa, even if the method is not the same. Hailey's comments on forced labour in South Africa are completely misleading.

"In the Union of South Africa", he says, "the use of compulsory labour is prohibited, but the labour of convicts serving sentences in the Prison Outstations is hired out to associations of farmers."[1]

Hailey does his best to make it all sound very reasonable and, in the general context of conditions in Africa, not at all exceptional. But it would be interesting to see the reaction on the faces of Africans if Lord Hailey were to make such a remark to a mass meeting in an African township in the Union—or, better still to the wretched victims of Bethal. For what Hailey does not explain is the ease with which an African in the Union can become a "convict", and the immense army of such "convicts" who are forced out to labour, under the most inhuman conditions imaginable, on the farms of the Europeans. In 1956, no less than 1,760,237 Africans in the Union were convicted of petty statutory offences. *The majority of these included contraventions of the pass and curfew laws.* The pass laws—"the hinge of labour control and consequently of white supremacy in South Africa", as Ronald M. Segal[2] has rightly said—have a dual purpose. They are not only intended as a means of controlling African labour; they also provide the pretext for mass arrests for alleged pass-law offences, and thus provide a steady flow of cheap, forced labour for European farms.

The figure quoted above, of some one and three-quarter million Africans convicted in 1956 for petty offences, does not tell the whole story. The number of arrests was considerably higher— and "an unknown number vanished between the charge office

[1] Hailey (Revised): op. cit., p. 1366.
[2] Segal: *New Statesman*, February 28, 1959, p. 295.

and the courts because they were given Hobson's choice, either to appear in court or to undertake farm labour".[1] One can therefore estimate that about one-fifth of the African people in the Union—and probably as much as a third of the adult males— are arrested annually, mainly for offences against the pass laws.

"These mass arrests", explains *Liberation*,[2] "are the government's reply to the revolt of the Africans against the feudal conditions which prevail on the farms. The dragnet is an attempt to prevent Africans from escaping from farm labour to comparatively better conditions in the urban areas. *There is very little which distinguishes these raids and arrests from the barbaric practice of raiding primitive communities for slaves. The purpose is the same: to satisfy the greed for cheap labour, of a heartless, selfish, and mean farming class.*"   [Own italics J. W.]

A large proportion of those convicted are naturally unable to pay their fines; and for them their destination becomes one of the thirty-odd farm prisons which have been set up by the farmers' associations with Government backing. Under this system the Department of Prisons undertakes to supply, through a contract with the local farmers' association, a steady flow of prison labour for employment at a fixed rate of hire to any farmer who provides a prison building. The number of these appalling farm prisons has doubled in the past four years, the Prison Department coffers have been swelled accordingly by £400,000 a year, and the farmers have obtained their cheap, forced labour.

Echoing the views of the official Year Book, Hailey has the audacity to claim that "The system is apparently appreciated both by farmers and *by prisoners in rural areas.*"[3] [Own italics— J. W.] One has only to look at the faces of these shackled convicts —"like victims of an eighteenth-century slave raid"[4]—on their way to the farm prisons to know what they think of this inhuman system of traffic in human flesh. And the name "Bethal"—a name which will go down in history along with the Bastille and Buchenwald—will long remain as a reminder of the foul, degrading

---

[1] *Liberation*, Johannesburg, March 1959, No. 35, p. 6.
[2] ibid.
[3] Hailey (Revised): op. cit., p. 626.
[4] *Liberation*, December 1958, No. 34, p. 3.

conditions under which convict labour in South Africa is compelled to work and live. Let Segal take up the story:[1]

"Those who read Michael Scott's exposure in 1947 of farm assaults and murders in the eastern Transvaal will remember the name 'Bethal'; will remember, perhaps, the description of African labourers dressed in sacks and clawing out potatoes with their bare hands: work under the hot sun and the sjambok, and nights in stuffy, windowless barns with fierce watchdogs outside to cut off escape. And Bethal, with its surrounding maize, wheat and potato farms, has changed little since it first flared into the news. Regular press reports testify to the perpetual beatings, the assaults sporadically turned to murder, and the increasingly desperate methods employed by the government to recruit labour for this notorious area."[2]

Segal further states that convicts are hired out to farmers at 2s. a day, while short-term offenders are hired out at only 9d. a day.

Yet, despite this whole system of forced labour, "the demand for farm labour", says Segal, "remains unquenched. And the labour bureaux, run by the government's Department of Bantu Administration and Development, use the machinery of the pass laws to squeeze what they can from the urban labour force."

Daily in the Union Africans are subjected to police pressganging. No African, when he leaves home in the morning, can be certain that before dusk he will not have been picked up by the police and, with no trial and for no offence even, spirited away to work on a farm. *New Age* has given countless individual examples of this. Its issue of January 8, 1959, describes two typical cases. One concerns a younger brother of the treason trial victim, Alfred Hutchinson, who is now in Ghana.

The report states that George Hutchinson was arrested on December 23, convicted for being in possession of liquor and sentenced to a fine of £3 or four weeks in jail. When friends tried to contact him, the prison authorities said that he had been "sold" as a labourer to a farmer named Stals. It was only after

[1] Segal: op. cit., p. 295.
[2] For further details on the shocking conditions on South Africa's farms, see *The Farm Labour Scandal* by Ruth First (*New Age* pamphlet, Johannesburg, July 1959).

the most strenuous protests by Hutchinson's attorneys, and their threat to apply to the Supreme Court for an order of *habeas corpus*, that Hutchinson was "found" and released.

George Hutchinson's freedom was only regained by dint of exceptional vigilance and speedy action by his legal representatives. But for every such case revealed there are many more which pass undiscovered.

The same issue of *New Age* also reported the case of a thirteen-year-old boy, Veldman Mtekeli, who was shanghaied in the Transkei and later found working on a farm at Kinross, in the potato belt in the eastern Transvaal, notorious for the farmers' harsh treatment of their labourers. Subsequent enquiries revealed that a number of other young boys from the Umtata area in the Transkei were working on this farm; and *New Age* revealed on May 7, 1959, that young African girls of only nine years had been similarly hired or shanghaied into farm slavery.

An extraordinary case was revealed in the *New Statesman*, at the end of 1957—the case of Nelson Langa.

Nelson Langa, a street cleaner employed by the Johannesburg City Council, was stopped by plain-clothes police one evening, and asked for his pass. Like all African street cleaners on duty, he did not have his pass with him (for fear of losing it, or getting it dirty), but he produced for the police his embossed municipal disk giving his official employee number, which was proof of his legitimate employment.

Despite this, the police took him and he was sent under guard to Bethal, where he was forced to work in the fields. Again vigilance and an application for *habeas corpus* had their effect and Nelson Langa was freed. What is striking about this case, however, was the revelation in court that according to an arrangement between the Secretary for Native Affairs, the Department of Justice and the Commissioner of the South African Police, *Africans arrested for pass irregularities are not charged, but are passed on to the Native Affairs Department.* An administrative circular of the Department, in 1954, which was quoted in court, actually states that Africans arrested in this way should be "offered employment" in rural areas, and that "priority should be given to farm labour". Those declining to accept such employment are not released but "returned to the South African police for prosecution".

In commenting on this enormity, the *New Statesman* points out that signing a farm-labour contract means working from three to six months for 2*s*. a day, whereas the usual penalty for a pass offence should be a week in jail or a fine of £2. What happens in so many cases is that the choice between a week in jail or six months' serfdom is not put before those arrested. Without their consent they are simply shanghaied off to Bethal, or similar dreaded farm areas.

In commenting on the case of Nelson Langa and others, the *New Statesman* says that "the use of convict labour, quartered on the farmer's land and in his sole charge, has become common. In the Bethal area, which has a particularly small locally available labour force, it is estimated that one farmer in four is dependent on convict labour".

George Hutchinson and Nelson Langa were fortunate. In both instances legal representatives were contacted, and thus it became possible, by exerting considerable legal pressure, to secure their release. But for countless others there is no such escape; there is only Bethal or a farm jail in another area, forced labour of the most degrading kind, accompanied by beatings and other brutalities. According to incomplete statistics, in the first six months of 1958 more than 30,000 illegally arrested Africans were sent to European farms in the Transvaal.

Following the scandalous case of James Musa Sadika in 1959 and his revelations of murder, brutality and slave-labour conditions on a European farm in Heidelberg (for further details, see *New Age*, April 30 and May 7, 1959), public protests against the whole system of forced labour on South African farms became so powerful that in June 1959 the Government was compelled to announce the suspension of the scheme, and in December 1959 its complete abandonment. In reality, however, as Mr. James Fairburn has pointed out,[1] while the forcing of *unconvicted* pass offenders to "offer" themselves for farm labour is now officially ended, the leasing of short-term *convicts* to private farmers, who pay them 9*d*. a day plus the minimum of food, clothing and shelter, continues. More significant still, this use of convict labour has grown enormously in the past few years, from 100,000 in 1953-4 to 199,312 in 1957-8.[2]

[1] Fairburn, James: "The New Serfdom," *New Statesman*, July 18, 1959, p. 70.
[2] First, Ruth: op. cit., p. 16.

To people in the West the constant use by Africans of the word "slavery" when protesting against their appalling conditions may appear a sweeping exaggeration. But to those who care to acquaint themselves with the realities of the African scene, to learn of the conditions under which Africans first came to labour for Europeans and of the indignities, humiliations and brutalities under which they are still compelled to work, the word and its use are fully justified.

CHAPTER FOUR

THE WANDERING AFRICAN

In January 1960 a total of 429 Africans lost their lives in the terrible mining disaster at Coalbrook, in the Union of South Africa. Of these 429, only two were believed to be indigenous to the Union. Of the remainder, half came from the British Protectorate of Basutoland and half from Portuguese East Africa.

When African miners went on strike in the Wankie Coalfields in Southern Rhodesia, in 1955, they were sacked and sent home—to Northern Rhodesia.

When African building workers went on strike on the Kariba dam in Southern Rhodesia, in 1959, they were sacked and sent home—to Nyasaland.

The dead miners of Coalbrook and the workers dismissed from Wankie and Kariba were, in part, victims of the migrant-labour system of Africa.

Migrant labour is not a phenomenon restricted to Africa. Even from highly developed countries like Britain thousands of workers emigrate every year. Yet, for the most part, these latter workers emigrate for good; they usually emigrate as workers, with a trade at their disposal, and in the land to which they migrate they normally take up work in their own trade for which they are qualified.

From Asia, too, under the impact of imperialist conquest and exploitation, vast armies of people have emigrated—from China to Malaya, Thailand and Indonesia; from India to Ceylon, Burma and Malaya, and even to parts of Africa. These emigrants have, in the main, settled down in the land of their adoption, forming more or less permanent, stable communities, national minorities—and all the usual class and occupational divisions have soon arisen, some becoming workers, some traders, some acquiring land and becoming farmers, some taking up professions, and a few even forming a local bourgeoisie.

Labour migration in Africa, although it shares many of the characteristics common to all societies going through a process of the break-up of pre-capitalist forms of agriculture and the development of wage-labour, yet has certain distinctive features of its own which merit special attention. First, it is a migration *almost overwhelmingly of adult males*, single men, or husbands unaccompanied by their wives and children, who have been left behind in the ruined countryside. Secondly, the migrants usually *take up employment for a strictly limited duration*—six months, a year, two years, but seldom longer. Thirdly, *the migration is repeated again and again in the life of the individual peasant-worker*, his career consisting of numerous short terms of employment alternating with periods at home in his village or the Reserve. Fourthly, whether he migrates from the countryside to a town or mining area within the same territory, or whether it is a question of "alien migration" across frontiers, it is usually a case of *travelling enormous distances, often on foot*. Fifthly, it is frequently *connected with various forms of labour recruitment* which sometimes tend to be disguised forms of forced labour. *And sixthly, it is on such a scale and of such a character that it produces a completely disproportioned population both in the towns and in the rural areas, aggravates terribly the already acute agrarian crisis, and leads to a total disharmony of the economy of the African territories most affected by it.* From the standpoint of labour it has three further results; the constant change of personnel in employment which arises from this system *makes difficult the acquisition of labour skill, creates enormous difficulties for trade-union organisation, and tends to depress wages.*

The reasons for the extent of migrant labour in Africa have already been indicated in the earlier chapters to this book. Compelled through land starvation, taxation, and forms of compulsion to take up wage labour, the African has had to travel from his own restricted and poverty-stricken, soil-eroded land to areas where he can obtain work for wages. This has meant in the first place to the mining areas, and to the farms and plantations owned by Europeans. Since Africa has been largely divided into urban and rural areas for whites, with the Africans pushed away into Reserves or other restricted areas by various land laws, Africans in search of work have had to travel from their own villages to the European areas offering employment. In many cases there is no European farmer, mine-owner or factory-owner near at hand. Thus long-distance travel has become a necessity.

Immense Scale

The scale of this migration is really enormous.

Hailey says[1] that in 1946 out of 305,410 African workers employed in industries represented in the Witwatersrand Native Labour Association in the Union of South Africa "only 41½ per cent originally came from within the Union". On the basis of the 1936 census it had previously been estimated that *half* of the total labour force in the Rand mines came from outside the Union. Figures for 1957 show that two-thirds of all African miners in the Union of South Africa came from other African territories.

The effect of the migrant-labour system *inside* the Union is even more marked.

Mr. John Burger[2] says:

". . . as many as sixty per cent of the adult male population from any one area may be absent at work in European areas; on the day that the 1936 census was taken twenty per cent of the total male population, of all ages, was absent from the Reserves of the Union."

The 1949 *Handbook of Race Relations in South Africa* refers to a study of seven territorial divisions of the Union which showed that there was a ratio of absentees to total males of *all ages* amounting to an average of thirty-two per cent. If the ratio were calculated in relation to men of working age instead of all males, it said, then it might reach *nearly a hundred per cent in certain districts*.

European farming and mining in the Union have become an almost bottomless pit for migrant labour from neighbouring— and even distant—African territories. In fact, some of them have been turned into virtual reservoirs of cheap labour for white employers. From the High Commission Territories of Basutoland, Bechuanaland and Swaziland some hundred thousand migrate to the Union every year. The *Agricultural Survey* for Basutoland published in 1952 estimates 77,000 males and 22,000 females as being away from their villages at any one time. This means, says Hailey,[3] that *the whole territory is deprived of fifty to sixty per cent of*

---

[1] Hailey (Revised): op. cit., pp. 1377–8.
[2] Burger, John: *The Black Man's Burden*, p. 52, London, 1943.
[3] Hailey (Revised): op. cit., p. 1379.

its able-bodied men every year.[1] For Bechuanaland, figures for
1938–40 showed some 27½ per cent of adult males away from the
Protectorate, while for Swaziland the figure was twenty-five to
thirty per cent.

Bechuanaland is an instructive example of the steady increase
in labour migration in the last fifty years. In his *Migrant Labour
and Tribal Life*, I. Schapera provides the following table:[2]

TABLE II
BECHUANALAND NATIVES EMPLOYED IN LABOUR DISTRICTS,
UNION OF SOUTH AFRICA, 1910–1940

Year				Number
1910	..	..	..	..	2,266
1920	..	..	..	..	2,578
1925	..	..	..	..	3,820
1930	..	..	..	..	4,712
1935	..	..	..	..	10,314
1940	..	..	..	..	18,411

(The present writer has omitted the percentage increases provided
by Schapera, since they are not relative to the point being made here.)

These figures show quite clearly the steady increase in labour
migration over the thirty years covered. In his book, which was
published in 1947, Schapera, who undertook his study for the
Administration, urged a number of steps to slow up, if not halt,
the pace of migration which, he showed, was having serious
economic and social consequences.

The figures given in the Bechuanaland Annual Reports for
the last ten years show, however, that far from the pace being
slowed up (let alone halted), the drain of manpower away from
Bechuanaland becomes ever greater.

TABLE III

Year				Number of Men Leaving Bechuanaland
1947	..	..	..	..	9,300*
1948	..	..	..	..	14,000†
1949	..	..	..	..	17,000†
1950	..	..	..	..	17,500†
1951	..	..	..	..	17,000†
1952	..	..	..	..	24,000
1953	..	..	..	..	23,000
1954	..	..	..	..	21,000
1955	..	..	..	..	21,000
1956	..	..	..	..	15,000

* To go to work in South African mines.
† Left for the Union of South Africa.

[1] The 1960 general election in Basutoland showed forty-three per cent of all
the eligible voters were absent, working in the Union.
[2] Schapera: op. cit., p. 32.

The annual average for the first five years of the period covered in this table is 14,960. For the second five years it is 20,840— an increase of nearly forty-three per cent in a relatively very short period despite the quite considerable decline in its last year. (A small part of the indicated increase in the latter five years may be due to the fact that in the period up to 1951 the figures provided were for the Union of South Africa only; but since the over-whelming majority of emigrant workers from Bechuanaland go to the Union, the percentage allowance for this discrepancy should not be very great.)

Migrant labour from Mozambique has always played an important role in the Union of South Africa's economy, especially in the mining industry. In 1954 there was a known total of 173,433 Mozambique workers employed in the Union. Because of the conditions in Mozambique, already referred to in an earlier chapter, labour migration from this territory is directly linked with forced labour. The recruiting schemes under which Mozambique carries out its long-standing agreements to supply the Union with 100,000 mining recruits each year are naturally also part of this system of forced labour.

A recent study[1] reveals that the actual number of Mozambique workers in the Union is considerably more than this agreed figure. In 1954 an additional 21,596 illegal migrants were identified by the Portuguese native affairs and tax-collecting authorities operating on Union soil. Harris, in the study referred to above, states that: "There is every reason to believe, however, that substantial numbers of clandestine migrants remain undetected." Examining the Thonga ethnic group, the one most affected by this migration, Harris shows that even according to the Portuguese authorities forty per cent of the active Thonga males are working in the Union of South Africa. He continues:

"Since these calculations fail to take into account many additional thousands of Thonga men who are away in the Union under illegal circumstances unknown to the *Curadoria* (Portuguese tax collectors in the Union) we may feel confident that the direction of probable error is towards minimising rather than exaggerating the total movement."[2]

[1] Harris, Marvin: "Labour Emigration Among the Mozambique Thonga", *Africa*, January 1959, **xxix**, No. 1, pp. 50–65.
[2] Harris: op. cit., p. 51.

If one takes into account also the large number of males away from their homes working inside Mozambique itself on farms and plantations, on the roads and railways, in factories and in commerce, "it seems safe to conclude . . . that during any given year *well over fifty per cent of the active Thonga population is away from home working for wages in the employ of Europeans.*"[1]

[Own italics—J. W.]

Under a government agreement, Mozambique also recruits 15,000 African workers each year for employment in Southern Rhodesia.

The 1951 census for Southern Rhodesia gives the number of indigenous Africans in employment as 271,000; the immigrant labour force is put at 247,000. This shows to what extent Southern Rhodesia is dependent on outside labour for its farms, mines, plantations and new secondary industries. This immigrant labour force in 1951 was mainly composed of 102,000 from Mozambique, 86,000 from Nyasaland, and 48,000 from Northern Rhodesia; the remainder came from Angola, Belgian Congo, Bechuanaland and South West Africa.

In Northern Rhodesia, according to the 1955 Labour Department Report, 22½ per cent of all African labour employed in the mines and in other undertakings employing 300 workers or more is migrant labour from outside the territory. Figures for 1953 show some 15,000 migrant workers entering Northern Rhodesia from Tanganyika, Angola and Nyasaland. In 1954 some 11,000 workers left Northern Rhodesia to work in Southern Rhodesia. This, of course, is apart from the large number of Africans in Northern Rhodesia who are steadily drained off from the villages to work in the mines and European farms within the territory. So considerable has this become that Hailey states:[2]

"It has been estimated that taking the territory as a whole at least one-third to a half of the able-bodied men are normally away from their villages"

—even rising to seventy per cent in certain outlying areas. Hailey adds:

[1] ibid., p. 51.
[2] Hailey (Revised): op. cit., p. 1381.

"It is generally agreed that the number of Africans now leaving their villages as wage earners is such as to be a serious menace to the development of rural areas."

Few African territories have been so denuded of their labour force as Nyasaland. *Of the 380,000 adult males suitable for employment in 1954, it is estimated that some 160,000 were employed outside Nyasaland; that is, over forty-two per cent.* No less than 100,000 of these are employed in Southern Rhodesia and 42,000 in the Union of South Africa. There are 10,000 in Northern Rhodesia. As Read has rightly remarked:[1]

"*The chief export of Nyasaland in the past fifty years has been men.*"

Some light on the reasons for this mass emigration is given in a sample survey conducted in 1949 in the Southern Province of Nyasaland. Some seventy per cent of those asked said they were emigrating in order to obtain money which they needed for clothes and other goods. As many as *seventy-two per cent said they would prefer to work in Nyasaland if higher wages were obtainable there.* But the higher wages at home are not available—and so the migration continues.

To travel outside Nyasaland an identity certificate is required of all Africans. The issue of these certificates is a partial indication (not complete because numbers leave without a certificate) of the numbers leaving Nyasaland each year. The 1957 Annual Report for Nyasaland shows unmistakably that the trend is for labour migration to increase from year to year.

TABLE IV
ISSUE OF IDENTITY CERTIFICATES FOR AFRICANS LEAVING NYASALAND

From Nyasaland to Country of Destination	Annual Average 1946–50	Annual Average 1951–55	1956	1957
Southern Rhodesia	22,853	40,662	50,760	49,248
Northern Rhodesia	1,309	4,145	5,638	6,671
Union of S. Africa	9,295	10,089	15,516	18,045
Other territories	395	619	390	382
Totals	33,852	55,515	72,304	74,346

Source: *Annual Report for Nyasaland for 1957.*

[1] Read, Dr. Margaret: "Migrant Labour in Africa", *International Labour Review*, June 1942, **xlv**, No. 6, p. 606.

Much play has been made on the remittances sent back to Nyasaland by these migrant workers. In fact, Hailey has referred to them as forming "an important element in the economy of Nyasaland,"[1] adding that in 1954 the total amount remitted in various ways to Nyasaland by these absent workers was £670,000. Yet this works out at about £4 4s. a year from each worker; and if one estimates the family as comprising four persons (a modest estimate), it means that the remittances provide one guinea per head per year for those families in Nyasaland whose breadwinner is temporarily away working in another territory. *Not even three-farthings a day.* If this is alleged to constitute "an important element in the economy of Nyasaland", then it merely serves to expose the depths of poverty to which these people have been plunged.

Even since Federation the much-talked-of remittances have increased only to a slight degree. Total remittances sent home by some 150,000 migrant workers from Nyasaland in 1957 were £1,500,000. Even if one discounts the £250,000 poll tax annual increase introduced since Federation, and ignores the increased cost of living, the additional revenue from labour migration means for the average migrant breadwinner's family an increase from three-farthings a day to a little over 1½d. In percentages it may look quite considerable—nearly 100 per cent!—but in terms of real hard cash it is completely negligible.

Uganda is another British-held territory in which migrant labour is a marked feature. Some 60,000 leave Uganda every year, and about 100,000 immigrate into the territory. The overwhelming majority of these workers coming into Uganda emigrate from Ruanda-Urundi or the Belgian Congo; and some come from the Nyanza Province of Kenya. The 1957 Annual Report of the colony, which reveals that as many as 133,000 workers immigrated into Uganda in 1956, says ". . . *the great majority of the employed population are migrant workers*". It attributes the decline in migrant workers in 1957 to *improved conditions* in Ruanda-Urundi, the main source of supply, thus confirming that it is the poverty of the rural areas which drives Africans across the face of their continent to seek wage labour. Uganda's dependence on alien migrant labour is noted by Noon,[2] who points out that "immi-

[1] Hailey (Revised): op. cit., p. 1382.
[2] Noon: op. cit. p. 96.

grant workers provide ninety per cent of the employees in cotton ginneries, forty-two per cent in mines and twenty-nine per cent in the sugar, timber and sisal enterprises".

To Tanganyika, too, come some 40,000 workers a year, mainly from Ruanda-Urundi and Portuguese East Africa. A number leave Tanganyika every year, too, to seek work outside; Noon, for example, estimates that "between 25,000 and 30,000 Africans are engaged in work abroad".[1]

In West Africa, migration for work is common, though for a number of territories it is mainly seasonal, for agricultural purposes. In Ghana, Nigeria and, to some extent, in Sierra Leone, a considerable proportion of the labour force comes from outside, or constitutes internal migration from rural areas. Firth has estimated[2] that some 100,000 foreign workers are engaged in the mines in Sierra Leone, Ghana and Nigeria. Hailey has pointed out that the *majority* of unskilled labourers in commerce and industry in Ghana is drawn from the north-western territories and the French colonies to the north and west. The 1946 census for the Gold Coast showed 121,000 foreign immigrants—52,000 of them from British territories. "In 1953", says Hailey, "391,000 persons crossed by the ferry on the Volta River travelling south, and 378,400 returning northwards."[3] This is a really considerable figure and shows that migrant labour, far from diminishing over the years, has increased. Noon, for example, writing of an earlier period, says: ". . . in 1942—63,809 workers travelled southward over the Volta ferries to find agricultural employment. . . ."[4]

In French West Africa, too, one can see the same rivers of humanity flowing back and forth across frontiers in search of work, though much of it is seasonal. In 1951 some 50,000 migrated, on six-month contracts, from the Upper Volta to the Ivory Coast to work on farms or in forestry; and another 130,000 to Ghana (the Gold Coast). Ghana also receives about 25,000 a year from Niger.

The Belgian Congo does not rely on migrant workers from outside. It has a big enough population to be able to meet its labour

[1] ibid., p. 106.
[2] Firth, R.: "Social Problems and Research in British West Africa," Part II, *Africa*, July 1947.
[3] Hailey (Revised): op. cit., p. 1384.
[4] Noon: op. cit., p. 57.

requirements from its own impoverished countryside. In fact, it has been estimated[1] that over two and a half million Africans are now living outside their original village areas.

In other words, labour migration in the Belgian Congo takes place on a similar scale as in other territories, but in this case it is overwhelmingly a migration from countryside to towns and mines within the confines of the same territory.

Why They Go

It should be abundantly clear from the Keiskammahoek example, as well as from the other facts given above in this and previous chapters, that migrant labour in Africa has its roots in the impoverishment of the peasantry, that it is, above all, compelling economic necessity, supplemented by the poll tax, which drives these millions from their homes to seek work far afield.

Nevertheless, it is often argued that there are other reasons for this labour migration. The hoary "African custom" has even been pressed into service by some authorities. Others claim that it is the "spirit of adventure" or the "monotony of tribal life" which is responsible. Harris, in his recent valuable survey of labour emigration in Mozambique,[2] refutes such views, indicating quite clearly his opposition to "the widely disseminated notion that the migratory current to the mines is motivated largely by the desire of the African male to see the wonders of Johannesburg and to enhance his stature in the eyes of the people at home, especially the women."

Schapera, in his well-known study on the emigration of labour from Bechuanaland, makes much play with non-economic factors, including desire for adventure, escape from the dull and empty life at cattle posts, a wish to impress the girls, escape from domestic control, and so on. Yet, as already indicated earlier in this book, Schapera's own facts and figures refute his own theories and show, as Professor Mitchell has recently said[3] in

[1] Malengreau, G.: "Recent Developments in Belgian Africa," *Africa Today*, 1955, p. 343.

[2] Harris, Marvin: op. cit., *Africa*, January 1959.

[3] Professor Mitchell, "Factors Motivating Migration from Rural Areas": *Present Interrelations in Central African Rural and Urban Life*, Proceedings of Eleventh Conference of Rhodes-Livingstone Institute for Social Research, held at Lusaka, Northern Rhodesia, January 14–17, 1958. Ed. by R. J. Apthorpe, Rhodes-Livingstone Institute, February 1958. (Referred to hereafter as "Apthorpe Report".)

commenting on Schapera's views: "*A far more universal and important cause is economic necessity.*"

The same conclusion has been drawn by Dr. Richards[1] in a survey of 200 males on a migration route into Buganda. In reply to questioning, seventy-five per cent said they were coming for economic reasons. Dr. Richards sets little store on the explanation that this migration might be the result of habit or adventure, and says that "most spoke of the sheer economic necessity". She notes, too, the general absence of "desires to see European life, get a reputation for sophistication or similar motives given by Schapera". Of significance, too, is Dr. Richards' remark that "evidence from other parts of Africa tends also to show that Africans rarely travel long distances if they can make money under satisfactory conditions at home". (The same point has already been noted above in relation to Nyasaland.)

Further confirmation that economic hardship is the spur behind labour migration is provided by Dr. Gulliver, whose analysis[2] of 2,500 journeys made by Ngoni migrant labourers in southern Tanganyika shows that ninety per cent of these journeys were for economic reasons. Again we find that almost all the migrants said they would have preferred to stay at home if there had been reasonable and reliable opportunities to earn sufficient for their needs.

Gulliver's study of south-western Tanganyika[3] comes to similar conclusions. "The basic and overwhelmingly important cause of Nyakyusa labour migration", he writes, "is an economic one."

On the other side of Africa, in north-western Nigeria, R. M. Prothero has found that ninety-two per cent of migrations are on account of economic causes.[4] No less than sixteen per cent were migrating *in search of food*, a clear sign of extreme economic hardship.

Mitchell makes the telling point[5] that where alternative cash sources are available the rate of migration tends to drop. Among the many studies which confirm this, Gulliver's is particularly useful. He shows that in the northern uplands of the area he

[1] *Economic Development and Tribal Change*, Ed. by Dr. A. I. Richards, 1954.
[2] Gulliver, Dr.: *Labour Migration in a Rural Economy*, 1955.
[3] *Rhodes-Livingstone Journal*, No. 21, 1955.
[4] *Apthorpe Report*, p. 16.
[5] ibid., p. 19.

studied, only twenty to twenty-two per cent of his sample were absentees; and the reason he hazards is that the uplands are valuable coffee lands with less land scarcity. On the alluvial flood plains, where there is not sufficient land for cultivation, he records thirty-three per cent absentees. Dr. Southall's material on the Alur of Buganda[1] reveals the same trend: fifteen per cent absent from Okoro district where no cotton will grow, six per cent from Jonam where cotton is cultivated, but on a limited scale, and only two per cent from the Padyere area where more intensive cotton cultivation is possible.

These figures are valuable and the conclusions drawn from them are confirmed by other reports indicating that in all parts of Africa waves of migration tend to increase whenever there is an abnormally bad situation in the countryside—a bad harvest, or a drop in prices of cash crops grown by Africans.

It can be rightly argued that not all the economic reasons given by migrants as the cause of their journeys are ones of sheer desperation, that there are, in fact, other economic reasons, such as the desire to purchase cattle or a bicycle or some other particular commodity. That may be true in some cases, but in the overwhelming majority it is undeniably economic hardship or even economic disaster which is the spur behind migration.

Further light is thrown by Argyle[2] on the role the impoverishment of the African peasantry plays in causing labour migration. Citing figures for the Rufunsa Valley, about a hundred miles east of Lusaka, he shows that some seventy per cent of the adult male population is away from the valley. Yet in Lusaka itself, forty per cent of the Africans earn less than £3 per month. With wages at such a level, it is obvious how dire must have been the economic situation in Rufunsa Valley to drive so many men away from home.

Professor Irving[3] has claimed that: "Migration is a necessary condition of development of industrialisation and urbanisation. It is no more a psychological whim of the African to go to town any more than it was for the nineteenth-century Englishman leaving the land to settle in the Lancashire textiles areas or in the industrial cities." This analogy, however, is misleading. Nine-

---

[1] *Economic Development and Tribal Change*, Ed. by Dr. A. I. Richards, 1954.
[2] Argyle, W. J.: *Apthorpe Report*, pp. 48–50.
[3] Irving, Professor James: *Apthorpe Report*, p. 61.

teenth-century England was becoming rapidly industrialised and Englishmen were drawn off the land to become permanent workers in a developing industrial economy, to become, in fact, an industrial proletariat.

In twentieth-century Africa, however, apart from the Union, one cannot talk about industrialisation taking place, despite some industrial development here and there. The African economy is still a colonial economy. And an essential factor in this economy is the African worker-peasant, the circulating or wandering African, moving constantly from village to town, from field to mine. He does not leave the land to *settle* in the town, as did Professor Irving's nineteenth-century Englishman, but lives a rootless, vacillating life, for ever uprooting himself to leave his home to seek work, or abandoning his work on European farm or in European mine or factory to return home.

The distinctive character of the African migrant worker as a perpetual migrant or constantly circulating worker-peasant, dividing his time between wage labour for Europeans and returning regularly to his village home, is well established in the case histories compiled by the Keiskammahoek Rural Survey.[1] For reasons of space, it is not possible to quote more than one example of these labour histories though its relevance is shown by the survey's statement that it "is typical of many".

"Sex: Male.
Born: 1892.
Education: Standard·1.
First went out to work: 1908 (age 16).
Feb. 1908 to March 1909: Worked for German West African Railways, S.W. Africa.
Mar. 1909 to Sep. 1911: At home.
Sep. 1911 to Apr. 1912: Mine worker, Premier Mine, Pretoria.
Apr. 1912 to Dec. 1912: At home.
Dec. 1912 to Sep. 1913: Mine Worker, Witwatersrand.
Sep. 1913 to Nov. 1913: At home.
Nov. 1913 to Sep. 1916: Mine worker, Witwatersrand.
Sep. 1916 to Mar. 1917: At home.
Mar. 1917 to Sep. 1917: Mine worker, Witwatersrand.

[1] *Keiskammahoek Survey*, 1952, op. cit., pp. 120–4.

Sep. 1917 to Nov. 1917: At home.
Nov. 1917 to Nov. 1919: Mine worker, Witwatersrand.
Nov. 1919 to Feb. 1921: At home. (He was married during this period.)
Feb. 1921 to July 1921: Domestic servant, Convent, Cape Town.
Jul. 1921 to Sep. 1923: At home.
Sep. 1923 to Jun. 1924: Worked for building contractor, Cape Town.
Jun. 1924 to Nov. 1924: At home.
Nov. 1924 to Nov. 1925: Milk delivery boy, Royal Dairy, Cape Town.
Nov. 1925 to Feb. 1928: At home.
Feb. 1928 to Nov. 1930: Worked at Dunswart Steel Works, Benoni.
Nov. 1930 to Oct. 1931: Worked at Silverwright Electric Works, Johannesburg.
Oct. 1931 to Sep. 1932: Domestic Servant, Drill Hall, Johannesburg.
Sep. 1932 to Feb. 1937: At home.
Feb. 1937 to Mar. 1938: Mine worker, Witwatersrand.
Mar. 1938 to Nov. 1939: At home.
Nov. 1939 to May 1940: Mine worker, Witwatersrand.
May 1940 to Nov. 1943: Mine worker, Johannesburg.
Nov. 1943 to May 1945: At home.
May 1945 to Nov. 1945: Mine worker, Witwatersrand.
Nov. 1945 to date: At home."

Thus this unnamed African had a working life as a migrant worker from the age of sixteen to fifty-three. During these thirty-seven years he worked as railwayman, miner, domestic servant, builder, delivery boy, steel worker, and electrician, finding employment in Cape Town, Benoni, Witwatersrand, Johannesburg, Pretoria and S.W. Africa. Thirteen times he returned home and on sixteen separate occasions he took up fresh employment. And this case, says the survey, is "typical of many".

No comparable detailed labour histories are available for the whole of the Union, let alone the whole of Africa; and it would be erroneous to argue, from the Keiskammahoek Survey alone, or from the case cited above, that this is the normal pattern of migrant labour. Yet, closer acquaintance with the lives of migrant workers in other parts of Africa reveals that, in essence, their experience is not dissimilar, even if the number of occupations followed, the number of towns in which employment has been secured and the frequency of visits home, may be less. For all African migrant workers, whatever the variation in detail, their working life is one of continual shift and change from the village to wage-labour, and from wage-labour back to the village.

"... their Need must be Very Great..."

When one realises what this migration of labour means in terms of human endurance, hardship and suffering, bitter indeed must be the lot of the Africans and desperate the plight which drives them in such quantities and so relentlessly to abandon wife, children and home, to set out from their accustomed plains and hills, to travel hundreds of miles over tiring, barren land, to slave from dawn to dusk for a foreign farmer, or enter the darkness of mines to dig gold, tin or copper for a European master.

An investigation made in Uganda in 1937,[1] in commenting on the long and difficult journeys undertaken by these migrant workers, says:

"... it surprises me that any of them travel at all; it shows that their need must be very great for them to undertake the hazards of the present journeys."

Writing of the reluctance of many Africans to migrate under various recruitment and contract-labour schemes, and of their preference to "go it alone", Noon[2] says:

"The African under this system generally travels on foot to the place of employment, saving the employer the expense of transportation and the fees paid for the services of the recruiting agency. . . . Many workers exhaust their resources before

[1] *Report on an Investigation into Conditions affecting Unskilled Labour and the Supply thereof, within the Protectorate*, by J. R. McD. Elliot, District Officer, Uganda, 1937.
[2] Noon: op. cit., pp. 37-8.

reaching their destination. *Frequent mention is made* in the
Colonial Reports of West African territories *of Natives found
either dead or starving along the migration routes* . . . a worker who
has voluntarily migrated has spent fifteen to twenty per cent
of his earnings to cover the expenses of the journey. He has
also lost from three weeks' to a month's wages if not more while
travelling."   [Own italics—J. W.]

And still they come, in ever-increasing armies, in their search
for work and for cash to pay the tax, to purchase some clothing,
to save themselves and their families from complete starvation
and misery. Across the whole continent, in a never-ending and
ever-increasing flow, rolls this tidal wave of Africans, victims of
an imperialist system of exploitation which can exist only on the
basis of turning the African into a wanderer on the face of the
earth.

"They travel many hundreds of miles to look for a job," says
David Niddrie, in a special study on the journeys of these African
migrant workers.[1] "These walks", he says, "may be from a
hundred to *fifteen hundred miles in length*, depending on the destination of the labourer." Merle Davis[2] has also recorded the long
distances walked by Africans to seek work. A Nyasaland report
in 1935 stated that *as many as ninety per cent of the Nyasaland
labourers going south walked, as they had not sufficient cash to pay the
rail fare.* Even on the return journey, after they have completed
their spell of wage labour, the majority walk.

Buell,[3] too, has noted the long journeys. Writing of an earlier
period he refers to Africans in Northern Rhodesia having to
"walk three or four weeks" to obtain work.

Schapera, in his study on migrant labour leaving Bechuanaland,[4] quotes a local District Commissioner's memorandum of
1943 which states "any native desiring to seek employment away
from home at a European centre has to travel at least three
hundred miles by motor lorry *or on foot*, or, if he comes from the

---

[1] Niddrie, David: "The Road to Work: A Survey of the Influence of
Transport on Migrant Labour in Central Africa," *Rhodes-Livingstone Journal*,
Manchester, 1954, No. 15, p. 32.
[2] Davis, Merle: *Modern Industry and the African*, p. 156, London, 1933.
[3] Buell: op. cit., p. 240.
[4] Schapera, I.: op. cit., p. 74.

Kabamokoni area, about five hundred miles." [Own italics—
J. W.] Roper,[1] too, says that: "A surprisingly large number of
workers in West Africa travel long distances in search of work."

This tendency to travel by foot is in part a consequence of the
increased trend shown in favour of seeking work independently
of the usual recruiting agency. Recruitment has been an important source of enrichment for the agencies and individuals concerned with this human traffic, but despite the increase over the
years in the number of workers migrating in Africa, the *proportion*
going via the recruiting agencies continues to fall. G. N. Burden,
a colonial administrator, has noted[2] that "a large number of
migrants from Central Africa to the Union prefer to proceed
independently and choose their own employer".

The same point is made by the *Annual Report for Nyasaland*
for 1957, which states that "the majority of migrant workers
elect to go uncovenanted. The greatest number of these migrants
go to Southern Rhodesia, for the Nyasa is a prohibited immigrant
into the Union of South Africa, unless he is recruited for work in
the gold mines." One scarcely has to read between the lines to
detect here an official admission that, given a choice, Nyasas,
even when compelled to migrate to seek work, prefer not to work
in the South African mines.

There is no doubt that one of the reasons for the huge amount
of *unrecruited* migrant labour, apart from a disinclination in many
Africans to work in the mines, is simple economics. Migrant
workers, including those recruited, are expected to pay their
bus or lorry fares. Rail fares are generally paid by the recruiting
agency, but the workers often have to travel such long distances
to reach the railway station that the free rail fare only meets part
of their problem. Recruited workers' bus fares are normally
debited from the point of recruitment and then deducted from
the first month's wages.

For Bechuanaland, Schapera gives some examples of the fares
involved—ranging from 2s. 6d. up to 30s. for a journey of 320
miles. It should be noted that this latter figure is well above the
average mineworker's monthly pay, or that of many agricultural
workers. Evidently this expense (a month's pay for the average

---

[1] Roper, J. I.: *Labour Problems in West Africa*, p. 32, London, 1958.
[2] Burden, G. N.: *Labour Migration in Africa*, part 1, Corona III, p. 56,
February 1951.

British industrial worker would be £45–£50) is an important reason why so many migrants walk these long distances, and why they prefer to seek work outside of the official recruiting schemes.

Recruited workers usually have to pay the cost of their own repatriation—and if they return home once a year, as most of them do, one can see what a heavy economic burden this can be.

Africans have many other complaints against the recruiting system. Speaking of the recruitment of migrant workers for the mines in West Africa, Roper[1] says that it provides a "distressing record".

He mentions, in particular, the "deceit" and "violence" which has so often accompanied recruiting, the lack of food on the long journeys to the places of employment, the dishonouring of contracts and promises by employers and recruiting agencies, and the "oppressive conditions of employment".

Schapera[2] describes the similar treatment of migrant workers from Bechuanaland, and although he is apparently persuaded that such treatment belongs to a past period and that these days, with officially recognised recruitment agencies, abuses do not exist, there are few African workers who would share his opinion. Roper, evidently, is not at all convinced that abuses have disappeared, and in fact argues that without trade-union organisation and the "collective protection" which it can afford to migrant workers, "it is, indeed, difficult to ensure that abuses do not arise in the labour contracts of migrant workers".[3] Among the type of abuses which still exist, Roper mentions deductions from wages, and bad housing and medical conditions. The complaint from Tanganyika, cited in an earlier chapter, again reveals the abuses attached to recruiting systems.

Turnover of Labour

An inevitable accompaniment of migrant labour is the terrific and wasteful labour turnover.

The mining industry in the Gold Coast recorded in 1949 that the overall turnover of labour was nearly eighty-five per cent of the labour force, and for underground workers it was nearly a

[1] Roper: op. cit., p. 35.
[2] Schapera, I.: op. cit.
[3] Roper: op. cit., p. 36.

hundred per cent. Figures for Nairobi in 1953 showed that forty-eight per cent of the workers had less than one year's service in the undertakings in which they were employed at the time of the survey; eighty per cent had been employed not longer than two years; only three per cent had a record of employment exceeding ten years. An investigation into Uganda tobacco factories[1] showed that, for a six-month period during which the study was made, the *monthly* labour turnover was 7·6 per cent. A report from Salisbury[2] says that seventy-six per cent of the labour force remains on an average less than four and a half months in each job.

A study of labour turnover in the Cape[3] showed that the average annual percentage labour turnover for the period 1949–54 was no less than 138. In 1954, for even regular work it was as high as 139, while for irregular or seasonal work it reached 191. The study also revealed that eighty per cent of all those leaving had worked in the job for less than a year, and even where work was of a regular character this was true of three-quarters of those leaving.

This study further revealed that forty-one per cent of the African workers whose wages it had been possible to ascertain received between £2 and £3 a week; three-quarters received under £4 per week. Dr. S. T. van der Horst shows that low wages are directly related to high labour turnover, and she produces evidence to indicate that working conditions, social amenities, training and promotion also play their part. She concludes that her study "suggests a positive relationship between wages and other conditions of work and labour turnover, namely that labour turnover diminishes as the advantages of a given employment improve."[4]

In their study on labour turnover on the railways in Kenya,[5] Northcott and Goss show that nearly a third had less than a year's service, nearly forty per cent of those who left in 1946 had been less than twelve months with the railway, and over seventy per

---

[1] Elkan, W.: *An African Labour Force*, East Africa Studies No. 7, Kampala, 1956.
[2] *Annual Report of the Secretary for Native Affairs, 1953.*
[3] Van der Horst, Dr. Sheila T.: "Native Labour Turnover in the Cape", *The South African Journal of Economics*, December 1957, **xxv**, No. 4.
[4] ibid., p. 288.
[5] *African Labour Efficiency Survey*: Ed. by C. H. Northcott, London, 1949.

cent of those who left had less than three years' service. Summarising the situation, they say "a great flood of African labour is flowing in and out of railway employment".[1]

As to why there is such a big turnover, enquiries revealed that "In the majority of cases the workers leave to return to their Reserves", sometimes because of health, sometimes in order to look after their parents' affairs, sometimes to have "a rest from work", or they leave to "seek lighter work or better pay". It is also of significance that the enquiry revealed that "men usually return for re-employment". This is one more confirmation of the extreme mobility of African labour, and the consistency with which this "great flood", as Northcott and Goss call it, flows back and forth from the Reserves.

It is true, as some commentators point out, that many of these workers are what are known as "target workers"; that is to say, they seek work for a specific target—cash to pay taxes or to buy clothes or some other necessity beyond minimum subsistence—and having achieved that target, return home to the countryside.

But this is by no means the whole story. The European employers themselves, especially in mining and agriculture (two sectors of the economy which largely determine the *colonial* pattern of exploitation), maintain a system of short-term contracts.

Noon,[2] for example, says: "It has been the general policy in African dependencies to limit the term of labor service contracted for by legislative enactments"—six months, a year, two years, or even three years (in the Belgian Congo). Once the contract is over, the worker is sent back home, often a worn-out wreck. In Nyasaland and the Ciskei or the Transkei one can see many of these tubercular, crippled, blind, used-up hulks which once were men, completely burned-out by their labour in mines or plantations, a heavy economic burden to their already poverty-stricken relatives.

Search for Security

The African worker, it must be realised, is usually unable to bring his family with him when he comes to work for a European

[1] ibid., p. 74.
[2] Noon: op. cit.

company. It is inevitable that, under such conditions, he will not stay away from his native village longer than is absolutely necessary. In addition, it is vital for the African to have some security, not only for old age, but also in case of loss of employment, illness or becoming incapable of working. Thus he strives to keep one foot on the land, to maintain his rights in tribal land tenure—and this necessitates his constant return.

Social surveys conducted by the Rhodes-Livingstone Institute show that 37·3 per cent of adult males in Northern Rhodesian towns intend to return home when their working days are over, because they hanker after security which the towns cannot give them. Another 54·7 per cent are "target workers", who will also return home. Only eight per cent said they had no intention at all of leaving the towns.

Commenting on these figures, the CCTA report on *Human Factors of Productivity in Africa*[1] declares that they are "intimately bound up with the question of security". The African can find this security on his tribal lands, says the report, but "in few places in the European economy can similar occupational security be found, housing being in many cases dependent on the retention of employment". It adds that the "same preoccupation with 'security' is seen in several British territories as the root problem to be solved before any long-term policy of improving the productivity of labour can be undertaken. Migrant labour may be said to be—almost of necessity—unattached; unreliable, unskilled because untrained, untrained because untrainable. Uncounted man-days are wasted on long, often exhausting, journeys between tribal Reserves and areas of employment; in the degree that detribalisation occurs, it tends to create at the unskilled level a rootless proletariat swarming in shanty-towns and breeding social problems faster than they can be tackled."

Low wages, too, are a factor preventing Africans from becoming stabilised and compelling them to move constantly between urban areas and their own villages. Noon points out that:

". . . the wages which they would earn at the mines were often too low to permit them to sever entirely ties with their

[1] *The Human Factors of Productivity in Africa*, Inter-African Labour Institute: Commission for Technical Co-operation in Africa South of the Sahara (CCTA), Bamako, 1956, pp. 46-7.

Native village. It is one thing to look on wages as a supplemental income to afford the means of meeting a passing obligation . . . while a considerable share of the family income is still produced by the labour of the wife and children who till the land. It is an entirely different situation when the worker must rely on wage earnings as the sole source of income for himself and family."[1]

Between Two Worlds

Though security is not to be found through wage labour in the towns, neither is it to be found in the rural areas, for that, too, was never imperialism's intention. The entire land and agricultural policy of the Europeans, as already pointed out, was precisely to prevent the emergence of a flourishing African agriculture, not only in order to stifle a potential economic rival to European farmers and plantation companies, but also to reduce the African to such dire economic straits that he would be compelled to leave his land periodically and sell his labour power to the European mining companies and farming interests.

Thus, by maintaining a poverty-stricken economy in the countryside as well as poverty wages, slums and lack of security in the urban areas, imperialism prevents the African finding economic security in either and so brings about the constant cycle of African movement from African subsistence farming to European employment, from European employment back to the countryside, which is such a marked feature of Africa today. The African is unable to maintain himself and his family without wage labour during part of his life. Neither does wage labour allow him to keep his wife and family. He is thus crushed between the millstones, and cannot escape in either direction.

"In South Africa the African is neither given the chance to become a stable peasant nor a stable city dweller. . . ."[2]

In East Africa, the Royal Commission of 1953-5 noted that the African worker in farm, plantation or town *"has found no permanent security for himself and his family. He has lived with one foot in his place of employment and one in his Reserve."*[3]

[1] Noon: op. cit., p. 36.
[2] Mphahlele, Ezekiel: "The Dilemma of the African Elite," *The Twentieth Century*, April 1959, **clxv**, No. 986, p. 319.
[3] EARC: op. cit., p. 27.

An observation obtained from one of the interviews carried out by C. H. Northcott during his enquiry in Kenya in 1947[1] runs:

"A porter in the goods shed on the minimum wage. Joined the service eighteen months ago to pay his poll tax and to get clothes. Brought his wife with him from North Kavirondo but soon found he could not support her and had to send her back."

Inevitably this poor porter must return home if he is ever to live with his wife again. Yet, just as inevitably, he must abandon her after a while "to pay his poll tax and to get clothes". And so the circle of movement continues.

Such is the system of migrant labour which impoverishes the African whether he remains a peasant or becomes a worker.

The policy frequently advocated in official and semi-offical studies is the gradual abolition of the migrant-labour system and its replacement by a permanent, stabilised, urbanised working class which has severed its ties for good with subsistence farming; and, as a counterpart to this, the forcible break-up of the African communal-land-holding system and its replacement by individual freehold, with the buying and selling of land. Though both these ideas have been advocated with growing frequency for at least twenty years, *migrant labour, far from declining, is maintained and even growing in most territories.*[2]

Why is it that the traditional pattern of cheap, migrant-labour persists with such stubbornness? The migrant-labour system is a basic element of colonial exploitation in Africa, which was founded on the exploitation of African mineral wealth and agricultural resources. The continent of Africa, after some sixty years of imperialist rule, remains unindustrialised, and its labour requirements, therefore, continue to be, in the main, the seasonal needs of European farms and plantations, and the unskilled

[1] Northcott: op. cit., p. 82.
[2] A recent U.N. study, referring to the "large-scale migrations which . . . are in the main a phenomenon of the African labour situation", adds that: "The most recent information indicates the continuation of these movements." It makes it clear, too, that among the main causes for this are the insufficiency of land and "the spread of economic and social insecurity". (NSG, p. 128.) See also *African Labour Survey*, pp. 127–38, I.L.O., 1958.

labour needs of European-owned mines. Even in the Union of South Africa, where the highest degree of industrial development in the continent has taken place, labour migration on an immense scale still prevails, the majority of workers remain unskilled (though there is a growing number of skilled and semi-skilled in manufacturing), and mines and farms remain the biggest consumers of labour even though manufacturing now produces annually more in value. It is colonialism's vested interest in maintaining a plentiful supply of cheap, migrant labour for the farms, plantations and mines that explains why the system still persists.

One has only to consider some of the figures again, in summary, to realise the extent to which the colonial economy of Africa is based on migrant labour. *Two-thirds* of the miners on the Rand come from outside the Union. Nearly *half* the Southern Rhodesian labour force is immigrant labour. A *majority* of the Uganda labour force is immigrant labour. About *half* the unskilled labourers in Ghana are drawn from other territories, and the *majority* employed during the important cocoa harvest season are migrants. A *quarter* of the African mineworkers in Northern Rhodesia come from outside the territory. A *majority* of the million African mineworkers in the continent are migrant workers.[1]

The traffic in the opposite direction is just as emphatic. *Over half* the able-bodied manpower of Basutoland leaves the territory every year. From Bechuanaland and Swaziland, some *twenty-five to thirty per cent* of adult males are absent from home. *Over forty per cent* of all Nyasaland adult males suitable for employment are employed outside the territory. *Well over fifty per cent* of southern Mozambique's adult male population is away from home working for wages in the employ of Europeans outside Mozambique.

But even these figures do not tell the whole story, for in addition to the immense volume of alien migration there is a similarly large volume of migration within each territory, from countryside to European employment. Thus it is that surveys of different territories find so often that *60, 70, 80 and even 100 per cent* of adult males are absent from villages.

> "*The vast majority of wage earners south of the Sahara are probably migrants.*"[2]

[1] See *Economic Survey of Africa Since 1950*, p. 61, U.N., 1959.
[2] ibid., p. 42.

It should be obvious, therefore, that *in Africa migrant labour lies at the very heart of the labour system.* Noon has said, with considerable justice, that migrant labour is *"the end result of all the problems which confront African labour today"*. It is migrant labour which provides the mechanism through which imperialism can best maintain a steady supply of cheap labour. Naturally enough, if one is concerned with securing abundant and continual supplies of cheap labour, it is scarcely likely that simultaneously vast sums are going to be spent on providing the housing, social security, pensions, family wage, education and training and employment in skilled jobs which are inevitable accompaniments, indeed requirements, of a labour stabilisation policy.

"White employers on the whole are ready to put up with migrant labour provided the supply is constant, for the important reason that migrant labour is likely to be cheaper in the long run than permanent labour. Apart from a rising scale of wages, a permanent labour force would require social amenities, such as housing and recreation, of a more extensive and costly type than the migrant labourer will accept. Even more costly, whether at the employers' or the Government's expense, would be the necessary provision for old age and unemployment. The white employers, provided they can get their labour at what they consider to be 'reasonable wages', do not, naturally, concern themselves with the problem of whether the African by working for them is undermining the economic life of his own village."[1]

Official reluctance to break with the migrant-labour system and to provide the necessary forms of social security essential for any policy of labour stabilisation was noted by the East Africa Royal Commission, 1953–5, which found the governments in Kenya, Tanganyika and Uganda "anxious to preserve among Africans that form of security which prevailed where each individual had access to land in his own tribal area for subsistence purposes. They were also anxious to avoid the emergence of a landless class which had lost the traditional form of security in sickness and old age."[2]

[1] Read, Dr. Margaret: op. cit., p. 608.
[2] EARC op. cit., p. 50.

In other words, the colonial governments in East Africa prefer to throw on to the poverty-stricken peasantry all the burdens of providing security in sickness and old age, though elsewhere in the report the Royal Commission has to admit that *"poverty still characterises the condition of nearly all the inhabitants of the three territories"*.[1]

Some emergence there might well be in certain centres (the Union of South Africa, the Belgian Congo, Northern Rhodesia, for example) of pockets of stabilised labour; and it is true, too, that these pockets are steadily growing larger. But they do not, nor can they within the colonial system obtaining in Africa, change the dominant pattern. It is the European mining and farming interests, and their related trading, shipping, banking and insurance concerns, which call the tune. The very money which flows into Africa from Wall Street, the City of London or the Bourse is attracted precisely by the abundance of cheap labour which is created by continual migration.

Nor are there only economic reasons for maintaining the migrant-labour system. There is a fundamental political reason, too; and that is the desire to prevent or at least retard the formation of a permanent working class, completely alien to the limited outlook and political horizons of village life, and capable of maturing into a powerful, cohesive, modern proletariat which knows where it is going and is strong enough to reach its goal. It has not escaped the notice of the imperialists that it is in the urbanised labour areas where the biggest challenges to imperialist exploitation and rule are being made. As elsewhere in the capitalist world, it is the working class which is the grave-digger of imperialism. Fear of this growing force erupts constantly between the lines of official reports. Warnings are repeatedly made of the "social dangers" arising from the "severance of Africans from their traditional tribal society" with no "stabilising factors" to replace "tribal ties and customs".

Schapera[2] states that in Bechuanaland it is a common complaint (presumably of British officials and of chiefs) that migration makes young people "disrespectful and insubordinate", that they are "often insolent towards the chief" and tend to be "rebellious" as shown by their "failure to pay tax". It is said—and this has

[1] ibid., p. 28.
[2] Schapera: op. cit.

some significance—that migrant workers "have come into contact with all sorts of new influences and ideas" and that when they return home they come "with the idea that they are more enlightened". New conceptions have arisen, says Schapera, as to "the relationship between ruler and subject, especially in regard to matters like forced labour".

It is clear that what the forces of reaction recognise here and fear is the growth of political understanding with its accompanying determination not to submit to the old order of things.

> "The dilemma is clear," warns a Central African Federation Report quoted in *The Human Factors of Productivity in Africa*. "On the one hand migrant labour is grossly inefficient, and to improve its quality and efficiency stabilisation in the area of employment is essential; *on the other hand the retention of a link with the tribal background has great advantages in the plane of family cohesion, and general morality, and hence for social peace and political stability.* This point is stressed in the report from Ruanda-Urundi, itself a large exporter of migrant workers to the Congo and East African territories, especially Uganda. It is also brought out in British reports and other sources."[1]
>
> [Own italics—J. W.]

It is significant that at the height of the emergency in Kenya the Government carried out "Operation Anvil" in Nairobi, an operation specifically aimed at removing from this urban centre thousands of African workers, in order to break up what it regarded as a dangerous concentration of proletarians. Similarly, when the clash with imperialism became acute in Leopoldville, Belgian Congo, at the beginning of 1959, the Government immediately removed thousands of workers back to the country-side. In the Union of South Africa, too, the whole drive behind the Bantustan conception is to force the African proletariat out of the towns to the countryside, to deny him education through the Bantu Education Act, and thus to plunge him back to the ignorance, superstition and obscurantism of his former life.

Migrant labour has often been called the curse of Africa, but amid the welter of African studies which describe this system, frequently from a critical standpoint, one scarcely finds a word

[1] CCTA, 1956, op. cit.

to explain that migrant labour in Africa is part and parcel of colonialism, is, in fact, a system devised and fostered by imperialism. Useless, therefore, are all the appeals, however well-meaning and however backed up with arguments favouring greater efficiency in production, to the imperialist authorities to abandon the migrant-labour system in favour of labour stabilisation. Migrant labour and slave wages will be eliminated only when colonialism itself is overcome, when the African people obtain their freedom and, through the control of their own resources, are able to transform their lands from agrarian and mineral appendages of Western metropolitan countries into lands possessing a modern industry, a flourishing agriculture and a stable, prosperous population in both sectors.

CHAPTER FIVE

AN AFRICAN REVOLUTION?

I⊤ is fashionable these days to talk about an "African revolution". Great, indeed, are the changes sweeping like storm clouds so hurriedly over this vast continent; yet *The Economist*[1] and others are wrong in their basic contention that Africa is undergoing a fundamental economic and industrial revolution.

According to this theory Africa is passing through the same process that Britain went through in the nineteenth century, when millions of workers were driven off the land to enter the new factories and mills. Africa, we are told, is becoming industrialised and her people are being changed into a stable, urbanised proletariat, acquiring labour skills and becoming completely cut off from their former life on the land.

It is necessary to look a little closer at this question, for our interpretation of what is happening in Africa today and our examination of the roots of the present national resurgence engulfing the whole continent depends to a large extent on our understanding of the character of the African working class and the degree to which the African people are, in fact, becoming proletarianised.

The size and character of the working class in any country is obviously determined by the character of its economy and the form of its society. It is in the industrially developed countries that the main concentrations of the modern proletariat are to be found, while in the under-developed areas the overwhelming majority of the people are peasants and live off the land. Africa is no exception to this rule. Moreover, facts confirm the Marxist contention that those areas of the world which are politically and economically dominated by the Western imperialist powers remain as the main non-industrialised areas, with only limited industrial developments being permitted to take place.

[1] "The African Revolution", *Economist* Special Supplement, December 13, 1958.

A recent Unesco report[1] points out that in Africa, apart from the Union of South Africa, "industry of any kind, in the sense of production with power-driven machinery and a considerable labour force, is very recent and still confined to a few widely dispersed centres. . . . *The vast majority of industrially manufactured goods are still imported from overseas and local activities are still largely confined to their assembly, distribution and maintenance.*" [Own italics—J. W.]

Thus industry in tropical Africa, apart from mining and assembly, "is mainly concerned with initial processing of agricultural produce for export, the plants for which are again dispersed in comparatively small units on plantations or in the ports or rail centres of the various territories".

Further more, as this report comments, these very limited ranges of industrial activity "do not call for a large and diversified body of highly skilled labour".

The Unesco report goes on to point out that African wage earners continue, for the most part, to maintain their connections with their indigenous subsistence economies, and that the main characteristics of African labour are its temporary basis, low wages, lack of training or continuous experience and limited openings to acquire skill. Where there has been extensive European settlement and the establishment of Reserves, as in South Africa, the Rhodesias or Kenya, the problem has become aggravated, the African people finding it more and more difficult to support themselves and being increasingly compelled to depend on the export of unskilled labour as their main source of livelihood.

"*Industry in Africa has accordingly been built up with comparatively low mechanisation and high consumption of low-paid unskilled labour, and this pattern, once established, has acquired an inertia often reflected in the economic policies of the enterprises and in the social attitudes of Europeans.* In urban areas the effect in general has been to produce large floating populations with low and insecure incomes, little differentiation in skills and education, and very limited means for material and social advance.

"Urbanisation is correspondingly recent and restricted in scale and scope."[2]   [Own italics—J. W.]

[1] *Social Implications of Industrialisation and Urbanisation in Africa South of the Sahara*, p. 11, Unesco, 1956.   [2] Unesco, op. cit., p. 12.

The report comes to the conclusion that "both industry and urban life in Africa are . . . still in an early and limited phase of development."[1]

Even if this Unesco report tends to underestimate the extent of wage labour in certain areas of Africa today, basically its assessment is correct.

A similar view regarding the lack of industrialism and urbanisation of Africa is expressed by Irving:[2]

"Africa has not yet attained the high levels of concentration attained elsewhere. . . . As long as man is the basis of power and not factory organisation, no concentration of men in large aggregates is possible. The new age demands concentration of men and concentration of machines. . . . [The process] is still embyronic in Africa. This is one of the primary sources of African problems."

But to deal adequately with the question of the "African revolution" it is not sufficient to pose one opinion against another. It is, after all, facts which will really provide the answer.

And among the facts which help to provide the answer are the size, composition and character of the working class.

It attempting to answer the questions: How large is the African working class? What proportion does it constitute of the total population? and What are its main characteristics? one comes up against a considerable difficulty. It is recognised on all sides that there is a woeful lack of accurate statistical material available regarding the size of Africa's population and of the different classes it comprises; and even though some improvements have taken place in the past few years in the collection and compilation of such information, the inadequacy of the earlier statistics makes it difficult to define with exactness what trends are taking place or to make any comparisons.

Only the more recent decisions to step up the exploitation of Africa and her people has motivated the authorities to carry through a more careful sifting of the facts, to ascertain the size

[1] ibid., p. 13.
[2] "Ecology of city growth in the African context": paper read by Professor James Irving, Rhodes University, Grahamstown, Union of South Africa: *Apthorpe Report*, op. cit.

of the population, the potential labour force, the potential market and so forth. Yet even now the general contempt of many colonial officials towards Africans leads them to make general and rather wide assumptions based on tax returns. One is reminded here of Kuczynski's reference[1] to the *Report of the Census of the Colony of Hong Kong, 1931*, which calculated the population in the following bizarre fashion:

"... the amount of night-soil now being collected approximates to nearly 4,000,000 taels, which at three taels per head gives a population of over 1,300,000 without allowing for wastage."

No doubt somewhat similar "scientific" methods of computing populations were used by Europeans with regard to China before her liberation in 1949. This may account for the fact that European estimates—or those of the Chiang Kai-shek Governmen guided by Western advisers—never gave China more than 500,000,000 people. When a proper calculation was made after the founding of the Chinese People's Republic in 1949 it was discovered that China had well over 600,000,000 people.

In the light of such experience it is as well to regard figures for the population of African territories as being, in most cases, only approximate estimates.

TABLE V

POPULATION BY COUNTRY AND ETHNIC COMPOSITION, 1956*

(Thousands of persons)

Country	African	European	Asian	Other	Total
North Africa					
Algeria[1] ..	8,570[2]	1,050[3]	—	—	9,620
Egypt (UAR)[4] ..	23,887	121	—	18	24,026
Libya[5] ..					1,092
Morocco:					
Northern Zone ..	...	...	...	...	1,068
Southern Zone ..	7,979	460	—	141[6]	8,580
Tunisia ..	3,442[2]	255	—	86[7]	3,783
South Africa					
Basutoland	...	...	...		643
Bechuanaland ..	...	...	...	...	327
Union of South Africa ..	9,306	2,907	421	1,281[8]	13,915
South West Africa	449	62	—	—	511
Swaziland ..	...	...	...	...	237

[1] Kuczynski, R. R.: *Colonial Populations*, 1937.

Country	African	European	Asian	Other	Total
Tropical Africa					
Central Africa:					
Belgian Congo	12,698	102	11	—	12,811
Rhodesia and Nyasaland (Federation of)	6,980	251		30	7,260
Northern Rhodesia	2,110	66	7[9]	—	2,180
Southern Rhodesia	2,290	178		13	2,480
Nyasaland	2,580	7		10	2,600
Ruanda-Urundi	4,427	6	—	—	4,433
East Africa:					
Ethiopia	20,000	...	...	...	20,000
Kenya	5,902	58	185[10]	5	6,150
Madagascar	4,846	72	—	—	4,918
Mauritius	...	...	...	...	569
Mozambique[1]	5,923	66	17[11]	35	6,040
Réunion	...	...	...	...	296
Somaliland, British	...	...	...	...	650
Somaliland, French	...	...	...	...	67
Somaliland, Italian administration	...	...	...	...	1,300
Sudan	10,263	—	—	—	10,263
Tanganyika	8,329	28	93[10]	6	8,456
Uganda	5,527	8	56[10]	1	5,593
Zanzibar	...	...	...	...	280
West Africa					
Angola[1]	4,222	110	—	30	4,362
Cameroons, French administration	3,171	16	—	—	3,187
French Equatorial Africa ..	4,854	24	—	1	4,879
French West Africa	18,842	88	—	—	18,930
Gambia	...	...	...	...	285
Ghana	4,684	7	—	—	4,691
Liberia	...	...	...	...	1,250
Nigeria	31,824	10	—	—	31,834
Sierra Leone	...	...	...	...	2,100
Togoland, French administration	1,084	1	—	—	1,085

* *Economic Survey of Africa since 1950*, p. 13, United Nations Department of Economic and Social Affairs, New York, 1959.

[1] 1955.
[2] Moslems.
[3] French.
[4] 1957.
[5] 1954.
[6] Jews.

[7] Algerians and Tripolitanians.
[8] Coloured, mainly Cape coloured.
[9] Including coloured.
[10] Indians and Arabs.
[11] Mixed.

How Many African Wage Workers

Special difficulties have to be faced when ascertaining the size of the African working class. On the basis of official figures, estimates and, in some cases, census figures, Hailey arrives at the following table:[1]

[1] Hailey (Revised): op. cit., p. 1360.

TABLE VI
AFRICAN WAGE WORKERS

1953	South Africa..	..	..	2,240,000
1951	Southern Rhodesia ..		..	488,450
1954	Northern Rhodesia ..		..	258,340
1954	Nyasaland ..	..	..	106,900
1954	Tanganyika ..	..	..	439,094 (gainfully employed)
1953	Kenya	..	..	359,000
	Uganda	..	..	224,500 (estimates say 300,000)
1948	Zanzibar	..	..	107,800
	Nigeria and Br. Cameroons			500,000
1953	Ghana	..	..	216,300
1952	Sierra Leone	..	..	90,000
1951	Gambia	..	..	5,400 (plus casual dock labour)
1951	French Equatorial Africa	..		216,500
1947	French West Africa..		..	232,000
1951	Belgian Congo	..	..	1,030,900
1951	Ruanda-Urundi	..	..	110,000
1954	Angola	..	..	800,000
1954	Mozambique	..	..	110,000
	Liberia	..	..	25,000 (on rubber estates only)

This gives a grand total of 7,554,384 African wage earners.[1]   There
is no doubt that this figure is an underestimate, apart from
being based, in many cases, on rather old sources. Hailey
himself says:[2]

> "The figures which it has been possible to quote refer for
> the most part to the number in regular employment by
> companies, individual European or Asian employers, or in
> Government undertakings. In most cases they exclude the
> more casual wage-earners and those in the employment of
> Africans, who in some areas (as in Uganda) employ labourers
> for cash wages. . . ."

It should perhaps be borne in mind that official statistics for
African wage earners are usually based on the returns from firms
employing ten or more workers. This means that the large numbers

[1] If one includes North Africa one must add another 2½ to 3 millions. More
recent figures for the number of African wage workers, provided in the recent
U.N. Economic and Social Department *Economic Survey of Africa Since 1950*
(New York, 1959), show, for certain territories, that the number of workers
has increased since Hailey compiled his table (Belgian Congo by 100,000,
Southern Rhodesia by 120,000, Nyasaland by 60,000, Kenya by 200,000 and
Ghana by 50,000); but in most cases there is little change. Hailey's table has
been preferred because it includes far more territories than the U.N. report
does, the latter excluding the Union of South Africa, Nigeria, Angola, Mozambique, Liberia and the whole of the French Community and Guinea.
[2] Hailey (Revised): op. cit., p. 1361.

of African workers employed by African farmers and traders, especially in West Africa, are not included in the official figures. It is interesting to note, in this connection, that Professor Potekhin, on the basis of a personal investigation made in Ghana, comes to the conclusion that the number of wage workers in Ghana is probably twice the official figure.[1] There is no doubt that much of what he says on this point has a relevance for Nigeria, too.

The recent *Economic Survey of Africa since 1950*[2] also draws attention to the inadequacy of statistics relating to the African working class, and claims that "Wage employment among Africans is far more widespread than a hasty consideration of the available statistics . . . might suggest."

Noon is most critical of official statistics on the number of African wage workers,[3] stressing in particular the tendency to ignore the number of Africans working for African employers, as well as the number of seasonal workers, employed by both Europeans and Africans, and the number employed in domestic service. He even estimates the number of Africans employed by Africans in agriculture in the French Cameroons as exceeding the number employed by Europeans.[4] There is often confusion, too, he indicates, between agricultural workers, squatters and peasants.

On the basis of the above considerations, Noon provides the following figures:[5]

TABLE VII
MANPOWER AND EMPLOYMENT IN AFRICA

	Potential Manpower			Total Employment	% of manpower
	Males	Females	Total		
West Africa	13,180,979	15,314,533	28,495,512	571,836	2
Central Africa	5,798,625	5,914,001	11,733,477	613,120	5·23
East Africa	6,873,075	7,960,002	15,050,853	1,108,172	7·36
South Africa	3,355,284	3,343,410	6,703,294	5,849,125	87·26
Total	29,207,963	32,531,946	61,983,136*	8,142,253	13·14

* The total manpower exceeds the figures given for males and females since it was not always possible to provide separate figures for male and female workers.

[1] *West Africa*, p. 1061, November 8, 1958.
[2] ECSA, op. cit.
[3] Noon: op. cit., p. 56 et seq.
[4] ibid., p. 71.
[5] ibid., p. 135.

It is interesting to note here that Noon's figures, worked out
a decade earlier than Hailey's, give a total of *8,142,253 compared
with the latter's 7,554,384,* although it should be borne in mind
that Hailey does not include all the territories listed by Noon
(e.g. Sudan). Noon points out that his figures are by no means
accurate, but that they are *an underestimate* since "the employment
figure represents with few exceptions the manpower utilised by
European enterprise".[1]

In this connection it will be noted that it is the white-settler
areas where the proportion of Africans engaged in wage labour
is greatest, and West Africa, which is characterised mainly by
the African farming of cash crops for export, where the proportion of wage labour is lowest—though, in the light of the remarks
above, it is clearly not as low as official figures indicate.

The numerical strength of the African working class cannot be
determined with any degree of scientific accuracy. But taking
into account all the shortcomings indicated above in the methods
of compiling official statistics of African wage labour, and making
some allowance for the further growth of the working class since
the above calculations were made, *one can probably put the figure
today at somewhere between ten and twelve million*—that is, *between six
and seven per cent of the total African population south of the Sahara.*

This, of course, is by no means a weak force. Moreover, it is
growing and will continue to grow.

It should be borne in mind, too, that the figures given above
represent the number of Africans engaged in wage labour *at any
given time.* As a consequence of the migrant-labour system the
number of Africans who, at some period in their lives, have had
experience of wage labour or who repeatedly re-enter the labour
market, is considerably greater than the figures for the total
labour force indicated by official statistics.

In Bechuanaland, for example (admittedly very much a labour
reservoir for the Union of South Africa) Schapera[2] found that
among 1,172 men whose labour record was investigated, *no
less than 83·9 per cent were either away working outside Bechuanaland,
or had done so.*

In 1947, it was estimated that *almost every adult Ngoni male* in
the Eastern Province of Northern Rhodesia had, at one time or

[1] ibid., p. 136.
[2] Schapera: op. cit.

another, emigrated to find work, in most cases outside Rhodesia.[1] A report on South Africa[2] states that "with the exception of cripples and disabled persons, *nearly all males* are employed outside Bantu areas at one or another stage between the fifteenth and fiftieth birthdays".

Even if one concedes that such high percentages are not reached in every African territory, there is no doubt that over the past two decades the *majority of African males have had some experience of wage labour*, even if only for a few months. The significance of this will not be lost on the reader.

The Nature of Employment

Where workers are in a state of constant movement between village and town, mine, or plantation, clearly one cannot talk about a modern proletariat in the full sense of the term.

In fact, the disposition of the African working class as between the main fields of employment—as one might expect—shows that it bears all the usual hall-marks of a working class in a colonial economy.

A recent U.N. Report[3] provides the following instructive table. (See page 118.)

Leaving aside for the moment the key question of agriculture, which is not included here, what are the distinguishing features of the African working class which clearly emerge from this table? One has only to subtract from one's analysis the number of Africans engaged in manufacture in the Union of South Africa (the one area of the African continent where basic industrialisation has made some headway), to find that less than 450,000 workers are so employed in the rest of Africa, and of these no less than 167,312 are accounted for by the Belgian Congo, leaving a balance of some 280,000 for the remainder.

It is indicative of the character of the African economy that the largest numder of Africans is engaged, according to the accompanying table, in domestic and other services, which take up no less than 1,500,000 workers, about thirty per cent of

---

[1] Quoted in NSG, op. cit., p. 110.
[2] *Summary of the Report of the Commission for the Socio-Economic Development of the Bantu Areas within the Union of South Africa*, Government Printer, Pretoria, 1955. (Quoted in ECSA, op. cit., p. 42.)
[3] *World Social Situation*, U.N., 1957.

TABLE VIII

DISTRIBUTION OF AFRICAN WAGE EARNERS BY PRINCIPAL OCCUPATION

Territory and Year of Reference		Extractive industries	Manufacturing	Building and construction	Transport	Commerce	Domestic and other services	Public administration	Total
French West Africa	1954	12,419	39,779	42,670	33,134	51,210	21,123	107,626	298,961
French Equatorial Africa	1953	20,333	12,188	22,089	14,292	12,626	15,329	16,800	113,657
Sierra Leone	1954	4,901	—	10,963	5,004	4,962	2,688	11,162	39,680
Gold Coast	1952	41,037	11,776	44,700	18,511	23,498	18,328	33,352	191,202
Nigeria	1952	57,688	17,923	35,392	42,335	20,579	13,129	53,181	240,227
Belgian Congo	1954	103,518	167,312	128,915	84,468	77,399	318,741	—	880,353
Angola	1953	21,809	—	—	—	—	—	—	21,809
Mozambique	1953	5,025	29,866	—	—	—	—	—	34,891
Madagascar	1953	12,920	25,312	11,138	7,677	16,900	36,997	55,343	166,287
Southern Rhodesia	1951	63,805	55,729	48,971	17,813	—	131,033	—	317,351
Northern Rhodesia	1953	46,100	18,650	25,500	8,150	6,810	73,820	37,450	216,480
Nyasaland	1953	—	1,400	4,300	5,800	1,800	3,200	19,100	35,600
Uganda	1954	7,922	24,414	45,448	7,625	6,245	28,486	48,408	168,548
Tanganyika	1954	15,453	19,669	16,373	34,262	11,428	50,946	76,334	214,465
Kenya	1954	5,448	42,754	19,411	34,355	22,080	44,274	103,709	272,031
Union of South Africa	—	491,900	436,029	107,593	98,367	109,600	830,900	—	2,074,389
TOTAL	..	910,278	893,801	563,463	401,793	365,137	1,588,994	562,465	5,285,931

Source: *World Social Situation*, U.N., 1957.

the entire labour force (less agriculture). It is striking that almost the whole of that figure is accounted for by the main areas of white settlement—South Africa, Northern and Southern Rhodesia, Kenya, Tanganyika, the Belgian Congo. In West Africa, where white settlement has been at a minimum, only a small number of workers comes within this category.

A further significant fact revealed by this table is that the second largest consumer of African labour after "domestic and other services" is the extractive industries, of which mining is the most important. The extraction of minerals is one of the twin bases of the imperialist exploitation of Africa (the other being agriculture); and it is interesting to note that even in the industrially developed Union of South Africa more Africans are engaged in mining than in manufacture. Transport and commerce, which are closely connected with the extractive industries, account for another 767,000, not far off the figure for manufacture. And more than half a million are engaged in building and construction, and the same in public administration—both being categories of labour connected with the existing colonial system. Much of the building is devoted to constructing main roads, warehouses, harbours, airfields, commercial offices, and the like (so essential for drawing off the wealth of Africa), as well as constructing prisons, police barracks, and government buildings of various kinds from which the colonial authorities conduct their colonial administration. Building devoted to the needs of the African people takes up a very small proportion of the labour force.

What is striking, too, as far as the structure and disposition of the working class is concerned, is the dominance of agriculture. A U.N. report,[1] based on figures up to about 1951 and covering a selected group of countries, shows over 1,000,000 workers engaged in agriculture and forestry, about 390,000 engaged in mining, and some 2,000,000 engaged in all other sectors of the economy, including 370,800 in industry.

This means that in the ten selected territories agriculture and forestry account for 32 per cent of the total labour force, and mines for another 11 per cent. Among the individual territories, agriculture accounts for 52 per cent of the total number of workers in Tanganyika, 48 per cent in Kenya, and 39 per cent in Southern

[1] *Enlargement of the Exchange Economy in Tropical Africa*, pp. 23-4, U.N., 1954.

TABLE IX

Employment of African Labour,[1] by Major Categories
(Thousands of workers)

Columns *Domestic and other services*, *Public administration*, and *Miscellaneous* fall under the grouping heading **Other Employment**.

Territory and year	Agriculture	Forestry	Mining and quarrying	Electric power production	Building and Construction	Industry	Commerce	Transport	Domestic and other services	Public administration	Miscellaneous	Total	Overall Total
Belgian Congo .. 1950	238·8	—	113·8	—	84·8	134·9	62·1	62·1	—	—	255·5	609·4	962·0
French Equat. Africa 1950	44·3	22·0	27·1	—	17·1[2]	14·2	9·1	5·6	8·2	44·4	0·7	99·3	192·7[3]
French West Africa 1947	50·0	10·4	4·7	—	—	41·1	39·9	18·4	—	50·8	28·9	179·2	244·3[4]
Gold Coast .. 1950	20·0	—	44·3	1·7	33·7	10·1	19·2	15·2	9·7	30·5	—	120·0	183·3[4]
Kenya 1950	201·9[5]	—	8·3	1·4	16·3	34·7	19·3	5·2	—	95·1	38·5[6]	210·5	420·8
Nigeria 1957	55·0	—	70·6	0·8	—	10·0	—	28·7	32·0	92·1	—	131·9	257·5
Northern Rhodesia 1949	32·4	—	37·0	—	43·0	21·0	—	3·9	—	9·7	36·0	102·6	172·0[7]
Southern Rhodesia 1950	177·0	—	59·5	3·7	45·0	52·0	19·0	10·0	{— 93·0 —} (combined domestic & administration)		0·8	221·5	458·0[8]
Tanganyika .. 1951	232·7	4·4[5]	18·3	—	34·5	28·4	19·9	24·1	51·1	31·2	—	200·2	455·4
Uganda 1950	29·5	3·6[5]	5·8	—	—	24·4	2·5	6·4	7·2	39·3	—	132·2	171·2[9]
TOTAL ..	1,122·0		389·4	7·6	274·4	370·8	191·0	179·6	108·2 / 93·0	393·1 / 93·0	360·4	2,006·8	3,518·2

[1] Including extra-territorial workers.
[2] Building and public works.
[3] Including 3,200 Europeans.
[4] Of these, 77,375 were employed by the Government and 106,963 by private enterprise.
[5] Including fishing.
[6] Including domestic service.
[7] Including 36,000 migrants from other territories.
[8] Including 253,000 migrants from other territories.
[9] Including 18,000 Africans employed in cotton ginning, which provides only seasonal employment.

Source: *Enlargement of the Exchange Economy in Tropical Africa*, p. 24, U.N., 1954.

Rhodesia. (It is interesting to note that in the Union of South Africa, too, agriculture is the area of the economy in which the majority of African workers are engaged, there being in 1953, according to Hailey,[1] some 700,000 African wage workers employed on farms in the Union.)

Secondary industry provides employment for approximately ten per cent of the total number of wage-earners in the ten territories, the Belgian Congo and Southern Rhodesia alone accounting for about half of the total. It should be borne in mind, however, that secondary industry in Africa is almost everywhere light industry, is often connected with the preliminary processing of agricultural goods or minerals, and that much of it is small-scale. Scarcely any large heavy-engineering exists, nor iron and steel, motor-car manufacture (as distinct from assembly), nor machine-tool making. The Union of South Africa is, of course, an exception to this rule; and an iron and steel industry is being developed in Que Que in Southern Rhodesia.

In general, however, statistics strikingly confirm that the main characteristics of the African working class are those of a colonial working class, working within the sphere of a colonial economy and scarcely touched by the breath of industrialisation. It is a working class which is mainly unskilled, largely migrant and, as we shall see later, only partly urbanised. It works in mines, farms and plantations producing the goods which the imperialists require for export. It works on the railways, roads, docks and airfields in order to transport the wealth from Africa to the West, and to distribute the manufactured goods sent in from the West for sale on African markets. It builds roads and administrative and commercial buildings to facilitate the exploitation and administration of the territories. In government offices and in commerce it helps to perform the clerical and administrative labour essential for colonial rule. And in hotels, clubs and private houses it waits on the white man, mixes his drinks, cooks his meals, washes his children, and launders his clothes.

In every direction it turns the African working class comes up against the realities of the colonial system—the exploitation by big foreign companies and the arbitrary rule of colonial authorities.

The African working class has grown considerably, especially

[1] Hailey (Revised): op. cit., p. 1360.

in the last two decades. As we have seen, it probably numbers ten to twelve million and is still growing. It is significant that its growth is proportionately more rapid than that of the African population as a whole. Furthermore, in certain territories there has been a growth of manufacturing industry and the emergence of an African stratum of semi-skilled, and in some cases skilled workers, and this section, too, is growing. In the Union of South Africa, for example, by 1951 no less than sixty-seven per cent of all semi-skilled work was being performed by Africans.

Yet basically the African working class remains a cheap, unskilled, migratory labour force, employed in mining and agriculture and the ancillary trades, and connected by every thread and fibre of its being to the system of colonial exploitation.

Urbanisation

Another partial test which has been applied to ascertain the rate and degree of change taking place in Africa, and as a basis to argue the conception of the "African revolution", is that of the urbanisation and stabilisation of labour. Much of the confusion which has arisen is due to a certain looseness with which the terms have been employed. The words "urbanisation" and "stabilisation" have been used often interchangeably, although they concern two quite distinct yet not unrelated phenomena.

Furthermore, there has been a tendency in some quarters to exaggerate the extent to which urbanisation has taken place, and somewhat sweeping conclusions have been drawn regarding its significance. An additional difficulty has been the different criteria used to determine the degree of urbanisation. Finally, general declarations from official quarters in favour of creating a stable, permanent, urbanised working class have often been accepted at their face value even though the governments and employers in the different African territories have continued, in all essentials, to carry out the same economic and social policies which have so far prevented the emergence of a large, modern, stable and urbanised proletariat.

Naturally enough, there has been a growth of towns in Africa in the past twenty years or so, and a considerable increase in their African populations.

The following table, based on figures provided by Hodgkin,[1] gives some indication of this rapid growth:

TABLE X
GROWTH OF TOWNS

Dakar			Bangui		
1936	..	92,000	1945	..	25,000
1955	..	300,000	1955	..	100,000
Bamako			Lagos		
1941	..	22,000	1931	..	126,608
1955	..	100,000	1955	..	270,000
Leopoldville			Enugu		
1940	..	46,884	1939	..	15,000
1955	..	340,000	1953	..	60,000

Elizabethville
1940 .. 26,789
1955 .. 120,000

A recent Unesco study[2] provides the following figures for some of the other main towns in Africa:

TABLE XI
GROWTH OF TOWNS

Nairobi		.109,000 (1951) (of which about half African)
Douala	..	51,000
Freetown	..	64,000
Accra	..	136,000
Port Harcourt		50,000
Kumasi	..	78,000
Ibadan	..	459,000
Kano	..	130,000
Brazzaville	..	64,000
Matadi	..	53,000 (1953)
Stanleyville	..	49,000 (1953)
Mombasa	..	85,000 (of which 43,000 African)
Dar es Salaam		70,000 (1948) (of which 51,000 African)

There is no doubt that African towns have grown still further since these figures were compiled. This is certainly true, for instance, of Southern Rhodesia. The Plewman Commission Report[3] shows, in fact, that the number of adult males in employment in the seven municipalities and suburbs of Southern Rhodesia increased from 97,314 in 1946 to 198,542 in 1956—an increase of more than a hundred per cent in ten years:

[1] Hodgkin, Thomas: *Nationalism in Colonial Africa*, p. 67, London, 1956.
[2] Unesco, op. cit.
[3] *Report of the Urban African Affairs Commission*, Salisbury, 1958, Plewman Commission Report, p. 16.

TABLE XII
NUMBER OF AFRICAN MALES IN SOUTHERN RHODESIAN TOWNS

	Salisbury	Bulawayo	Umtali	Gwelo	Gatooma	Que Que	Fort Victoria	Total
1936	20,010	15,070	3,523	2,125	1,697	3,213	. —	45,638
1946	45,216	32,413	6,353	7,141	2,385	3,806	. —	97,314
1951	73,594	54,392	10,569	10,021	4,462	4,843	2,735	160,616
1956	99,131	63,906	13,254	10,315	4,117	4,626	3,193	198,452

(Source: Central African Statistical Office.)

An estimate[1] given in this same report for the ·total African population in these seven municipal urban areas—men, women and children—shows an increase from 248,000 in 1951 to 324,700 in 1956.

TABLE XIII
TOTAL AFRICAN POPULATION IN SOUTHERN RHODESIAN TOWNS

			1951	1956
Salisbury	..	.. ..	104,000	151,000
Bulawayo	..	.. ..	90,000	116,000
Umtali	..	.. ..	15,000	22,000
Gwelo	..	.. ..	18,000	21,000
Gatooma	..	.. ..	6,600	6,900
Que Que	..	.. ..	7,500	7,800
Fort Victoria	..	..	6,900	—
Total ..		..	248,000	324,700

On the basis of regarding all municipalities and townships, including neighbouring suburbs and mine townships, as "urban" if they had non-African populations of more than 1,200 at the time of the 1956 census, the Plewman Commission concludes that "thirty-seven per cent of the total number of Africans were working in urban areas as so defined".

TABLE XIV
SUMMARY OF THE URBAN-RURAL DISTRIBUTION OF AFRICANS
IN EMPLOYMENT IN SOUTHERN RHODESIA: 1951 AND 1956 CENSUSES

1951 Census			1956 Census		
Urban Areas	Rural Areas	Total	Urban Areas	Rural Areas	Total
183,582	346,621	530,203	224,905	385,048	609,953

Whether one accepts the rather sweeping criterion adopted by the Plewman Commission or not, the *trend* towards urbanisation is apparently clear. And the trend is equally revealed by the earlier figures quoted above.

[1] ibid., p. 17.

Equally significant trends are shown in several other territories. In Senegal 18 per cent of Africans were living in towns of over 20,000 inhabitants, by 1943.[1] A later report,[2] which states that urbanisation "has gone further in Senegal than in any other part of French West Africa", gives an estimate of 500,000, or about 25 per cent of the population, as living in towns, with 250,000 in Dakar, 39,000 in Saint-Louis, 39,000 in Laoloack and 39,000 in Thies. In the Belgian Congo, returns for 1952 and 1953 indicate about 500,000 Africans—a number equal to a little less than half the labour force—now living in towns. In the Middle Congo (1953) 16 per cent were living in Brazzaville and Pointe Noire alone.

It is, of course, in the Union, the most industrially developed region in Africa, that African urbanisation has made most headway. At the time of the 1921 census 508,000 or 13 per cent of the total African population were classified as urban. By the time of the 1951 census the figure had risen to 2,312,000, or a little over 27 per cent; and today it is estimated at some 3,500,000, or about 35 per cent. In Johannesburg alone, by 1946 the number of Africans, 357,175, was greater than the total number of Africans resident in all urban centres in the Union in 1904.

The trend towards urbanisation of Africans is also clearly shown by figures given in the *Economic Survey for Africa since 1950*.[3] In French Cameroons the percentage of Africans living in towns increased from 2·4 per cent in 1937 to 5·5 per cent in 1957; in French Equatorial Africa, from 1·7 per cent in 1936 to 4·4 per cent in 1956; in French West Africa, from 1·1 per cent in 1936 to 4·1 per cent in 1956; in Madagascar, from 3·9 per cent in 1936 to 5·6 per cent in 1956; in the Central African Federation, from 4 per cent in 1951 to 5·5 per cent in 1956; in South West Africa, from 5·9 per cent in 1936 to 9·4 per cent in 1951; in French Togoland, from 1·8 per cent in 1936 to 3·7 per cent in 1956.

Nevertheless, compared with the other under-developed areas of the world, such as Asia and Latin America, the African towns are still relatively small. Moreover, the number of Africans living in them remains a considerable minority of the total African

---

[1] Balandier, Professor Georges: Paper in Unesco Report, op. cit.
[2] Mercier, Dr. P.: Paper in Unesco Report, op. cit.
[3] Source: Table I–II, page 14, ECSA, op. cit.

population. In fact a U.N. report on the world social situation[1] states that whereas 75 per cent of the 4,000,000 Europeans and 70 per cent of the 700,000 Asians and Arabs living in Africa south of the Sahara are city-dwellers, only 6 per cent of the total African and non-African population live in towns of 20,000 or more inhabitants. This means that *the number of Africans south of the Sahara living in towns of 20,000 or more inhabitants is only about 6,000,000—or a little under 4 per cent of the total African population.* This is a striking figure not only in relation to industrialised countries—such as England and Wales (1951), 69 per cent; Australia (1951), 57 per cent; United States (1950), 43 per cent; and the U.S.S.R. (1959 census), 35 per cent—but is far below that of other underdeveloped countries—India (1951), 12 per cent; Iran (1950), 21 per cent; Egypt (1947), 29 per cent; Cuba (1950), 33 per cent; Mexico (1950), 24 per cent; and Ceylon (1946), 11 per cent.

Clearly sweeping generalisations about African urbanisation are somewhat premature.

That such an extremely small number of Africans live in towns is a further confirmation of the colonial character of the African economy. Real urbanisation in society is a factor connected with industrialisation, especially factory production. Generally speaking, however, apart from certain exceptions, factory production on any considerable scale is not a characteristic feature of Africa; and consequently even the towns that have developed are not, in the main, industrial towns or manufacturing centres.

The *World Social Situation* points out that many of the cities in Africa "were established in a colonial framework, for the use of non-Africans, and were originally conceived as administrative, military and trading posts, or mining centres, which were not meant to include a large permanent African population".[2]

Hodgkin,[3] pointing out that in parts of Africa important urban communities existed before the coming of Europeans—for example, Kano, Timbuktu, Gao, Jenne and Walata—stresses that such ancient centres had nothing in common with the new towns, which are essentially a product of the colonial epoch.

[1] *World Social Situation*, op. cit., pp. 18 and 93.
[2] ibid., pp. 95–6.
[3] Hodgkin: op. cit., p. 64.

"These new African towns are as unlike Timbuktu as Stoke-on-Trent is unlike Chichester."

Hodgkin himself subsequently makes clear that even his reference to Stoke-on-Trent is a little misleading, since African towns such as Dakar or Lagos are something quite different from the industrial centres of Britain.

"The cause of their existence, the basis of their economic life, is not factory industry but commerce. They have been brought into being to meet the needs of European trade. Their main function is to drain out of Africa its groundnuts, palm products, coffee, cocoa, cotton, minerals; and to pump into Africa European consumer goods—cloth, kerosene, bicycles, sewing machines. Their focal points . . . are the warehouses of the great European commercial houses."[1]

Describing the character of Kaolack, a port in Senegal, Richard-Molard says:

"It is to groundnuts that the town owes its whole existence."[2]

In the same way, Kampala is primarily a market for cotton, Kumasi for cocoa, Elizabethville for copper, and so on.

Since African towns are usually linked with commerce, with the export of African raw materials and the import of European manufactured goods, they are also closely connected with transport and communications. Many of them are important sea towns—Dakar, Sekondi-Takoradi, Accra, Lagos, Mombasa, Dar-es-Salaam—or river ports such as Brazzaville and Leopoldville, or else important centres of road or rail transport.

Added to their function as commercial and transport bases, or as market-towns, a number of African urban centres have taken on the functions of administration. This, of course, is partly the consequence of the colonial character of the exploitation, the need to safeguard foreign monopoly interests in its key commercial centres as well as the necessity of constructing an apparatus of

[1] ibid., pp. 64–5.
[2] Richard-Molard, J.: "Villes d' Afrique Noire", *Présence Africaine*, No. 15, 1954. Quoted in Hodgkin.

repression based on the main lines of communication.[1] To meet the needs of the administrative class, almost entirely European, which is the consequence of colonial rule, and to cater for its various activities, a considerable building programme has been carried out—government offices, telephone exchanges, post offices, club houses, hotels, together with all the usual social services and public utilities which the imperialist bureaucracy expects as its right. The new towns, points out Hodgkin, "are thus partly the consequence of the demand for bigger bureaucracies and more African labour to man the building industry".[2]

There is a further type of town which should be mentioned, and that is the mining township. These are usually small, scattered communities, very unlike, in character, the usual urban centre. Since most African mineworkers are migratory, the townships tend to possess all the makeshift characteristics which one would associate with hostels for temporary workers, rather than the more stable institutions, social functions and other facilities that one would expect in a town. The mining townships are again a typical expression of the colonial system; they consist mainly of a barrack-like compound in which the African workers are compelled to live under a semi-military discipline. Apart from the mining operations themselves, very little economic activity is carried on; and, as can be readily imagined, social conditions and facilities for culture and recreation are all of a piece with this economic basis.

There are also a number of railway camps which, in many ways, share the characteristics of the mining townships.

Another section of workers who are not accounted for in the surveys of the main urban centres is that employed in European (and to some extent African) agriculture. Agricultural workers are largely seasonal, living sometimes on the farm or in plantation lines.

It is evident that neither the growth of towns in Africa nor the increased number of African town-dwellers is any proof of an industrial revolution in Africa. Admittedly the fact that some

[1] The present author recalls being informed before the war by a highly placed British officer in the Indian Army how the whole machinery of repression in case of revolution was based on the railways, with the railway depots combining their normal passenger and freight functions with those of arms depots.
[2] Hodgkin: op. cit., p. 66,

six million Africans live in towns of twenty thousand people or more does denote the drawing of Africans into a money economy and, as part of that development, the involvement of African peasants in wage-earning activities. And in certain areas, as we have seen, this is taking place fairly rapidly and on a considerable scale. But with only four per cent of Africans living in African towns and with the towns themselves being mainly centres of commerce, transport and administration rather than of manu-facturing industry, the so-called "urbanisation" of Africans is obviously a process that has not yet developed very far.

"To Minister to the Needs of the White Man"

One major reason why the urbanisation of Africans has not made more headway is that in the principal areas of white settlement it has been deliberate government policy to keep the Africans out of the towns, which have been regarded as specially privileged areas for the white man.

The rigid exclusion of the African people from the European-populated areas of the towns or even from the towns altogether, finds its sharpest expression in the Union of South Africa and in Southern Rhodesia.

"The Native should only be allowed to enter urban areas, which are essentially the white man's creation, when he is willing to enter and minister to the needs of the white man, and should depart therefrom when he ceases so to minister."

Thus declared Mr. Stallard, chairman of a commission on local government in South Africa. The Native (Urban Areas) Act, introduced by the Smuts Government in 1923, embodied these shockingly racialist principles. Urban Africans in the Union are thus confined to certain defined areas, their numbers there limited, and their residence elsewhere controlled to ensure that the African lives not where he wishes but where the European decides.

"In urban areas", explains Hailey,[1] "specially proclaimed for this purpose the entry of Africans is prohibited except in

[1] Hailey (Revised): op. cit., p. 567.

accordance with prescribed conditions. . . . Every male
entering such an area must obtain a document certifying that
he has permission to be there, and permits may be refused if
there is already a surplus of labour. Employers must obtain
permission before introducing Africans into the area, and must
undertake to repatriate them on the termination of their
employment."

Hailey argues that much of this legislation "was obviously
intended largely as an indication of policy; it can never have been
thought possible that it should be fully implemented in practice".
Yet, in fact, successive governments in the Union have tried to
impose this policy in practice, the practice becoming more severe
with each passing year, and being supported with an increasing
range of additional legislation. It has, of course, found its most
extreme form in the "Bantustan" conception, which has now
passed into law.

The deliberate racial segregation which is an essential part
of the policies pursued by white governments in Africa results
also in the development of separate African townships several
miles from the European town. As the European town expands,
so more and more are encroachments made on African-occupied
territory, the African townships cleared and the African people
pushed still farther away from the European towns. This has
been done in the Union as a result of the Group Areas Act of
1950 and the 1954 Natives Resettlement Act. Under these laws,
ostensibly passed in order to concentrate scattered locations into
single areas, thousands of Africans have lost their homes. In 1955,
for example, 70,000 Africans were removed from the western
areas of Johannesburg (Sophiatown, Maryinclare and Newclare)
to a site several miles farther out of town.

The problem is not dissimilar in Southern Rhodesia. Leys[1]
has pointed out that since, according to the land Apportionment
Act, Africans cannot own land, they cannot own it in the towns
as these are all in the European area. As a consequence, Africans
can only reside in the European area on the premises of their
employers, or in the native urban locations or African townships
adjoining the towns. For the African people, the results of these
restrictions are little short of disastrous.

[1] Leys, Colin: *European Politics in Southern Rhodesia*, London, 1959.

"As it is much cheaper to provide accommodation for single men than for families, the urban locations, like the domestic servants' quarters in the suburban gardens, become a kind of barracks rather than homes. The bulk of the labour force moves continuously back and forth between these locations and the country, seldom long enough in any one job to begin to do it efficiently; for although most Africans no longer come merely to earn their tax, their family life must usually be left behind in the Reserves, and naturally it draws them back there again."[1]

But both in the Union and in Southern Rhodesia, as well as in other areas of white settlement, the policy of the government is frequently in conflict with the harsh realities of economic development and the requirements of European employers. Casual and migrant labour may well suit the needs of the farms and mines, but the newer manufacturing interests have need of a certain number of more skilled African workers.

"The greater industrial areas", says de Kiewiet,[2] "are, in fact, engaged in an active process of economic integration between the races." This process, he points out, is dictated by industry's inescapable need for labour—labour which is increasingly required to be "more experienced, more adjusted to the habits of modern industrial society". Consequently, there is "a fundamental quarrel between the natural integration of urban life and the unhistorical effort to impose 'disintegration' upon the vital centres of South African economic prosperity."

Thus Africans are becoming integrated into industry and, despite government regulations, a considerable degree of urbanisation has taken place. It cannot be emphasised too much, however, that the growth of African urbanisation is not, in the main, the result of government policy. On the contrary, it has happened despite government reluctance that it should do so.

Stabilisation—Fact and Fancy

As already indicated above, the question of urbanisation is very much linked to the question of the stabilisation of labour.

[1] ibid., p. 29.
[2] De Kiewiet, C. W.: "Fears and Pressures in the Union of South Africa", *Africa Today*, 1955.

Urbanisation figures indicate how many Africans are resident in towns at any given time; whereas stabilisation figures reveal the extent to which those Africans are abandoning their pattern of continual migration between town and country and are settling down, with their wives and children, as permanent dwellers in urban areas.

For many years now official reports and government commissions have repeatedly drawn attention to the wastefulness of the migrant-labour system and emphasised the necessity of encouraging the establishment of permanent African labour forces in the main urban areas and centres of economic activity.

"It is now widely believed that stabilisation in urban areas is the essential prerequisite for the creation of an effective African labour force."[1]

But has such stabilisation, in fact, taken place? Many commentators, pointing to the example of the Belgian Congo, the Union of South Africa, Southern Rhodesia and the Northern Rhodesian Copper Belt, would answer in the affirmative. The most significant comment that could be made regarding such claims is simply that only some four per cent of Africans live in towns of twenty thousand and over—and that even among this four per cent a substantial proportion are not even workers, let alone stabilised workers.

It should, however, be said that although the overall picture for Africa as a whole does not denote any *decisive* shift towards the stabilisation of the labour force, there are partial exceptions to this, as in the Union and the Belgian Congo, and to a lesser extent in Northern and Southern Rhodesia, though even in these cases, too, the trend towards urbanisation and stabilisation is by no means entirely, if at all, due to official policy. On the contrary, it has to be said that despite the constant pleadings of social workers and commission, neither governments nor employers in Africa have displayed exceptional enthusiasm for the idea of stabilisation for reasons we have indicated in the previous chapter. Hailey, with his customary restraint, admits that "in certain instances the principle of stabilisation has become a controversial issue of State policy".[2] He is compelled to

---

[1] *World Social Situation*, op. cit., U.N., 1957.
[2] Hailey (Revised): op. cit., p. 1388.

add further that: "In Northern Rhodesia both the government and the copper-mining companies appear to have entertained at one time some doubts regarding the advisability of adopting the principle of stabilisation. The presence of a large force of stabilised African employees might create a serious responsibility for the State if there should occur again a period of depression such as that from which the mines at one time suffered."

This reference to depression in the mines is to the period before the war, which witnessed the clash in the Copper Belt in 1935. The same problem arose in 1940. Such fears of the Government and the copper companies can readily be understood in the light of the events in Leopoldville at the beginning of 1959 when, through a fall in the copper price, a temporary crisis arose in the mines, and 50,000 unemployed African workers took a key part in the demonstrations which then rocked the Belgian Congo.

No doubt such considerations play a big part in determining the attitude of imperialist interests in Northern Rhodesia. In fact, one of the leading spokesmen of these interests, Sir Ronald Prain, speaking at the Duke of Edinburgh's Study Conference at Oxford in 1956, made special reference to the "unwillingness of the Government of Northern Rhodesia in 1941 to commit itself to the policy of establishing a permanent industrial African population on the Copper Belt'.[1]

Some light is shed on this reluctance by the fact, mentioned in the Apthorpe Report, that the copper resources being worked by Roan Antelope are estimated to be sufficient only for another twenty-five years, and those of Rhokana Corporation for about forty. In their greed to extract the utmost from these fast-dwindling reserves, the copper companies have in the past fifteen years exploited the African miners to the utmost, combining absolute ruthlessness with scientific efficiency.

It is understandable that these companies are unlikely to be interested in sinking capital into schemes of labour stabilisation considering that they will no longer require the labour itself in a few decades. It is only their recognition that the efficient exploitation of the copper mines requires a substantial proportion of semi-skilled African labour that has resulted in a modification in their attitude to stabilisation. In one mine the average length of service of Africans in employment increased from 25 months

[1] See paper read by H. A. Fosbrooke, *Apthorpe Report*: op. cit.

in 1942 to 33 months at January 1950, and to 50 months at December 1954.[1] Clearly some degree of stabilisation of labour is taking place on the Copper Belt.

And yet as recently as 1957, of the 12,834 African miners (about a third of the entire African labour force) who left the mines that year, no less than 49·1 per cent returned to the village, while as many as 52·2 per cent had been employed in the mines for less than one year. At the same time, of the 12,597 men taken on for work in the mines in 1957, as many as 21·9 per cent came direct from the village without previous mining experience, and a further 37·5 per cent came from the village but with previous experience of work in the mines.[2] Thus it is abundantly clear that, despite all that has been said about the growth of stabilisation on the Copper Belt, migrant labour still predominates, and stabilisation is making only slow progress.

Northern Rhodesia has been the subject of many studies on the stabilisation of labour. In his well-known survey of Broken Hill, Wilson,[3] on the basis of the four categories he adopted for the purposes of his investigation, concluded that *8·6 per cent of the population were peasant visitors* (i.e. had spent less than a third of their time in town since first leaving their villages); *20·5 per cent were migrant labourers* (i.e. had spent between a third and two-thirds of their time in town since first leaving their villages); *69·9 per cent were temporarily urbanised* (i.e. had spent over two-third of their time in town since leaving their villages); and *only 1 per cent were permanently urbanised* (i.e. men born and bred in town).

Wilson's particular emphasis is on the 69·9 per cent temporarily urbanised, though other social investigators have challenged Wilson's findings. Yet even Wilson's figures reveal a high degree of unstable labour, and he himself stressed that, at the time of his investigation nearly twenty years ago, the considerable disproportion between the number of able-bodied men in town and of women, aged people and children in the country had resulted in the perpetual circulation of population between town and country.

[1] ibid.
[2] All figures in this paragraph taken from the *Northern Rhodesia Chamber of Mines Year Book, 1957*, pp. 56, 60, 61, Kitwe, 1958.
[3] Wilson, G.: *The Economics of Detribalisation in Northern Rhodesia*, Rhodes-Livingstone Institute, 1941.

"Circulation of population", says Wilson, "is the keystone of the unstable arch of present-day Northern Rhodesian economy."

Clyde Mitchell[1] has subjected Wilson's findings to a critical examination, and, on the basis of an analysis made by the Rhodes-Livingstone Institute, 1951–3, into the Roan Antelope copper mines, other Luanshya areas, Broken Hill and Ndola, has produced the following findings:

TABLE XV

	Other Luanshya	Roan Antelope	Ndola	Broken Hill
Labour migrants	53·3	54·5	54·7	55·5
Temporary stabilisation ..	38·8	39·0	22·6	37·9
Permanent stabilisation ..	7·9	6·5	12·7	6·6

Mitchell used a different method of analysis from Wilson's, and therefore one cannot make a strict comparison between the two sets of figures. Yet even allowing for this it is really striking that Mitchell's analysis, based on an investigation made ten years later than Wilson's, reveals that, despite the evident existence of a considerable pocket of partly stabilised workers, the *majority are still migrant workers* and only a relatively small proportion can as yet be classified as permanently stabilised.

In his study of the African Centre at Elizabethville, Grevisse[2] found that some fifty-five per cent of the population had lived there less than five years. His conclusion is that the stabilisation of the African urban population is only relative, and that most Africans maintain contact with their rural homeland to which they periodically return. Even those who have lived in towns for 20, 30 or 40 years, he says, expect to return home when they retire. (This phenomenon, noted more than ten years ago by Grevisse, has often been remarked on by commentators in other African territories.) Most investigations, however, show that in the Belgian Congo, especially in the Katanga copper region, there has been a quite strong trend towards the establishment of a more stabilised, urbanised working class. By 1950 about 46 per cent of all workers in the Katanga copper mines had 10 years'

[1] Mitchell, Dr. J. Clyde: paper on "Urbanisation, Detribalisation and Stabilisation in Southern Africa", Unesco, op. cit.
[2] Grevisse, F.: Unesco, op. cit.

continuous service, and only 24 per cent had worked for less than 3 years.[1] The growth of family life—another index of stabilisation—is shown by the increase in the number of children to every 100 workers, from 9 in 1927 to 56 in 1939 and to 146 in 1949.[2] Significant figures given by Davidson[3] show that in 1925, the year before the policy of stabilisation was introduced into the Katanga, the *Union Minière* had 13,849 workers accompanied by 2,507 wives with no more than 779 children. In 1940 there were 11,200 workers with 6,464 wives and 6,634 children; about one child for each wife. By 1952 there were two children for each wife. The trend towards stabilisation and urbanisation is to be noticed elsewhere in the Belgian Congo, though not so marked as in the Katanga.

Family Life

It is interesting to note that, according to Capelle[4] and to Comhaire-Sylvian,[5] the ratio of men to women in Leopoldville is in the neighbourhood of two to one. In Donda it is practically the same.[6]

As elsewhere in Africa, the uneven ratio of African men to women in the towns and the lack of children is the corollary to the devastation wrought to the African countryside, where old men, women and children predominate and young men are scarce; in both cases the extreme disproportion is a direct result of the migrant-labour system. The high ratio of men to women in the towns is an expression of the basic instability of the labour force; for the unnatural life which such a ratio imposes means that sooner or later the man will return to the countryside, either to be with his wife and family, or to find a wife and rear a family.

In Jinja, for example, according to Sofer, "the population is predominantly male".[7] A pilot survey[8] showed that in the 15 to

---

[1] Malengreau, G.: "Recent Developments in Belgian Africa," *Africa Today*, 1955.
[2] Bertiaux, R.: *Aspects de l'industrialisation en Afrique Centrale*, 1953.
[3] Davidson, Basil: *The African Awakening*, p. 112, London, 1955.
[4] Capelle, Emmanual: A study of Leopoldville, quoted in Unesco, op. cit.
[5] Comhaire-Sylvian, S.: Another study of Leopoldville, quoted in Unesco, op. cit.
[6] *World Social Situation*, 1957, op. cit.
[7] Sofer, Dr. Cyril: A paper on Jinja, Unesco, op. cit., p. 595.
[8] Sofer, C. and R.: A survey, Unesco, op. cit.

45 years age group men outnumbered women by 4 to 1. Only 2·3 per cent were over the age of 45, while 11·7 per cent were children under 15. Thus it was among the largest group— 86 per cent of the total—that the extreme unbalance between men and women occurred. Under such conditions it is understandable that little stabilisation can take place; and, in fact, the survey showed that 70 per cent of the population had been there less than 2 years. It is clear that what we have here is the familiar repeated migration. Sofer's findings tend to confirm this. "A large proportion of the African working population consists of migrant labourers who leave their families at their rural home-places, to which they plan to return after a spell in the town."[1]

The reluctance of Africans to have their children with them in urban areas is understandable when one realises under what terrible conditions these children are compelled to live. Even of Leopoldville in the Belgian Congo, which many superficial commentators (in the pre-January 1959 period) held up as a model of enlightened colonial policy and of African progress, it has been said: "Many children know hunger very early."[2] At the age of six the African child in Leopoldville is reckoned to have learned to fend for himself, and probably to "have learned to fast for up to twenty-four hours". Such a child, we are told, "will have an advantage over his comrades because it is at this age that 'hunger-training' starts in most poorer families. . . . On a conservative estimate, the proportion of undernourished children is about half." Because of their plight Bacongo children form sharing associations called *peka*, under which a dozen children of school age pool all the food they can get and share it equally. Many of them seek work; but even they "find living on a regular wage difficult. . . . It is not uncommon for small groups of three or four boys to be formed, who pool all their resources and assign them to one member each week in turn."

Much the same conditions exist for African children in other urban areas. Thus the African worker is torn: either to have his family with him in the towns, and watch them suffer and starve, or to leave them behind in the countryside and live a lonely, celibate life, anguished by the knowledge that his abandoned family is aching for his return.

[1] ibid.
[2] Unesco, op. cit., pp. 118–9.

In the Union of South Africa the same problem of family life exists. Rheinhallt Jones[1] has noted that in the Union "the ratio of men to women is very high in the urban areas". He found that in the age group 15–29 years there were 279 men to every 100 women; in the 30–44 group, 333 men to every 100 women; and in the 45–59 group, 221 men. He adds that the figures for males "are heavily weighted by the large number of mine Natives living under celibate conditions". This, of course, is not the choice of the African mineworkers. It is an essential part of the migrant-labour system on which mine labour in the Union is based, and is laid down in the miners' contracts. Even in the Free State gold fields where, it is alleged, a policy of the stabilisation of labour is favoured, the South African Department of Native Affairs "has allowed the undertakings concerned . . . to provide married quarters for only three per cent of their employees, not for ten per cent as originally proposed".[2]

Under such conditions stabilisation is more or less halted in its tracks. But in South Africa it is not only in the mines where the lack of family life is to be found. A survey of the Dunlop factory in Durban,[3] made some ten years ago, found that only six per cent of the workers had their wives with them in Durban. A further fourteen per cent said they would bring their wives to come and live with them if housing and other facilities existed.

The problem in South Africa has been well presented by Hellman.[4]

"The practice of employing migrant labourers, housed in compounds under conditions of single life, inaugurated by the mines more than sixty years ago, still prevails on the mines and in a number of other enterprises, such as brick and coal fields and municipal service departments. Large-scale mining development brought about the rapid growth of towns which meant, particularly as secondary industry developed apace in the main urban centres, a growing demand for native labour. Originally, domestic, commercial and industrial labour was

[1] Rheinhallt Jones, J. D.: "The Effects of Urbanisation in South and Central Africa", *African Affairs*, January 1953, lii, No. 206, pp. 37–44.
[2] *The Times*, December 13, 1954.
[3] *African Factory Worker*, A survey of the Dunlop Factory, Durban, by the Department of Economics, University of Natal, London, 1950.
[4] Hellmann, Dr. Ellen: Unesco, op. cit., pp. 726 et seq.

migratory and overwhelmingly unskilled. Gradually, with the expansion of industry . . . this situation changed. Africans began to enter semi-skilled and, in smaller numbers, skilled occupations; and with the increase in skill, which inevitably involves some degree of stabilisation of labour, the tendency towards permanent urban settlement under conditions of family life became more pronounced.

"The townward movement of Africans has, however, from the first been subject to conflicting pressures. An expanding economy, reflected in a greatly increased national income, required better trained and more productive workers and a more stable labour force. *But official policy has always considered Africans as being temporarily in the urban areas and the towns themselves as white enclaves in which Africans are to be permitted on sufferance. It has not encouraged or in any way facilitated African family settlement. Native urban areas legislation has repeatedly been amended with the object of stemming the native influx' into the towns and securing greater control over those Africans in the towns.*"

[Own italics—J. W.]

Rheinhallt Jones has clearly explained, beyond any possibility of confusion, why the government of the Union of South Africa is so violently opposed to the stabilisation of African labour:[1]

"Stabilisation leads to a demand for the abolition of the colour bar and, with wider opportunities, political consciousness grows in the community. Their old ways of life are dissipated and new modes of thought develop. So, I think, we had better face the likelihood that demands for political rights will increase and so, you will see, our Government is quite logical in its views. *If you abolish the colour bar and have stabilisation, it means greater demands for political rights and people are not prepared to face that at the moment.*"

[Own italics—J. W.]

Social Security

Coupled with its legal restraints on African workers becoming stabilised in the urban areas, governments and employers have followed economic and social policies deliberately designed to

[1] Rheinhallt Jones: op. cit., p. 44.

perpetuate the migratory-labour system. These policies have been based on discrimination in education and industry (limiting the entry of Africans into more skilled jobs or the professions); a cheap wage policy which provides only the lowest subsistence for a *single* man; completely inadequate housing (this, too, based on the "single man" concept); and denial of social services and of social security, including old-age pensions and unemployment benefit.

Later chapters deal, in some detail, with questions of skill and education, and with the colonial wage system. But here it is important to stress that the total effect of the economic and social policies pursued by the imperialists towards the African workers have left the African in the town completely devoid of security. He has no adequate housing. He lives on a starvation wage. He cannot "work his way up" the social scale, since racial discrimination has already decided to which rung on the ladder he can ascend. If he falls ill, his treatment is inadequate and usually he gets no sick pay. If he loses his job, he may lose his house; worse still, he receives no unemployment pay. And when he becomes old he must either try to live off his sons or literally starve; the only other thing left to do is to return to his village. Moreover, during all this time, his wife and children have been left behind and his family life more or less destroyed. Little wonder therefore that sociologists constantly note the feeling of insecurity which seems to weigh down on the urban African.

"The average urban African", says Gussman,[1] "is unhealthy, badly housed, uneducated, and he lacks any security in town even if he happens to have been born there."

Many reports make it clear that the authorities are well aware of the situation and understand what needs to be done to ensure the stabilisation of labour. The necessary steps, says the U.N. *World Social Situation* report,[2]

"are considered to include incentives in the form of higher wages, which would increase according to length of service

[1] Gussman, B.: "Industrial Efficiency and the Urban African," *Africa*, April 1953, **xxiii**, No. 2, p. 141.
[2] *World Social Situation*, op. cit., p. 125.

and improvement of qualifications; holidays with full pay for continuous service of twelve months; better housing; measures of family support; financial assistance for the establishment of newly wed couples; children's allowances; provision of more schools, hospitals, maternal and child-welfare centres, and recreational facilities. Systematic assistance to labour organisations to improve bargaining power and promote a sense of belonging, and vocational training and guidance to improve job fitness and promotion opportunities of the workers, are likewise considered essential."

The practice of the employers and governments of African colonial territories, however, shows only too clearly that these recommendations are more or less ignored. The official policy pursued today is, in essence, the same as that which has been followed for the past few decades. The attitude of colonial governments in Africa towards the question of social security has always been to take refuge behind the traditional custom of the African family to look after all its members.

"There is no organised provision for unemployment, old age and indigence as it is understood in the United Kingdom. The traditional social system, particularly the extended family system, provides for the assistance of the old, unemployed and infirm, and lays obligations on the whole family to look after the interests and welfare of each member."[1]

A Colonial Office Report for Uganda for 1950 bluntly declares:

"It is a cardinal point of Government policy to leave wherever practicable the relief of the destitute and disabled to the tribe, clan or family."

Similarly, the Tanganyika Report for 1957 states:

"The policy of the Administering Authority in matters of social security has continued to be one of reliance on the traditional welfare structure."

[1] *The Economic Survey of the Colonial Territories*, vol. iii, 1951; West African Territories, Col. No. 281–3, Section on Gold Coast, 1952.

The theory behind this policy was that the African worker would be partly subsidised by his wife and parents left behind in the Reserve or village. The worker would earn sufficient to maintain himself, while the family he had left behind would be able to maintain themselves as well as providing a haven and refuge for the worker when he became too old or too ill to work. (In fact, the family left behind in the Reserve is even expected to subsidise the town worker's wages, and the pretence that this could be done "has frequently been used" says Ibbotson,[1] "as a basis for arguing that urban wages should be kept low".) But so rapid has been the deterioration of African agriculture in the past three decades that it is to an utterly impoverished peasant family that the destitute or aged worker is expected to turn for succour and security.

Drawing attention to the gradual breakdown of this pretended form of "social security", Fosbrooke[2] says that "in Northern Rhodesia and Central Africa generally, the first generation of Africans in towns may live in a system of kinship social security, but the second generation suffers from its breaking up and the third generation may well be in total distress in this regard, and for them there can be no question that state-security schemes must be introduced".

Despite the apparent recognition in official and semi-official circles of the need to provide proper social security for African workers, in practice the working class has to fight bitterly for even the smallest concession. As recently as August 1959 one finds the Nigerian Workers' Union of the United Africa Company and Associated Companies including in its fourteen-point memorandum to the management of the U.A.C. demands for a housing scheme, pension funds, retirement benefits and other social demands.

It is, perhaps, in French West and Equatorial Africa that the biggest struggle for social demands has been waged. Strikes and demonstrations at intervals over a period of several years were waged to achieve the placing of the Labour Code on the Statute Book. A key aspect of this Labour Code was its provision for

---

[1] Ibbotson, Percy: Unesco, op. cit., p. 168.
[2] Fosbrooke, H. A.: "Can Labour be Stabilised Without Permanent Urbanisation and Concomitant Social Security Measures?", *Apthorpe Report,* p. 88 et seq.

children's allowances. Though the workers were successful in obtaining the Labour Code by 1952, they have had to conduct continual struggles ever since to secure the application of the Code in practice.

"Who Cares Where They Sleep?"

Equally essential to enable Africans to settle permanently in the towns is adequate housing. This, too, is admitted in all official and semi-official circles. Constant references are made in reports to the need to provide the African worker with decent housing, sufficient for his family and at a rental which he can afford. Once again, however, the words are more honoured in the breach than the observance.

The Carpenter Report admits[1] that as far as Kenya is concerned "in *all* urban areas, there is an *acute shortage* of housing accommodation, even on a 'bachelor' basis". In Nairobi, it says, there is an estimated shortage of at least 20,000 "bed-spaces", with 15,000 "bed-spaces" lacking in Mombasa. The result, states the report, is "appalling slum conditions".

The reasons for these shocking conditions are not merely the habitual consequences of low wages and poverty which face workers in many other parts of the world, but also, to quote the Carpenter Report again, that: "Most African housing programmes have, in the past, been planned on the assumption that the African labour force was, and would remain, one of *single* men." [Own italics—J. W.] A clear enough admission that the official housing policy was linked to the migrant-labour system. (In fact, the Carpenter Report itself states that of some 350,000 adult male African workers in employment outside the Reserves in Kenya, it is estimated that "more than half" are migrant workers, and that even among those who do not fall within this category "there is little *permanency* of employment".)[2]

The *East Africa Royal Commission Report* reveals that "the Mombasa riots in 1939 were mainly caused by bad housing".[3] Of Nairobi, it was reported in 1948 that African *employed* workers were sleeping "under the verandahs in River Road, in noisome

---

[1] *Report of the Committee on African Wages* (Carpenter Report), p. 95, Nairobi, 1954.
[2] ibid., p. 13.
[3] EARC, op. cit., p. 207.

and dangerous shacks in the swamp, in buses parked by the road-
side and fourteen to the room in Pumwani, two to a bed and the
rest on the floor".[1]

Such conditions, reveals the report, are not confined to
Kenya. "Settlements of closely packed African huts are to be
seen on the fringe of all the larger towns in East Africa."[2] Moreover, it states:

> "A study of official reports and the evidence of witnesses
> with knowledge of urban matters convinces us that conditions
> of life for the poorer Asian and the majority of the Africans in
> the towns have been deteriorating over a considerable period."[3]

That low wages are a major cause of the bad housing is
admitted.

> "The wages of the majority of African workers are too low
> to enable them to obtain accommodation which is adequate
> by any standard. . . . The high cost of accommodation relative
> to wages is, in itself, a cause of overcrowding, because accom-
> modation is shared in order to lighten the cost. This, together
> with the high cost of food in towns, makes family life impossible
> for the majority."[4]

The report quotes from the municipal African affairs officer's
report which states "in the course of a recent police investigation
at night no fewer than sixty persons were found sleeping in one
temporary single-storeyed house."[5]

In Dar-es-Salaam, in Tanganyika, "it has been calculated
that the average number of persons living in a room 16 ft. by
20 ft. is eight, and that in some rooms it is as much as twelve".[6]

So acute is the housing situation in Salisbury that on May 31,
1958, the Mashonaland Region of the African T.U.C. in Southern
Rhodesia led a procession of thousands of homeless people to the

[1] *Report of the Municipal African Affairs Officer*, p. 11, Nairobi, 1948. (Unpub-
lished, quoted in the *East Africa Royal Commission Report*, p. 207.)
[2] EARC, p. 207.
[3] ibid., p. 209.
[4] ibid., pp. 209–10.
[5] *Report of the Municipal African Affairs Officer*, p. 21, Mombasa, 1953 (un-
published).
[6] EARC, op. cit., p. 211.

offices of the Native Administration Department in the city.
Describing this important protest action, a Southern Rhodesian
trade-union leader has said:[1]

"The housing problem is one of the greatest facing African
workers in urban areas. In Salisbury, for instance, about
11,000 unmarried Africans are on the waiting list for accommodation, and about 5,000 married people are also on the
waiting list. These people are legally employed but the devil
knows where they put their heads at night. If they live with
friends, they are liable to prosecution if found by the police,
who frequently hold night raids. If they sleep in the open or
under a tree they are liable to prosecution if found.

"No employer cares. As long as they are present at work
every morning, who cares where they sleep, eat or rest at
night?"

Nor, apparently, do the employers care in other Southern
Rhodesian towns such as Bulawayo, Gwelo, Selukwe, Que Que,
Gatooma and Umtali, where Ibbotson[2] found conditions in
many of the compounds "appalling", and everywhere an acute
shortage of housing and serious overcrowding.

Of the Durban shack-dwellers who are unable to find normal
accommodation, the Unesco report says: "The majority of the
shack dwellers and all the casuals who are nightly admitted to
hostels cannot be regarded as housed at all."[3] The Dunlop
survey[4] found that of 260 workers interviewed, 74 were in
shacks, 73 in barracks, 34 in out-buildings, 3 in garages, and
10 in "undefined and possibly indefinable quarters". Only 66—
little more than 25 per cent—lived in houses or flats. In the
Poto-Poto "centre" in Brazzaville it has been ascertained that
over 45 per cent of the inhabitants live in housing units occupied
by 6 to 11 persons, and over 35 per cent in units occupied by
11 to 22 persons.[5] In Jinja, says Sofer,[6]

[1] Sithole, Edson F. C.: "The African Worker in Southern Rhodesia,"
World Trade Union Movement, October, 1950, pp. 19–20.
[2] Ibbotson, Percy: Unesco, op. cit.
[3] Unesco, op. cit., p. 203.
[4] *African Factory Worker*, op. cit.
[5] Balandier, Prof. Georges: paper in Unesco, op. cit.
[6] Sofer, Dr. Cyril: Unesco, op. cit., p. 598.

"more than half the African houses are small, one-roomed structures built of a combination of mud, grass and tins. The township estate consists of barrack-like rows of brick rooms. Fifteen per cent of all African houses lack latrines and over a third lack ready access to piped water."

Describing the "appalling congestion" which has developed among Africans in the towns of the Union of South Africa, Dr. Hellmann has stated that "Johannesburg still has a back-log of 30,000 families and 20,000 single Africans requiring housing, and the total number of dwelling units required for urban Africans was estimated at 167,328 in 1953".[1]

As de Briey has remarked:[2]

"In most cities the way the African population is huddled together in makeshift dwellings has to be seen to be believed."

Thus, neither the wages, the social security, nor the housing facilities—let alone the legal rights—are such as to encourage or facilitate the permanent settlement of African workers with their families in the urban centres. For the majority of Africans town life is a nightmare of poverty and persecution, a constant struggle against starvation and misery as well as against police harassment and brutality.

"The *leitmotiv* of Rooiyard life is the economic struggle," said Dr. Hellmann in her study of an African slum area.[3] "Daily activities are, to a large extent, motivated by the struggle of survival." There is a "deep feeling of unrest" in all African urban areas, says Malengreau.[4]

The Unesco report sums up the conditions of African urban populations in these terms:[5]

". . . they are characterised by a high incidence of poverty, malnutrition and disease, and live in overcrowded conditions. . . .

[1] Hellmann, Dr. Ellen: Unesco, op. cit., p. 728.
[2] De Briey, P.: "The Productivity of African Labour," *International Labour Review*, August-September 1955, p. 128.
[3] Hellmann: *A Study of Rooiyard—1935*, Rhodes-Livingstone Institute, 1941.
[4] Malengreau, Professor Guy: Unesco, op. cit., p. 629.
[5] Unesco, op. cit., pp. 211–12.

". . . there is a marked excess of men over women, which tends to make marriage unstable, and which also prevents the stabilisation of the population in towns. . . .

"Wage-earners cannot bring families to town when wages and housing are insufficient. Those married men who do bring their wives and children to town are in many areas poorer than single men, since no allowance is made for wage-scales. . . ."

This is the cold reality behind all the fine words about urbanisation and stabilisation.

It is, of course, important to detect the changes taking place in Africa. African agriculture and African village life are decaying, and the impoverished peasantry is disintegrating. A market economy has assumed dominance over the subsistence economy, and a polarisation of classes is developing in the countryside. Moreover, an African working class has been born, painfully and in misery. This African proletariat is growing steadily in numbers, and a section of it is acquiring some degree of skill. More and more Africans are being drawn into the wage-labour market. Towns are springing up and African urbanisation is increasing. There is a growth of stabilisation, and more Africans are coming to rely mainly, if not yet entirely, on their wages for their livelihood.

But all this is a trend, not yet the completion of a process. It is true, a profound change has come over African economy and the formation and growth of classes has proceeded rapidly over the past few decades. Nevertheless, this does not add up to an "*industrial* revolution". Economically speaking, despite the important transformations that have taken place, the continent of Africa remains essentially what it was twenty or thirty years ago—a colonial hinterland, an agrarian and mineral-supplying appendage of the metropolitan countries of Europe and increasingly of the United States, too.

Is there, then, no "revolution" taking place in Africa? There is certainly a *political* revolution sweeping over Africa, in the sense that the African people are in revolt against colonialism and, in a number of territories, political power is passing from the Europeans to the Africans. This is the essence of the African revolution of our times. But it is a revolution which has only begun.

The big European monopolies who went to Africa sixty years ago to exploit African resources and African labour still dominate the continent, still decide the policies of the governments in most of the territories, and almost everywhere still exploit the people and the natural wealth of their lands. In every aspect of African life the stamp of the colonial system is apparent—in the economy, the class structure, the political system, and the social pattern in general.

A profile of the African working class reveals the same colonial features.

The dominant thing about it is its continuing migratory character, rather than its stable settlement in the towns. What has happened is that the flood of migrant labour from the countryside to the towns—driven by the poll-tax system, recruitment and the impoverishment of the countryside, rather than attracted by industrial growth—has risen faster and higher; and each time that the flood has seeped back again to the villages the residue left behind in the urban areas has been added to, bit by bit. This residue is admittedly growing.

Small as it yet is, an African proletariat has been born. It is this new force, the working class, which is Africa's decisive force for the future. In its hands lies the destiny of this continent. It is the only force capable of giving the national liberation movement cohesion, consistency, and vision; and it alone is capable of carrying the African national liberation movement beyond the limits of political and economic independence to the creation of a new society based on social justice.

CHAPTER SIX

AFRICAN LABOUR EFFICIENCY
—MYTH AND REALITY

"THE peoples of Africa are poor because they do not produce enough."

Such is the argument advanced by de Briey,[1] and constantly used in official circles to justify African poverty and low wages.

"The dominant problem throughout East Africa", claims Orde Browne,[2] "is the deplorably low standard of efficiency of the worker."

If only the African would work harder, become more skilled, take more interest in his work, and co-operate with the management, then, we are repeatedly assured, productivity would rise, industry would thrive and it would thus become possible to pay higher wages and give better conditions to African workers.

To persuade the African worker—and the British public—as to the economic and political soundness of this argument, countless reams of paper have been consumed, articles written by the hundred, studies undertaken, conferences held, trade-union schools organised, and a combined onslaught made by government officials, employers, labour officers and trade-union advisers, Moral Rearmament representatives and missionaries. *And all to persuade the African that his wages and conditions are poor because his labour is poor; that it is he who is responsible for his poverty, and therefore it is in his hands that the remedy lies.*

[1] De Briey, P.: "The Productivity of African Labour," *International Labour Review*, August-September 1955, p. 123.

[2] Orde Browne, Major G. St. J.: *Labour Conditions in East Africa*, col. No. 193, p. 15, 1946.

"Since his output is low, his wage is low."[1]

Any impartial study of the facts, however, soon reveals that the very opposite is the case. *African labour is "poor" basically because the African worker's wages and conditions are poor.* Poverty and starvation, both physical and mental, of which starvation wages constitute the basic element, are a prime cause of low productivity.

Cheap Hands

Amid all the arguments about African labour efficiency are concealed three separate questions. Productivity of labour, in the strict sense of the term, is determined by the quantity and quality of the implements of labour used by the workers, in other words, by the level of technique. It is, however, often used widely to denote the worker's output—and this latter is determined not only by the level of technique available to the worker but also by the direct exertion of effort made by the worker, the quantity of muscular and nervous energy the worker expends in the process of production. Finally, there is the question of the worker's skill, his ability to use the technical equipment available to him.

It will be necessary, in order to deal with the whole question of African "labour efficiency" to examine all three aspects—level of technique, the worker's skill, and his capacity to work.

African labour, as explained in an earlier chapter, is basically cheap, migrant labour. Such labour, by its very nature, is bound to be inefficient, unskilled and less productive compared with highly paid, stable labour.

"The migrant-labour system has developed because to the great majority of the country's employers it has represented cheap labour. . . . The consideration that it has *appeared* cheap, and that it was available in apparently unlimited supply, has been sufficient to discourage employers from concerning themselves with such matters as individual productivity and the effective use of labour."[2]

[1] De Briey, P.: op. cit., p. 121.
[2] *Report of the Committee on African Wages* (Carpenter Report), p. 15, Nairobi, 1954.

Similarly, Orde Browne[1] has commented:

"A tradition of wasteful use of manpower has established itself in East Africa. . . . There is a tendency to deal with a lack of labour by an effort to find further supplies of untrained raw recruits from some distant area rather than by improving the performance of the labour force already available."

And coupled with the system of cheap, migrant labour goes, as has been seen above, a high degree of labour turnover. This, too, has a harmful effect on the acquisition of labour skill and on production and productivity. In fact Labouret[2] argues that:

"The chief difficulty raised by native labour is neither its low productivity, which can be remedied by education, nor the lack of employment opportunities in some territories or at certain seasons, but *above all its instability*."   [Own italics—J. W.]

Instability of labour, however, as shown above, is inevitable as long as African labour is based on perpetual migration and low wages. The fact that a stable, more skilled African working class is, at least in words, now regarded in some official circles as a desirable goal, should not delude anyone into thinking that there has been any change in the policies of governments or employers regarding their basic aim of the maximum exploitation of African labour. It is simply that under modern methods of production, with the spread of industry and mechanisation, some limited degree of labour stability and skill has become necessary, even in parts of Africa. Where the particular circumstances have made such a development possible, as in the factories of the Union of South Africa and in Southern Rhodesia, or in the Northern Rhodesian Copper Belt or in the Belgian Congo, employers have not been slow to ensure that their rates of profit are even greater than hitherto.

But though the creation of pockets of more skilled African labour may be necessary or may suit the special interests of sections of industry in some African territories, it is a relatively small section of the African working class which is drawn into this development. The big farming and plantation interests, the

---

[1] Orde Browne, Major G. St. J.: op. cit.
[2] Labouret, H.: *La Main d'Oeuvre Africaine* (Travail en Afrique Noire), p. 135.

mining companies, transport, building and government service, and employers of domestic labour, in other words the biggest employers of African labour and those whose interests largely decide official policies, are quite content to continue with the present system of untrained, unskilled, unstable, cheap, migrant labour.

This point of view finds expression in the report of a Northern Ireland official, reporting on the Kenya flax industry:[1]

"A most important consideration is the cheap and plentiful supply of labour. . . . I am quite satisfied that both the harvesting and scutching of the flax crop in Kenya *can be much more economically performed by manual labour than by means of flax-pulling and automatic flax-scutching machines which have in recent years been introduced in Western Europe.*"   [Own italics—J. W.]

The man and his hands in place of the beast of burden and the tool is a commonplace of all colonial countries. The present writer remembers in Kowloon watching women squatting on the ground, patiently and wearily breaking up large pieces of rock into small pieces of stone with another piece of stone; and then transporting the broken pieces with the aid of the traditional carrying pole with its two small, attached baskets. In India, during the hey-day of the white rajahs, it was possible to see an Indian gardener spending hours of backbreaking toil cutting his English master's lawn in front of a spacious, luxury bungalow with a pair of scissors. Or building workers on a site without even a hod; each brick was carried by hand. In the old tsarist empire, in the region now known as the Tajik Republic, even the wheelbarrow was unknown before 1917; the first wheelbarrow was actually flown in by aircraft.

Throughout Africa today one can witness the same appalling lack of tools and equipment. In building, porterage, agriculture and road-building, only the most primitive tools are available.

Writing as late as 1953, Heigham said:[2]

[1] Megaw, W. J.: *The Flax Industry in Kenya*, 1939, p. 4. (Quoted in *Crisis in Kenya* by S. and K. Aaronovitch, London. 1947.)

[2] Heigham, J. B.: *Labour Productivity in the Gold Coast*, 1953, Gold Coast Government (duplicated).

"In the Gold Coast thousands of men enter employment every year *who have never before seen a pick and shovel.*"

[Own italics—J. W.]

A friend of the present writer who visited Sierra Leone in 1958 said that he saw African workers spending wasteful hours chopping down huge trees with a simple axe. At the Jos tin mines in Nigeria, hundreds of labourers tramp all day up and down the inclines leading to the mines, carrying on their heads baskets filled with small supplies of ore, or work with the simplest of tools.[1]

Writing of the Ivory Coast, Vincent says:

"I have often had occasion to watch Africans from the bush at work for the Administration in small laterite quarries, near a bridge under construction. *These men know nothing of the technique of the shovel and wheelbarrow.* . . . . A wheelbarrow and shovel would have tripled the output of each of the five men in the team. *But for the Administration it wasn't worth while to teach them,* as they were only engaged for a few days or weeks."[2]

[Own italics—J. W.]

Human hands, arms, feet, head and back—where these are plentiful and cheap, what need is there for the European farmer or mineowner to sink funds in mechanisation and in training his labour? Furthermore, there is not only an absolute minimum of mechanisation and equipment introduced into the existing extractive industries of Africa; the complete lack of industrialisation, which flows from the imperialist policy of using Africa as a cheap raw materials base for Western industries, precludes the building up of a modern, stabilised, skilled working class equipped with all the most up-to-date machinery and technique.

Education and Training

To become a skilled worker one needs first of all a certain level of education and facilities for training or apprenticeship. Yet

[1] See, for example, the illustration in *The Times British Colonies Review*, First Quarter, 1960, p. 9.

[2] Vincent, J.: *Brief Study of the African Worker's Output in the Ivory Coast,* École Nationale de la France d'Outre-Mer.

figures compiled by Unesco for 1955 show Africa to be one of the world's blackest regions for illiteracy. Between 95 and 99 per cent of all African adults are illiterate in British Somaliland, French Equatorial Africa, French Somaliland, and French West Africa. For Gambia, Nyasaland, Sierra Leone and Zanzibar the percentage is 90 to 95. In Nigeria it is 85 to 90 per cent, in Swaziland 80 to 85 per cent, in Kenya, Bechuanaland and Northern Rhodesia 75 to 80 per cent, in Uganda 70 to 75 per cent, and the Belgian Congo 60 to 65 per cent.[1]

The paucity of educational facilities provided for Africans is so well known that it hardly seems necessary to refer to it. There are practically no State-run schools for African children in most African territories; it is the missions that run the schools, sometimes with limited grants from the governments. A large proportion of children receive no schooling at all. Less than twenty per cent of the five to fourteen age group in 1955 were enrolled in schools in British Somaliland, Gambia, Sierra Leone, Somalia, Sudan, French Equatorial Africa, French West Africa, Portuguese Guinea, Liberia, Mozambique, Tanganyika, Zanzibar, Angola and Ethiopia.[2] For Kenya, Northern Rhodesia, Nyasaland, Belgian Congo, Bechuanaland, Madagascar, Nigeria, Swaziland, French Togoland, Uganda, French Cameroons, Ruanda-Urundi and South-West Africa, the percentage was twenty to forty.

Most attend for two or three years only, and learn an absolute minimum. A small percentage continue their education after the age of eleven or twelve, but the percentage that receives any more advanced form of education is infinitesimal.

Official reports are fond of talking about the "progress" being made in the field of education. But any objective examination of the figures only reveals the continuing snail's pace rate of development with which this "progress" is taking place, and the enormous deficiencies which still exist. Much has been made, for example, out of the fact that there are now over two hundred thousand African children attending school in Northern Rhodesia. The Government's *Triennial Survey of African Education, 1955–7*, gives the following figures:

[1] NSG: op. cit., p. 190. (Table taken from special Unesco study: *World Illiteracy at Mid-Century*, 1957.)
[2] *U.N. Report on the World Situation, 1957*, p. 67.

TABLE XVI
ENROLMENT OF AFRICAN CHILDREN IN SCHOOLS IN NORTHERN RHODESIA

		Enrolment at 30.9.57	Estimated No. of School Age
Lower Primary (4 years)	..	191,484	215,000
Upper Primary (4 years)	..	39,579	170,000
Secondary (4 years)	..	1,600	145,000
		232,000	530,000

These figures show that only some 43 per cent of the African children of school age are at school. Nearly 76 per cent of those eligible for education after 11 or 12 years of age do not receive that education. And only 1·1 per cent of those who have reached the eligible age for secondary education receive it. Even at the primary level, most children do not complete their course.

The 1954 Report for Southern Rhodesia showed 350,000 pupils at school, 65 per cent of the school potential. But of these a half were in the two lowest classes, and only 231 in Standard VI. More recent figures give only 7 per 1,000 of the primary-school children getting into secondary schools.[1] The 1957 Report for Kenya shows 440,947 African children in primary schools, 59,390 in intermediate, and only 3,316 in secondary.

A report on education in Nyasaland,[2] based on the 1958 figures, states that the educational system "is in no sense a pyramid, but a Cleopatra's Needle set in a plain".

The meaning which the author of this report intended to convey by this metaphor is provided by the table he gives. This shows that 124,000 school children leave between the ages of 8 and 12, and a further 125,879 at 12. These 250,000 comprise the primary-school children. A mere 18,314 continue in senior primary, i.e. in Standards IV to VI, and they leave at 15 years of age. Only 768 continue in junior secondary school (up to the age of 17), and 421 complete full secondary education, taking Standard X, and leaving at about the age of 19. The total African population in Nyasaland is 2,600,000.

An estimate made by Monkhouse[3] ("approximate only . . . not statistically very satisfying") gives 0·45 per 1,000 of the population attending secondary school in Nyasaland, 0·81 in Northern

[1] Monkhouse, P. J.: "African Secondary Schools," Guardian, July 15, 1959.
[2] Taylor, Geoffrey: "The Half-Schooled Nyasas," Guardian, October 5, 1959.
[3] Monkhouse, P. J.: op. cit.

Rhodesia, 1·4 in Southern Rhodesia, 0·36 in Tanganyika, 0·66 in Kenya, 0·58 in Uganda.

In the Portuguese-held territory of Mozambique, the position is naturally far worse. According to Professor Marvin Harris,[1] out of 6,000,000 Africans in 1954, only 5,000 were in primary schools, 73 in secondary schools and 42 in industrial training classes. The 1950 census figures revealed no less than 99 per cent illiteracy!

"Although illiteracy runs high throughout all of Africa, Mozambique has the special distinction of lacking an educated *élite*. At the present moment there is exactly one African with a university degree among the 6,000,000 Negroes."

Professor Lewis[2] has emphasised that secondary education is "one of the keys to economic development" and has pointed out that even in Ghana, where considerable progress has been made in the field of education, "less than two per cent of the generation enters secondary schools". While it may be argued that Lewis puts too much emphasis on the role of secondary education as a factor in economic development, there is no doubt that the present imperialist policy of limiting education in Africa to the most elementary forms of the three "Rs" cannot but hamper the development of the African people and act to the detriment of their becoming more skilled.

It is therefore of importance to note that in all African territories it is only a relative handful of African children who go on to secondary school. This lack of educational facilities is a natural consequence of regarding Africans as the hewers of wood and the drawers of water. What makes this neglect even more scandalous is that independent efforts by Africans in colonial territories to try to make up for the shortage of schools and teachers by organising their own schools, financed with their own funds which they have collected with great difficulty and self-sacrifice, yet with considerable enthusiasm, invariably meet with repression. Thus one of the first acts of the authorities in Kenya, after the declaration of the emergency in 1952, was the closing down of the schools run by the Kikuyu Central Schools Association. (The same fate, incidentally, overtook the independent Chinese-language schools in Malaya and Hong Kong.)

[1] Harris, Marvin: *Portugal's African Wards*, American Committee on Africa—Africa Today pamphlet.
[2] Lewis, Professor W. Arthur: Letter in *Economist*, January 10, 1959.

There is probably no people anywhere who have shown yearning for education more than the people of Africa. In her study on Stanleyville[1] Nelly Xydias has painted a vivid contrast of the people's desire for education on the one hand, and the sadly lacking facilities on the other.

". . . on enrolment day the parents queue up at dawn outside the director's office to make sure of a place for their children. . . . *To a far higher degree than in Europe*, the young folk of all ages are fired with a keen desire to learn."

[Own italics—J. W.]

One schoolboy wrote in an essay:

"I think the happiest event in my life was the day when my father told me to go to school."

Another one wrote:

"The most unfortunate thing that could happen to me would be to have had no education, or to be sent away from school now, for then all my life would be wasted. . . . I should be happiest of all if I could continue my studies. I think of this every night as I lie in bed counting the leaves in the roof of the room, I think of it all the time. . . . I shall take up teaching as a career. Our Congo today is still in darkness, but the Congo of tomorrow will certainly be in the light. When I think of the vocation of teaching my little racial brothers, I feel my heart overflowing with joy."[2]

Yet, as Xydias shows, the tragedy is that for such zealous potential pupils the ratio of primary to post-primary places is sixty to one. Further, there is almost a complete absence of any sort of equipment in the schools. Physics and chemistry, when taught, is based entirely on books; there are no practical demonstrations. There is not even kindergarten equipment for the younger children.

---

[1] *Stanleyville Survey*, by V. G. Pons, N. Xydias and P. Clement. See *Social Implications of Industrialisation and Urbanisation in Africa South of the Sahara*, Unesco, 1956.

[2] Unesco, op. cit., p. 333.

Alongside this miserable lack of normal educational services there is a woeful shortage of industrial training facilities.

"Labour efficiency", points out Noon, "is affected by both the general educational level of the labour force and its specific vocational instruction for skilled occupations. A large part of African labour must be judged to be insufficiently trained in both respects but more deficient in the latter. *This is no reflection on the capacity of the African to profit by such training but instead constitutes a serious indictment of the present administration of African territories by the various colonial powers.*"[1]   [Own italics—J. W.]

In the whole of Kenya, in 1957, only 1,002 pupils were attending trade and technical schools, and only 227 apprentices completed their training.[2] Yet the 1957 Annual Report admits that "the number of applications received for admission to the technical and trade schools was far in excess of the number of places available."

Noon's comment quoted above that the lack of trained workers in Africa is no reflection on the African workers but rather an indictment of colonial rule, finds confirmation in Roper's remark that "*In Nigeria, where African workers have been trained for skilled mechanical work, as in the Ibadan cigarette factory or the Sapele plywood mills, they have achieved high standards of skill. . . .*"[3] [Own italics—J. W.]

Even the limited vocational training facilities that do exist tend very often to place emphasis on crafts which are dying, rather than on industrial purposes appropriate to the second half of the twentieth century.

Xydias in her study on Stanleyville in 1951 found facilities for the technical education of Africans sadly lacking. Not more than 5,000 boys were undergoing technical education, and of these 1,500 were attending rural schools. The majority of children leave school, she says,[4] "untrained for any particular trade" and have difficulty finding a job of any significance and so "under pressure of dire necessity" the young job-seeking African takes "a job as an unskilled labourer".

[1] Noon: op. cit., p. 18.
[2] *Annual Report for Kenya, 1957*, Colonial Office, London.
[3] Roper: op. cit., p. 43.
[4] Xydias, Nelly: Unesco, op. cit., p. 324.

Skill—and the Industrial Colour Bar

In territories where European settlement has been considerable, Africans are deliberately prevented from acquiring skill.

This industrial colour bar operates notably in the Union of South Africa and the Rhodesias, where official policy has aimed at maintaining a privileged position for European workers, preserving for them the positions requiring skill or carrying supervisory responsibilities, and leaving for the Africans the most menial and unskilled jobs. This policy is not just a question of unwritten colonial practice; it is reinforced and imposed by actual legislation and statute.

In the Union of South Africa, for example:

". . . the Mines and Works Amendment Act contains a provision enabling the Government to make regulations providing for the issue of certificates of competence in mines or works where electrical power is used, and to limit the issue of certificates to European or Coloured[1] persons. The Native Building Workers Act of 1951 made it illegal to employ Africans to perform skilled work in the building industry in urban areas. The Group Areas Act of 1950 was amended in 1956 to provide for the compulsory removal of Africans from any urban area; this can be applied to protect European labour from competition. Under the Industrial Conciliation Act of 1956 the Minister is empowered to issue a determination reserving certain work for persons of a specific race."[2]

This latter Act is already being applied in the Union, and in fact was the subject of widespread protests in 1957 when the Minister proposed its application to the clothing industry.

Apprenticeship systems, too, act against the training of African workers. According to Hailey[3] the practical result of the operation of the Apprenticeship Act of 1944 in South Africa "is to exclude non-Europeans from apprenticeship and thus to restrict their entry into the range of more highly paid employment".

[1] The term "Coloured" in South Africa denotes people of mixed racial origin, and excludes Africans.
[2] "Interracial Wage Structure in Africa," an article in the *International Labour Review*, July 1958.
[3] Hailey (Revised): op. cit., p. 1433.

Dr. S. T. Van Der Horst has pointed out[1] that:

"Although the Apprenticeship Act does not ostensibly differentiate between the different racial groups, in fact, it operates to exclude non-Europeans from becoming qualified artisans. In the first place, the educational standards laid down are high for non-Europeans. [High, that is, owing to the lack of educational facilities provided for Africans, and not due to any inherent inability on the part of the Africans—J. W.] Secondly, some employers, among them the South African Railways and Harbours, are reluctant to take on non-Europeans as apprentices, while some non-European employers have been precluded from taking on non-European apprentices. . . . Thirdly, facilities for the technical training of non-Europeans, which is compulsory either through the whole period of apprenticeship or during the first few years, are only available in a few towns."

In Northern Rhodesia Africans were not legally permitted into apprenticeship until May 1958; yet by January 1959, according to an official of the Northern Rhodesia Chamber of Mines at a meeting in London, no European employer, as far as his knowledge extended, had so far taken on any African labour for apprenticeship purposes. Once again, as so often happens in Africa, what is conceded by the imperial authorities in theory is often ignored in practice.

Skill, therefore, is not simply something which has been offered to the African worker on a plate and which he, because of his "inefficiency", has been unable to utilise. On the contrary, skill is an acquirement to gain which the African has had to surmount a hundred obstacles. He has been denied the level of education which is a necessary corollary to skill in industry. He has been denied—or even legally debarred from—proper apprenticeship. He has, in many cases, been specifically prohibited by law and excluded by social practice and pressure from acquiring skill or being employed in a skilled job. He has been given only the most limited training—and is often set to work with the most primitive of tools, sometimes with his hands alone. Confined to a pokey room in a shanty-town, or cramped "single

[1] *Handbook on Race Relations in South Africa*, p. 151, London, 1949.

man's" quarters in a compound, living on a "single man's" wage with no hope of security or pension in old age, he has little opportunity to become a stable, permanently urbanised worker but is condemned to the shifting pattern of the migrant, living a constant half-life between town and country, bachelor and husband, peasant and worker.

Is it surprising, then, if his skill is not of the highest order? What right, in the face of these incredible obstacles, has anyone to turn round and level the charge of "African inefficiency" to justify imposing on African workers such deplorable conditions?

No, the wonder is not the lack of skill. The wonder is how much the African has achieved in the face of everything.

Lack of skill, if it does exist, is no fault of the African. It is the fault of his poverty and of the colonial exploitation from which he and his country suffers. And all the talk about "African labour efficiency" is, in reality, a smoke-screen to cover up the truth of African exploitation, and to justify miserably low wages and wretched social conditions.

There is ample evidence at hand to expose completely this trick of using the African worker's alleged lack of skill as a pretext for paying him starvation wages.

A French report[1] says:

"Native workers, however unfamiliar they may be with modern techniques, however backward they may appear, adapt themselves quickly to the work when they are guided, advised and trained with skill."

A report from South Africa[2] says:

"A large number of tests and records made in the Dunlop factory suggests that the more efficient type of Native takes about half as long again to learn a particular job as a European, and that his normal rate of output is about eighty-five per cent of the European's."

That an African—ill-educated or without education at all, untrained and coming from a peasant background—should take

[1] CCTA, op. cit., p. 87.
[2] ibid., p. 127.

longer to learn a job than a much better educated European, coming from an environment with 150 years' background of industrialisation, is understandable. What is surprising is that, despite the handicaps from which he suffers, the African should so rapidly acquire such skill that he can reach eighty-five per cent of the European's output. *Needless to say, he does not get eighty-five per cent of his wage rate.*[1]

This once again shows that allegations about African workers' "lack of skill" or "low productivity" are pretexts to justify slave wages—since if output or skill was really the determining factor in fixing African wage rates, then there is not an African worker throughout the continent who could not immediately claim a substantial wage increase. (In fact, as is explained at some length in the next chapter, the low wages of African workers are not determined by their skill or productivity but by very different considerations.)

Northcott refers to African workers "who put together, without direct supervision, and riveted into place the parts of a seven-ton crane".[2] He cites the fact[3] that out of 15,292 African workers employed on the Kenya Uganda Railway at the time of his investigation, 4,262 were skilled enough to work as fitters, fitters' mates, painters, machinists in metal and wood, carpenters, riveters, electrical fitters, firemen, loco and motor drivers, cranemen, etc. He points out that: "The semi-skilled force is unskilled labour which has been enabled to acquire skill and is itself skilled labour in the making. *The manual operations which this body of craftsmen yet in the making perform are done in other lands by men of long craft training.*" [Own italics—J. W.] And a recent report[4] on the Central African Federation describes African steel workers at the Que Que iron and steel plant in Southern Rhodesia handling glowing ingots "with a dexterity which would be admired in Motherwell or Sheffield".

A study of Kenya by Northcott and Goss says:[5]

[1] Mr. Julius Lewin has cited the fact that lorry-driving was performed at one Northern Rhodesian copper mine by Europeans for £30 a month, and at another by Africans for about £3 a month. (*The Colour Bar in the Copperbelt*, Johannesburg, 1941.)
[2] Northcott: op. cit., p. 24.
[3] ibid., p. 26.
[4] *The Financial Times*, March 15, 1960.
[5] Northcott: op. cit., p. 32.

". . . the potential efficiency of Africans . . . is to be seen in the list of varied occupations upon which they are employed. These include electric welding, handling of damaged carriage bodies, armature winding, the charging of batteries, installation of electric fittings into coaches undergoing repairs, riveting with hot and cold rivets respectively, repairing steam boilers and fire boxes, driving a gantry crane, using automatic drilling machines, foundry work, carpentry and joinery work with the mechanical equipment associated therewith, stonemason's work, plastering, cement making and so forth. In the joinery shop all the furniture and fittings required by the Kenya-Uganda Railway in its carriages and offices were made mainly by Africans."

In other words, when given the chance, the African worker has rapidly displayed his ability to do a skilled job. Noon[1] points out that in the four years 1930 to 1934 Africans employed at the *Union Minière* mines of the Belgian Congo "took over 1,360 positions which formerly only Europeans had been considered capable of holding". It had only needed a modification of official policy for it to be "discovered" that African workers were quite able to take on skilled jobs.

In the Belgian Congo Davidson found Africans "drilling charge-holes, setting charges, firing charges, clearing debris with mechanical shovels, operating conveyor belts, working cranes. . . ."[2] He pointedly comments:

"In South Africa and Southern Rhodesia *they are not allowed to do these jobs. In Northern Rhodesia they often do them without its ever being recognised that they do them, so that they are not paid for doing them.*" [Own italics—J. W.]

Even more telling is Noon's exposure[3] of what goes on in the South African gold mines.

"There", he writes, "it is not unusual for the African labour gangs to descend into the mines at around 3.30 a.m., although European supervisors do not report before 7 or 7.30 in the

[1] Noon: op. cit., p. 32.
[2] Davidson: op. cit., p. 124.
[3] Noon: op. cit., p. 17.

morning. *In the meantime the labour gang proceeds with the work of marking out the areas to be blasted, setting the charges and detonating them as efficiently as they would if the White boss were present. If Africans can perform these operations (which, after all, are considered by the 'civilised' labour laws of the Union to be beyond their capacity and therefore must be reserved for White labour) without supervision for four hours daily, their ability to continue throughout the remainder of the day in the same fashion is implied."*   [Own italics—J. W.]

African mineworkers in the Northern Rhodesian copper belt have more or less put the same point as regards their work in the copper mines. Lewin has pointed out:[1]

"Besides all the unskilled work, the Africans are doing a considerable amount of skilled and especially semi-skilled work. Some of them hold blasting certificates, handle pneumatic drills, drive electric haulers, assist shaft-sinking, drive lorries, and take charge of trucks. . . . The Africans are well aware of the value and importance of their work, more especially as some of the Europeans are inclined to slack and to leave the major share of all the hard work to the Africans. Many Europeans are simply supervisors. *During their strike* [i.e. in 1940—J. W.] *the Africans challenged the mine management to allow them to work a competitive shift against the Europeans, in order to demonstrate who really produces the copper.*"

[Own italics—J. W.]

Needless to add, the challenge was never taken up!

Starvation

"*The capacity to work depends on health, and health is very largely determined by diet and nutrition.*"[2]

Few people will quarrel with this assertion, yet a United Kingdom report submitted to the Inter-African Labour Institute of the Commission for Technical Co-operation in Africa South of the Sahara (CCTA) for the *Survey on the Human Factors of Productivity in Africa* in 1956 states:

[1] Lewin, Julius: op. cit., pp. 4–5.
[2] Northcott: op. cit., p. 17.

"All the information available suggests that the African worker's basic handicap is physical, and arises from malnutrition."

This report significantly goes on to quote, as still valid, the 1939 report of the Committee on Nutrition in the Colonial Empire, which declared:

"We have no doubt at all that there are few parts of the Colonial Empire where the diet of the majority of the population is at present anything like sufficient for optimum nutrition. Diets are frequently insufficient in quantity and still more insufficient in quality."

Of Africa this is especially true. "Laboratory rats fed on a typical African's diet", says the *New Scientist*, "will eat their own offspring."[1] Dr. Josue de Castro has no hesitation in stating that Africa is *"beyond question one of the darkest spots on the world's map of malnutrition and hunger."*[2] He significantly points out that it is the African agricultural and wage workers (as distinct from "the traditional society organised in family groups, living by primitive agriculture, stock raising, hunting and fishing") who "represent the lowest nutritional level of the continent and perhaps, according to F.A.O. experts, 'the lowest in the world'."[3]

"The establishment of plantation colonies originated by the English and afterwards imitated by the other imperialist countries", explains de Castro, "had a grossly disturbing effect on the African nutritional economy. The plantation system . . . implies the destruction of natural wealth—regional fauna and flora—as well as the suppression of local subsistence agriculture. . . ."[4]

It is, he makes clear, European colonisation which, by ruining native agriculture, cutting down on food production in favour of cash crops, ruthlessly exploiting the soil and causing erosion, and turning millions into lowly paid wage workers, is primarily

[1] *The New Scientist*, August 20, 1959.
[2] De Castro, Dr. Josue: *Geography of Hunger*, p. 192, London, 1952.
[3] ibid., p. 180.
[4] ibid., pp. 179–80.

responsible for the semi-starvation which is the lot of so many
Africans.

"Wherever the Negro's contact with the Europeans was
prolonged, one finds a notably deficient type of diet."

In their study of two districts in Equator Province of the
Belgian Congo, Doucy and Feldheim[1] describe how the African
diet has deteriorated. The hinterland of the villages has been
reduced, the game has fled, and few varieties of vegetables are
now grown.

"This is a normal development", they say, "due in large
measure to the 'very fact of colonisation'; the result may be
encountered all over Africa: the extremely varied native diet has
been replaced by the relatively limited European diet."

Yet it has sometimes been argued that although the condition
of the African people is lamentable, it used to be worse; that, in
fact, imperialism is doing everything possible to bring about
improvements, that gradually life for the African people is getting
better. Official reports, however, themselves expose these myths,
and demonstrate only too well that imperialist rule, far from
bringing about progress, has led to a catastrophic *decline* in the
standard of living of the African people.

De Castro points out:

"When the Dutch settlers first appeared in this area [i.e.
South Africa] they found native tribes of strong, healthy
people who lived by raising cattle, growing corn, and hunting
wild game. . . . Today the diet is almost exclusively corn."[2]

He cites the evidence of J. H. Dugard, Inspector of Schools in
Transkei, who reported that out of 11,000 children observed,
84 per cent had only one meal a day; 14·9 per cent had two;
and no more than 0·6 per cent received three meals a day. "In
all cases, the meals were made up of corn in one form or
another."

[1] A study paper by Professors A. Doucy and P. Feldheim, prepared for
Unesco, 1954. See *Social Implications of Industrialisation and Urbanisation in
Africa of the Sahara*, pp. 680–1, 1956.
[2] De Castro, op. cit., p. 191.

A report from Sierra Leone says:[1]

"In the seventeenth century the people [of Sierra Leone] were of fine physique and lived on a mixed diet and apparently had sufficient animal food. . . . The present dietary of the people is surveyed and the evidence shows that it is ill-balanced . . . resulting in malnutrition and disease."

In Basutoland, a 1939 report said:

"According to residents of long standing, the physique and health of the Basuto today is not what it used to be. Malnutrition is seen in every village, dispensary, school or recruiting office. . . ."[2]

Now, twenty years later, a World Health Organisation report by Dr. J. A. Munoz reveals that in Basutoland "the standard of living—always low—appears to be sinking even lower."[3] The researches of Dr. Munoz show that the birthrate, which was 30·6 per thousand in 1951, had dropped to 22 per thousand in 1957; and Dr. Munoz comments that it was lack of food that made the parents infertile. He also draws attention to the fact that the infantile mortality rate doubled between 1951 and 1957, when it reached 116 per thousand children (the death rate for children under one year of age).

Thus, in place of the vaunted progress and improvement, we find a steady increase in malnutrition and a progressive deterioration in African physique and in growth of population, a certain sign of worsening conditions.

In many parts of Africa children suffer from a disease, nearly always fatal, known as *kwashiorkor* or malignant malnutrition. "This is a typical manifestation of inadequate diet," says de Castro, "characterised by cessation of growth, oedemas, fatty diarrhoea, fatty degeneration of the liver, and sometimes bleaching of the skin and hair."[4]

[1] *Sierra Leone Review of Present Knowledge of Human Nutrition*, Freetown, 1938.
[2] *Summary of Information Regarding Nutrition in the Colonial Empire*, Cmd. 6051, London, 1939.
[3] Duncan, Patrick: *Contact*, January 9, 1960. Quoted in *Africa Digest*, February 1960, vil, No. 4, pp. 124–5.
[4] De Castro: op. cit., p. 186.

Malignant malnutrition is now generally recognised as a major cause of African fatigue. Dr. H. C. Trowell has explained[1] that African women often have a smaller pelvis than other peoples, and that this itself *"is due to malnutrition during the period of bony growth when the mother herself was a child"*. As a consequence, not only is childbirth attended by increased risks, but the size of the pelvis and malnutrition in pregnancy produce an exceptionally small baby, which, says Dr. Trowell, "suffers from under-development of certain internal organs . . . [and] fails to put on weight". Many other signs apparently accompany this condition of *kwashiorkor*, such as changes in the blood, in the serum proteins, in the digestion of all forms of food, in the liver and possibly in the pancreas and kidneys.

These changes, says Dr. Trowell, "probably reflect a failure of development and in addition the strain of malnutrition." How devastating this disease is to the organism is best told by Dr. Trowell himself.

"The whole weight of modern research suggests that many Africans pass through this state, that many die during it, and that those who survive never recover completely. Doubtless many have only burnt-out scars in the internal organs and may, if they receive a good diet, recover full efficiency of mind and body, but it appears probable that many never recover completely. These persons appear normal when examined by the usual clinical methods and many medical men would consider them normal. Ordinary persons find them apathetic, given to laziness and sloth, short and slight in build, and generally ineffective. Those who recognise the symptoms of malignant malnutrition believe that many of the internal organs are scarred and function poorly, and that the condition is possibly incurable." [Own italics—J. W.]

Available reports make it clear that this disease is common throughout Africa. Quite simply, it is a disease resulting from semi-starvation both of the mother and of the child—and with which the child, on becoming adult, still suffers owing to his continuing to live under conditions of semi-starvation.

And to think, after that, that so many "experts" on Africa are ever ready to urge the African worker to increase his output as the key to overcoming his poverty and his starvation!

[1] Northcott, op. čit., pp. 86-7.

Further light on the malnutrition of African workers is shed by what is known about their eating arrangements and the number of meals they normally eat; and this, of course, is determined by their low wages and relative poverty.

In reference to the wage pattern in Kenya, Northcott and Crampton Chalk[1] have stressed that the rations provided with the wages "are not at all identical with what his own home garden would have supplied, nor do they correspond either in quantity or quality with what he would buy if he were free to do so."

Dr. Trowell points out[2] that in Kenya African workers whose wives are not with them—and this applies to the majority of workers employed in most urban areas—usually leave home too early for much breakfast. This itself is a consequence of Africans being compelled to live in locations or townships far distant from their place of employment. At midday, says Dr. Trowell, "they have too little time to return home and eat a meal". Nor do their low wages "permit the expenditure of 30 cents daily for lunch at the municipal canteen". The rations of maize-meal and meat, he states, "are inadequate" for health. Significantly, he adds:

"My own private observations, however, lead me to believe that, given an adequate wage and free, well-stocked markets of food, Africans can feed themselves better on their own than by any system of rations; and, further, that our paternalism in this respect is very deeply resented."

The problem is, however, that Africans do not get "an adequate wage", nor are "well-stocked markets of food" available at prices within reach of the African worker's pay-packet. Dr. Trowell, in fact, says:

"Visits to the Railway locations early in the day confirmed the statements made by many men that *little food is usually taken before leaving home in the morning, and that in the middle of the day some labourers who receive only a low wage eat nothing.* For long periods of the day some men are unable to satisfy

---

[1] ibid., p. 59.
[2] ibid., p. 85.

hunger; this might make them weak, faint, sleepy and irritable."[1]   [Own italics—J. W.]

The present author recalls being told several years ago by the Ghana railwaymen's leader, Pobee Biney, that he never ate a midday meal. He just had *posho* in the morning, and *posho* again at night. (*Posho*, a form of maize meal, is described by Henry and Grant[2] as "the cheapest foodstuff available", forming part of the ration issue provided "for the lower-paid wage earners". This meal is usually made into a form of porridge or gruel.)[3]

The lack of meals taken by Africans finds further confirmation in the findings of Northcott.[4]

Enquiries made at the houses of 153 African railwaymen in Kenya, in the Makongeni location, revealed that *not even twenty-five per cent of the men had a full midday meal, and that a number of workers not only went without a midday meal but had only a cup of tea at 4.30 p.m. and waited for their proper evening meal until as late as 8.30 p.m.*

Vincent, describing the plight of the Ivory Coast urban worker, writes:

"*In the last days of the month he often takes an empty stomach to work. When his wage is spent, he eats very little and his output curve descends more steeply as the last pay-day recedes into the past.*"[5]

                    [Own italics—J. W.]

A survey made by the East Africa Statistics Department in 1950, showed that in Nairobi, in all cases in the sample of workers taken, approximately seventy-two per cent of all income was spent on food, i.e. half as much again as was allowed for in the minimum wage formula, and that *many workers had little or nothing to eat at the end of the month.*

Much play has often been made of the food rations provided

---

[1] ibid., p. 87.
[2] ibid., p. 99.
[3] *Posho*, says Gicaru, "is an invention of the settler—or perhaps I should say of the devil—to keep down the African at the lowest level humanly conceivable and yet with sufficient strength to turn up for the roll call in the morning". (Gicaru, Muga: op. cit.)
[4] Northcott: op. cit., p. 113.
[5] Vincent, J.: *Brief Study of the African Workers' Output in the Ivory Coast*, École Nationale de la France d'Outre-Mer.

to African workers by European mining and other companies, and the impression has been created that these rations are sufficient in quantity and balance to provide a healthy diet. This "full-belly" policy, as it has been called, takes no account, in fact, of the health needs of the worker, since its main aim is to obtain from him the maximum output.

"The native worker at the mine, mill or plantation may get a stomach full of rice, or corn, or manioc meal," says de Castro.[1] "But this sort of stuffing, rather than improving his overall state of nutrition, has the effect of greatly aggravating any specific deficiencies he may have. . . . The so-called full-belly policy greatly worsened the nutritional situation of the Negro in Equatorial Africa. Bigwood and Trolli[2] observed that the Negro showed more frequent signs of dietary deficiency— particularly beriberi in both its dry and dropsical forms—after entering the service of the colonisers than he had before. . . . The nutritional situation is especially precarious in the mining districts, where fresh foods are practically unknown."

Such is the result of the European employer's policy of providing Africans with enough food in bulk to provide a quantity of energy which the employer expects to get back in the form of increased output. As de Castro has rightly said:

"*What he is really providing is not better nutrition, but merely an abundance of fuel.*"

The workers' malnutrition is, of course, a direct result of sheer poverty. Dr. Trowell has noted that:

". . . sitting and talking with the workers in their homes, one became aware of a very grave discontent. . . . Their mood is one of resentment and disappointment, and has the appearance of being ominous. *When asked to state their grievances they return with monotonous regularity to the question of wages and poverty.*"[3]
[Own italics—J. W.]

[1] De Castro: op. cit., p. 188.
[2] Bigwood and Trolli: "L'Alimentation au Congo Belge", in *La Science de l'Alimentation*, Paris, 1937.
[3] Northcott: op. cit., p. 85.

The important subject of African wages and its relation to semi-starvation is dealt with more fully in the next chapter; but at this point it is useful to stress that the starting point is *low wages* and the social misery which accompanies it. Dr. Trowell, for example, talks about "the vicious circle of low work-output, low wages, malnutrition and poor living conditions". This is taking us back again to the argument that "low work-output" is the starting-point of this vicious circle. In fact, however, the starting-point is the exploitation of the African worker based on starvation wages. The circle is therefore more apparent than real. There is a real starting point, low wages, and it is this which must be changed if output and productivity are to increase, malnutrition be wiped out and living conditions radically improved.

In his *Conditions Géographiques en Afrique Tropicale* P. Gourou has no hesitation in stating that *undernourishment is the prime factor in low productivity*. A report to the CCTA from Ruanda-Urundi says that, according to the estimate of one employer, provision of a balanced meal led to output increasing by 30 per cent. A British report to the same body argues:

"It is the view of a research worker on one of the plantations that no medical or social provision will promote increased productivity where the physique of the worker is continuously being undermined by a sub-standard diet."

It should, therefore, be clearly established that malnutrition, a key factor as far as output is concerned, is widespread in Africa; and that the output of African workers is largely determined by their malnutrition, or, to use more colloquial terms, their semi-starvation.

A striking example of such undernourishment was revealed at the Dunlop factory in Durban, in the Union of South Africa. In order to examine how the nutritional state of African workers in this factory was affecting industrial efficiency, the management arranged for every second African worker in the factory to be clinically examined during the course of a nutritional survey. This is what the examination disclosed:

"No single case was passed as completely normal. The

commonest skin lesion was phrynoderma, which occurred in half those under thirty-five years of age and in approximately two-thirds of those over thirty-five. . . . It may be added that this evidence of malnutrition develops over a relatively long period of time and similarly takes a long time to disappear. There were other skin lesions indicative of malnutrition, as well as eye-lesions, of which the commonest were those due to chronic and long-standing malnutrition. . . . *The general conclusion is that malnutrition exists in the majority of the men. The lesions are largely the result of malnutrition in childhood which has continued into adult life. . . .*"[1] [Own italics—J. W.]

Lest anyone might be led to believe that the above example was an exceptionally bad case and not at all typical of the conditions of the average African worker, a rude shock awaits him, for the above study added:

"*. . . it must be emphasised that the Dunlop factory workers are among the healthiest and best paid urban workers in Durban.*"

[Own italics—J. W.]

Disease

It is not merely that malnutrition robs the worker of his energy. In addition it makes him a more ready prey to diseases—diseases directly due to undernourishment as well as those to which he succumbs precisely because his half-starved body is less able to offer resistance. Any small interest shown in the ill-health of Africans by colonial authorities and employers is motivated principally by its effect on profits, and not by any humanitarian consideration for the Africans. "Low paid as the African labourer may often be," Hailey says,[2] "*an ailing employee is expensive and ineffective*".

Yet, despite official protestations of concern, all the facts reveal that ill health and disease is the common lot of the African.

In the Union of South Africa, a report of the Socio-Economic Commission of 1956 cites a factory where a large incidence of

[1] *The African Factory Worker: A Sample Study of the Life and Labour of the Urban African Worker*, p. 6, by University of Natal, Department of Economics, London, 1950.
[2] Hailey (Revised): op. cit., p. 1105.

indications of nutritional deficiency was noted. On further examination it was found that 44 per cent of the workers had round worm, 12 per cent tape worm, and 2½ per cent tuberculosis. In many British-controlled territories various forms of enteric diseases are widespread. Malaria is the principal endemic disease, and in many regions respiratory diseases including tuberculosis have a high rate of incidence. The Nigerian Railways report ten to fifteen days lost per man-year due to malaria. A Gold Coast survey in 1950 of a typical cocoa village[1] showed malarial infection in no less than 32 per cent of its inhabitants, hookworm in 52 per cent, round worm in 76 per cent and yaws (active or quiescent) in 75 per cent. This survey concludes that the *normal African is "undersized, anaemic and disease-ridden"*.

A similar conclusion is drawn by Carothers,[2] who claims "it would be easy to find examples of persons infected concurrently with malaria, hookworm, bilharzia, ascariasis and taeniasis, with a haemoglobin level of about thirty per cent, and yet not complaining of ill health. 'Normality' in the African, even from the standpoint of infection alone, is a rather meaningless abstraction."

The British Aluminium Company, reporting[3] malaria in 20 per cent of its employees, yaws in 10 per cent, and ascariasis in 2 per cent, added:

"Altogether, it would seem that a very high proportion of Gold Coast citizens are ill from parasitic diseases, and *that almost all of them have such diseases at some time.* Parasitic diseases not only impair efficiency directly—they also reduce the nourishment obtained from food, and lead to anaemia."[4]

[Own italics—J. W.]

A Belgian Government medical report for the Belgian Congo and Ruanda-Urundi in 1953 gave the number of cases of malaria as 688,841; of sleeping sickness (old and new cases) 20,862;

[1] See the Transactions of the Royal Society of Tropical Medicine and Hygiene, vol. xliv, No. 3. Quoted in *The Human Factors of Productivity in Africa*, CCTA, 1956, p. 23.
[2] Carothers, J. C.: *The African Mind in Health and Disease*, pp. 32-3, World Health Organization, Monograph Series, No. 17, Geneva, 1953.
[3] CCTA, op. cit., p. 23.
[4] ibid., p. 24.

tuberculosis, 13,349; yaws, 225,413; and leprosy, 210,000, approximately.

For the urbanised African worker tuberculosis is without doubt a growing scourge. A report on tuberculosis in Kenya in 1951,[1] in answer to the question "Is tuberculosis increasing in Kenya?" said:

> "If any medical officer in Kenya was asked this question, there is little doubt that his reply would be an emphatic affirmative."

On the basis of an analysis of reports of directors of medical services in Kenya during 1930–47, it is revealed that the number of tuberculosis admissions to hospital per 10,000 of the African population rose from 2·16 for the three years 1931–3, to 6·1 for 1945–7—nearly treble.

This, however, concerns only cases admitted to hospital. The figures take no account at all of the cases which never get that far. And on this Dr. Haynes has some very pointed remarks to make. It is, he says, very rare if anything at all is done for non-surgical tuberculosis. "On the contrary, the usual practice is to discharge such patients as soon as the diagnosis is made." Africans know, "often from bitter experience, that it is useless to seek hospital treatment for this condition". Consequently, says Dr. Haynes, "there are probably a lower proportion of cases of tuberculosis in the hospitals of the Colony *and a higher proportion in their homes than is the case for any other major disease.*"[2] [Own italics—J. W.]

Hailey admits that tuberculosis in Africa is mainly a proletarian disease, the consequence, in fact, of bad housing, overcrowding and undernourishment, though it is rapidly spreading to the rural areas as a result of labour migration.

> "At the Mulago hospital in Uganda it has been demonstrated that immigrant labourers predominate among the patients treated for pulmonary tuberculosis, bad nourishment on the journey accentuating their susceptibility. . . . Most of the male population of the urban areas are engaged in heavy work, to which they must often walk considerable distances each day;

[1] Haynes, W. S., M.A., M.D.: *Tuberculosis in Kenya*, p. 115, Nairobi, 1951.
[2] ibid., p. 115.

they usually take a diet grossly deficient in protein and vitamins. In these conditions tuberculosis flourishes. . . ."[1]

Wiles[2] states that in some industrial towns in the Union of South Africa the death rate from tuberculosis among Africans almost doubled in eight years, reaching 10 per 1,000 per annum, a rate *thirty times as high as that among Europeans in South Africa.*

Speaking of Africa generally, Hailey says:[3] "Tests have shown that *in urban areas almost every person is infected in early adult life.*" [Own italics—J. W.]

Leprosy, too, is widespread throughout Africa. There are said to be 80,000 cases in Uganda, where the infection rate is 33·5 per thousand. In Tanganyika the rate is 26·5, in Gambia 25, in Nigeria 16 (up to 50–60 in some districts), in Nyasaland 14, and in Northern Rhodesia 12·6.

Another terrible scourge of Africa, as indeed of all colonial areas in the world, is blindness. In parts of Nigeria and the Union of South Africa there are close on 2,000 cases per 100,000 of the population. In one area of Ghana it is said to be 7,000 per 100,000. In Kenya ten per cent of adults are said to be blind in one eye. The 1953 annual report of the British Empire Society for the Blind quotes evidence showing that in Kenya at least fifty per cent of Africans suffer from trachoma, either active or quiescent. There is a similar high incidence in Uganda, Tanganyika and Zanzibar.

Despite such appalling health conditions, the provisions made for African health services are scandalous. Whereas the number of inhabitants per hospital bed is 65 in France, 76 in New Zealand and 101 in the United States of America, it is 700 in Nyasaland and French West Africa, 910 in Ruanda-Urundi, 1,100 in Sudan, 1,550 in Sierra Leone, 2,200 in Nigeria, 3,500 in Ethiopia, and 4,000 in Liberia.[4]

Half-starved, diseased and often half-blind, the African is clearly expendable in the view of the colonial governments and European employers who exploit him so terribly. And it is of Africans suffering from such conditions that the Europeans

---

[1] Hailey (Revised): op. cit., p. 1128.
[2] Wiles, T. J.: *Tuberculosis in the Commonwealth*, 1947.
[3] Hailey (Revised): op. cit., p. 1128.
[4] The figures are taken from the U.N. *Report on the World Social Situation*, 1957, but in most cases refer to the year 1952.

complain that their output is too low and that they lack enthusiasm for their work!

"Human Relations"

There is more than a touch of racialism in much of the "scientific" material in which the African worker is dissected, his outlook examined, his "cultural pattern" described, his "adaptability" assessed, and so forth—and all to provide an "explanation" as to the alleged "inefficiency" and "low output and productivity" of African labour.

Lack of industrial discipline, unfamiliarity with machines or with work routines—only to be expected in a labour force which is largely migrant, confined to unskilled jobs, and denied education, training and access to skill—are often imputed to the African worker as if these were particularly *racial* or *African* characteristics. Indeed, the Forster Commission Report actually speaks of "a radical change in racial characteristics" as being a pre-condition for African copper miners being given more skilled jobs with correspondingly higher pay.

Such arguments concerning the alleged "racial" deficiencies of Africans in the field of industrial production have been emphatically exposed in theory and practice. Moore[1] rejects the proposition that different "racial" or ethnic groups have different capacities for assimilating the skills required for industrial production, owing to "differences in hereditary biological constitution". Although this position, he says, "is commonly held as a comfortable explanation for Western domination of underdeveloped areas, it is supported by no anthropological evidence and may be dismissed as having no scientific basis".

There was a time when European attitudes to African workers could be summed up in the crude words of a Major Ewart Grogan, D.S.O.:

". . . we have our old friend, as we affectionately term him, 'the ape', the proletariat of the country, the native of the country, upon which everything fundamentally and finally depends. . . . You engage a dusky brother . . . who will be

[1] Moore. W. E.: *Industrialisation and Labour, Social Aspects of Economic Development*, p. 124, New York, 1951.

quite pleased to carry your boots about for you and do anything else for five or six rupees a month and a certain amount
of porridge."[1]

Today, fifty years after this enlightened declaration by an
unashamed apostle of colonialism, one can still find European
employers in Africa who speak the same language. Still, we
have moved on a little. The world has changed somewhat, and
Africa has not been unaffected. Nowadays all the emphasis is on
"co-operation" and "productivity"—and all the efforts of trade-
union advisers, employers, government departments, Moral
Rearmament representatives and psychologists are deployed to
bring about this result, so desired by the employers. "Human
relations" is the formula, though behind this term stands a
most *in*human relationship of white master and African servant.

In pursuit of this aim of "co-operation" every form of "joint
consultation" is fostered. Reports from employers make quite
clear in whose interests the "consultation" takes place. A report
from Uganda states: "The few employers who have started joint
consultative committees state that they are in favour of them . . .
one or two state that these committees have prevented stoppages
of work".[2]

Another report from Tanganyika speaks in praise of "domestic
councils" in agriculture and mining which, it says, "have had a
favourable effect on productivity by encouraging more amicable
industrial relations and by minimising the loss of working time
arising from stoppages of work due to trade disputes".[3] From
Sierra Leone it is reported that joint committees "promote general
contentment and the development of a team spirit".[4] In Kenya
joint consultative machinery is regarded as essential "to a
contented and stabilised labour force".[5]

But how successful, in reality, have these bodies been as a means
of enticing African workers to work harder, produce more and
pay less attention to their own interests, such as better wages and

---

[1] *Lecture on the East African Protectorate* by Maj. Ewart Grogan, D.S.O., delivered
at Caxton Hall, Westminster, July 8, 1919. (Overseas Settlement Office,
S.W.I.)
[2] CCTA: op. cit., p. 62.
[3] ibid., p. 63.
[4] ibid., p. 63.
[5] ibid., p. 63.

conditions? It would be foolish to deny that they had had any influence at all; but, in the main, they have been no more successful than similar bodies in Great Britain. The African working class may be relatively new, but, as a class, it has a shrewd idea as to where its interests lie. And behind the frequent complaints of European managers and government reports one can see the stubborn and determined resistance of the African workers to the blandishments of their employers, and their persistent fight to secure better wages and conditions for themselves.

Thus, a report from Southern Rhodesia[1] says:

"In both the Rhodesias efforts to establish systems of joint consultation have frequently failed, despite the highest intentions of managements and the efforts of labour departments, owing to a lack of understanding and trust, and ignorance, on the part of the workers. . . ."

Anyone who has discussed these questions with African trade unionists will have rapidly become aware that Africans' opposition to joint consultation is due not to any "lack of understanding" on their part but, on the contrary, to a very clear understanding as to where their real interests lie. Lack of *trust* there may well be, but taking into consideration the manner in which the white rulers of the Rhodesias have treated African labour, for what reason should the African workers put any trust in their European employers?

Kenya settlers have apparently had no better success than their counterparts in the Rhodesias. Kenya employers complain, in fact, that "joint consultative machinery is often treated by the African worker as a medium for presenting the most unreasonable and unrealistic demands. . . ."[2] A living wage may appear "unreasonable and unrealistic" to those who have become rich by exploiting cheap labour in Africa, but to the workers themselves—and to any really impartial observer—their demands are fully justified, reasonable and realistic.

African awareness of all the cheap tricks and snares used by the employers to entice them into increasing their own rate of

[1] ibid., p. 65.
[2] ibid., p. 65.

exploitation is shown in the following example given by Vincent in his study on the Ivory Coast.[1] A coffee planter, whose workers earned 105 francs for a daily task of two baskets filled (i.e. at a rate of $52\frac{1}{2}$ francs per basket), offered his workers an *extra 25 francs for each extra basket filled*. The workers refused, naturally enough. After all, how many British workers would, let us say, be prepared to do overtime if told by the employer that for each hour over-time they would receive *not time-and-a-half, not even time-rate, but half-time?* Yet this refusal of the Ivory Coast workers is actually cited by the CCTA, with an air of astonishment, as a proof that African workers are not really interested in more money after certain elementary needs have been satisfied, and that they will not easily respond to incentives!

Productivity—for whom?

In none of the numerous studies made on African "efficiency and productivity" has any author thought it necessary to answer the question, "Why should the African increase his productivity?" After all said and done, what is he working for? Who is going to get the benefit of his increased productivity? As Batten[2] has rightly commented, the African is only too well aware that any economic development in Africa "serves mainly to enrich non-Africans".

And for the African worker it is not only a personal question. He knows that all the immense wealth he produces—the gold, diamonds, copper, tin, cocoa, coffee, tobacco, palm oil, sisal, and so on—is not destined to enrich Africa. With what heavy heart must the African docker work, watching the natural resources his African fellow-workers have garnered from the soil of his native land being loaded on to British or French ships, destined to add riches to the pockets of millionaires in London, Paris, Brussels and New York.

Why should the African speed-up the robbery of his native land? Because that is, in fact, what the advocates of "higher productivity" are asking him to do.

The African worker has absolutely no incentive to work harder. He is generally on a scandalously low *daily* rate—and no

[1] Vincent: op. cit.
[2] Batten, T. R.: *Problems of African Development*, Part I, p. 171, London, 1947-54.

one is going to pay him a penny more just because he works harder.

Where the African worker has increased output he has seen that the benefits have gone only to the European employers. No matter how much gold the mineworkers in Witwatersrand produce, no South African or British or American mining company is going to say: "Thank you very much. Now you can have more pay." In the last twenty years, African mineworkers have steadily increased the output of copper in Northern Rhodesia. Did the employers show them generosity and turn round and give them higher wages? Of course not! Every penny of increased wages had to be bitterly fought for. Workers were shot in the struggle for more pay. A trade union had to be built and strengthened, and long, protracted strike struggles waged before higher pay was granted. Similar hard-fought battles for higher pay, in which many Africans fell victim or were imprisoned, had to be waged in other African territories.

The experience of Africa, like the experience of workers in all countries under capitalist rule, shows that it is not higher productivity which brings higher wages but the workers' struggle.

Yes, labour productivity in Africa could be higher. But it has always been known that slave labour was a very low form of labour, with a correspondingly low degree of productivity. That is why it had to give way to serf labour. Serf labour was an advance on slave labour—but that, too, was found to be inadequate. African labour, colonial labour, is a combination of slave and serf labour. The African is not really free, as in Western capitalist countries, to sell his labour power to the highest bidder; he is compelled by legal, physical and economic pressures to work for starvation wages for a foreign exploiter. Such conditions of labour are bound to result in low productivity. History shows that no appeals, however well-intentioned, to the imperialist rulers of Africa to give African workers better wages and conditions are likely to have the slightest effect. If labour efficiency is to be improved and productivity increased, then the first prerequisite is to end colonialism. Once the African worker is fully liberated from bondage he will perform wonders of skill and effort that will shake the world no less than did the feats of the liberated peoples of the Russian Tsarist Empire and of China.

It took the 1917 revolution to bring the wheelbarrow to the Tajik Republic and to end the travail of the Volga boatmen as beasts of burden. It took the 1949 revolution to destroy the Chinese rickshaw and the age-old carrying pole. Liberated Africa, too, will end the degradation of the worker and open the way to new feats of human endeavour. And when that hour strikes, the African worker will show that he is second to no man in his skill and efficiency, and in his enthusiasm for work.

CHAPTER SEVEN

"ASINAMALI"—"WE HAVE NO MONEY"

DURING the epic bus boycott in South Africa, in 1957, African workers proclaimed on their banners: "*Asinamali*"—"We Have No Money". This slogan was soon taken up, and became a symbolic cry of the wages movement launched by the South African Congress of Trade Unions. One leaflet distributed in Johannesburg factories read:

> "Why can't we pay bus fares?
> We have no money.
> Why are our families hungry?
> We have no money.
> Why do our children die?
> We have no money."

"We have no money" is, in fact, true for workers throughout Africa.

It is sometimes argued that African workers do not *need* higher wages since they are used to living at a lower standard than people in the West. Typical of this kind of thinking is the following cynical reply given by a settler to the questionnaire of the Committee appointed to make a Survey of Nutrition in Northern Rhodesia in 1938:

> "I hold the view that the fuss about vitamins, etc., will die away. I do not believe in feeding people on foods based on their chemical analysis. There is very little difference chemically between good sugar and good coals . . . the people who are most healthy are those accustomed to live mainly on one article of diet. Their whole metabolisms get accustomed to deal with it. . . . The African Natives get meal or maize or millet and a

little meat; they do not require green vegetables or anything else. . . . It can't be necessary to give growing children milk. . . ."[1]

This, of course, is the familiar "handful of rice" theory, of which one heard so much before the war in connection with attempts to justify the starvation wages of workers in India and China. "They can live on a handful of rice a day." So ran the theory.

This is really putting the cart before the horse. *Anyone* receiving wages of one or two shillings a day—and this is the wage often paid to workers on European farms in Africa—no matter whether he were American, European, Asian or African, would be compelled to live at such a low standard that the proverbial daily handful of rice would doubtlessly constitute the main element in his diet. The truth is that workers do not *live* at such a level. They merely exist, until death comes to claim them. And the average expectation of a life of thirty years and sometimes less—not to mention infantile mortality rates of 100 per thousand upwards—so common in Africa and Asia, shows how early death comes to make its claim on these underpaid and undernourished workers.

Any consideration of African wages must start from the standpoint that these wages are incredibly low, by any standards. They are, in fact, colonialism expressed in the sphere of wage rates.

How low these wages are can be seen from the table below.

TABLE XVII

WAGES OF AFRICAN WORKERS IN SELECTED TERRITORIES

Territory	Year	Category of Worker	Pay
Nigeria[2]	1956–7	Unskilled, agriculture	2s. a day minimum
		Unskilled, tin mining	2s. 8d. a day minimum
		Unskilled, coal mining	4s. 2d. a day minimum
Sierra Leone[3]	1957	Building, labourer	£1 9s. weekly, average
		Mining, labourer	£1 19s. 4½d. weekly, average
S. Rhodesia[4]	1956	Unskilled labourer	7d. an hour

---

[1] *Report of Committee appointed to make a Survey of Nutrition in Northern Rhodesia*, p. 2, Lusaka, 1938.

[2] *Annual Report for 1956–7*, Department of Labour, p. 32, Lagos, 1959.

[3] *Annual Report for 1957*, p. 14, H.M.S.O., 1959.

[4] *African Labour Survey*, table 25, pp. 682–5, I.L.O., Geneva, 1958.

Territory	Year	Category of Worker	Pay	
N. Rhodesia[1]	1957	Unskilled, agriculture	80s. a month (26 days)	
		Unskilled, other	100s. a month (26 days)	
Nyasaland[2]	1958	Unskilled, agriculture	1s. 6d. a day, minimum	
Kenya[3]	1957	Urban labourer:		
		Mombasa	82s. a month (plus housing allowance)	21s.
		Nairobi	85s. a month (plus housing allowance)	22s.
Uganda[4]	1956	Unskilled, agriculture	35s. a month, minimum	
Tanganyika[4]	1957	Sisal industry, weeder	31s. a month (30 tasks)	
French Equatorial Africa[5]	1956	Unskilled labourer	22 fr., CFA hourly average	
French W. Africa[5]	1956	Unskilled labourer	21 fr., CFA hourly minimum	
Union of S. Africa[5]	1956	Unskilled labourer	1s. 5·2d. hourly minimum	
Belgian Congo[6]	1958	"Ordinary" workers in Elizabethville	16 B.fr. daily cash minimum (plus 20·10 in kind)	
Angola[7]	1956	Agricultural workers	57·50 escudos monthly (plus food, etc.)	

Minimum wage rates of unskilled labourers and agricultural workers have been taken in the main, since these constitute the most common category of wage labour in Africa and their rates are close to the average for all other sections. Undue attention is sometimes paid in studies on African questions to the maximum pay earned by some African workers, but these maxima are received by only a small proportion of workers and are completely untypical.

Moreover, as the *Report of the Committee on African Wages*[8] (commonly known as the Carpenter Report) points out, the statutory minimum wage tends to become the *basic wage*, and the whole wage structure is built on the foundations of the basic minimum.

The rates given in this table indicate that the majority of African workers receive wages in the order of one shilling a day up to under five shillings a day. Or, to put it in another way, an African worker usually receives for a day's work less than a

[1] *Annual Report for 1957*, p. 12, H.M.S.O., 1958.
[2] *Annual Report for 1958*, p. 30, H.M.S.O., 1959.
[3] *Annual Report for 1957*, p. 11, H.M.S.O., 1958.
[4] *Quarterly Digest of Colonial Statistics*, No. 41, p. 67, April 1959.
[5] *African Labour Survey*, table 25, pp. 682–5, I.L.O., Geneva, 1958.
[6] *African Labour Survey*, table 26, p. 686, I.L.O., Geneva, 1958.
[7] *African Labour Survey*, table 28, p. 687, I.L.O., Geneva, 1958.
[8] *Report of the Committee on African Wages* (Carpenter Report), Nairobi, 1954

British worker is paid for an hour. It takes an African worker usually a year to earn as much as an average worker in Britain earns in a month.

A striking characteristic of African wages is the persistence with which these low rates have continued over long periods of time. Roper[1] gives the example of the Ghana labourer's daily rate which, for the lowest-paid section, was 9d. in 1883, 9d. in 1920, 8d. in 1930 (at the time of the world economic crisis), and 1s. in 1938. *An increase of 3d. in fifty-five years.* Buell[2] gives a similar example for the Union of South Africa, where the average wage paid in the mines in 1897 was about 2s. a day, and in 1926 only 2s. 2d. This would appear to be an increase of 2d. in 29 years, but in fact the wage in 1896 had been 3s., being cut by a third in 1897. Thus the 2s. 2d. in 1926, when Buell did his tour, was still 10d. below the figure of 30 years previous. Even in 1960 the rate of pay for African miners in the Union is still only 3s. 4d. a shift—4d. more than it was in 1896!

A more recent example is that of the wages movement in the Tanganyika sisal industry, where the basic rate of pay of the workers in the plantations remained stationary for the eight years 1951 to 1958.[3]

Artisans' rates show the same picture as that of unskilled workers. Thus, for example, the average daily rate of Ghana carpenters was 4s. 6d. in 1921. In 1938, 17 years later, it was still 4s. 6d.[4]

Many similar examples could be given; and if one takes into account prices, taxation and other factors, and calculates *real* wages, then the trend usually shows not merely that wages have stood still but have declined seriously over long periods of time.

Real wages of Sierra Leone labourers declined from an index of 100 in 1949 to 87 in 1954.[5] Ghana miners' real wages declined from 100 to 84 between 1941 and 1947.[6]

In Southern Rhodesia, says Leys in his recent book:[7]

"Such evidence as there is suggests that from the 1930s

---

[1] Roper: op. cit., p. 90.
[2] Buell: op. cit., p. 43.
[3] *The State of Industrial Relations in the Sisal Industry of Tanganyika*, Report by Professor D. T. Jack, 1959.
[4] Roper: op. cit., p. 94.   [5] ibid., p. 91.
[6] ibid., p. 91.   [7] Leys, Colin: op. cit., p. 26.

until about 1950 there was no rise in African real wages—
indeed, during the years 1939–48 there may have been a slight
decline—and what made this possible was large-scale recruitment of labour from other territories."

African real wages in Johannesburg, too, show a serious
decline between 1944 and 1954, as the following table indicates.

TABLE XVIII
WAGES AND EXPENDITURE IN JOHANNESBURG

Monthly expenditure			1944 £ s. d.	1950 £ s. d.	1954 £ s. d.
Food, rent, fuel, light, cleaning, transport, clothing, tax	..	..	12 18 6	17 14 4	23 10 4
Average family income	..	..	9 18 1	12 16 6	15 18 11
Monthly income deficit	..	..	3 0 5	4 17 10	7 11 5

(Source: *An Analysis of Proposed Increases in African Taxation*, Fact Paper of
South African Institute of Race Relations, No. 1, 1958.)

The gap between income and essential expenditure has
widened still more since 1954, being estimated today by Segal[1]
at "probably almost £10 a month".

Minimum Wage

Before coming on to consider the cause of these low wages and
the reasons for their continuation over such long periods, some
general observations need to be made.

In his classic explanation of wage-labour, Marx[2] shows how
the price of labour is determined "by the cost of production, by
the labour time necessary to produce this commodity—labour
power", and goes on to point out that the cost of producing
labour power "is the cost required for maintaining the worker
as a worker and of developing him into a worker. The less the
period of training, therefore, that any work requires, the smaller
is the cost of production of the worker and the lower is the price
of his labour, his wages. In those branches of industry in which
hardly any period of apprenticeship is required and where the
mere bodily existence of the worker suffices, the cost necessary

[1] Segal, Ronald: *The Agony of Apartheid*, p. 4, Christian Action, London, 1960.
[2] Marx, Karl: *Wage Labour and Capital*. (See *Marx and Engels, Selected Works*,
vol. i, p. 82, London, 1950.)

for his production is almost confined to the commodities necessary for keeping him alive and capable of working."

Since the majority of African workers are employed in unskilled or, at best, semi-skilled jobs, the period of training is negligible; in fact in most cases there is none at all. This helps to explain why an African worker receives wages merely sufficient "for keeping him alive and capable of working". This question of skill or lack of skill raises a number of other questions to which attention is drawn later in this chapter.

There is a further general consideration to bear in mind. Marx explains that "the manufacturer in calculating his cost of production and thereby the price of the products takes into account the wear and tear of the instruments of labour. . . . In the same way, in calculating the cost of production of simple labour power, there must be included the cost of reproduction, whereby the race of workers is enabled to increase and to replace worn-out workers by new ones. . . . The cost of production of simple labour power, therefore, amounts to the *cost of the existence and reproduction of the worker*. The price of this cost of existence and reproduction constitutes wages. Wages so determined are called the *wage minimum*. . . . Individual workers, millions of workers, do not get enough to be able to exist and reproduce themselves; *but the wages of the whole working class* level themselves out within their variations to this minimum."[1]

Now, there is no doubt that the majority of African workers today are among those who "*do not get enough to be able to exist and reproduce themselves*". The Carpenter Report says:[2]

"We have seen, in our study of the Colony's wage structure, that the minimum wage has become very much a *real* wage, that a considerable proportion of the Colony's unskilled workers have been caught in its 'net', and that for many others the net has acted like a magnet to hold down wages. . . . *We have found very few witnesses prepared to say that the present minimum wage is adequate to cover the cost of living of a single man living under urban conditions. Many, on the other hand, including witnesses with some claim to 'expert' knowledge, have had no hesitation in condemning it as being definitely inadequate.*"   [Own italics—J. W.]

[1] Marx, Karl: op. cit., p. 82.
[2] Carpenter Report: op. cit., p. 55.

A recent study on "Interracial Wage Structure in Africa", published in the *International Labour Review*,[1] admits that the aim of establishing a minimum wage sufficient to maintain "the purchasing power of the lowest-paid workers at least equal to the cost of a minimum standard of living, at or above the subsistence level, so far as this is economically possible", has not always been achieved.

"Moreover, minimum rates of wages were, until recently, and in most cases still are, fixed at a level sufficient only to maintain *the minimum standard of living of the worker alone, and would not meet the cost of supporting a family.*"

[Own italics—J. W.]

Thus there is no doubt that in most parts of Africa wages are minimum wages, and that these minima are so low that they mean the most wretched poverty and misery for African workers.

In the light of the points already made, it is instructive to note how clearly official methods for calculating wage minima for African workers completely confirm the theories of Marx. In their general propaganda, employers of African labour as well as colonial government officials, claim, as we have seen in the previous chapter, that wages of Africans are low because their output and skill are low. But when it comes actually to calculating how much, or rather how little, they should pay an African worker, all references to basing the wage on the worker's output vanish, and instead we are immersed in icy cold, inhuman calculations as to what is the minimum wage which will enable the African worker to "exist and reproduce himself", as Marx put it.

Minimum-wage calculations in Africa are generally based on minimum diet requirements. Explaining the dietary aspect of the statutory minimum wage, Case[2] says:

"Foodstuffs, the constituents of a diet, must discharge three primary and essential functions. Firstly, they must provide

[1] *International Labour Review*, July 1958, p. 50.
[2] Case, Dr. E. M. (Medical Department, Kenya): Appendix G to the Carpenter Report, p. 193.

energy both for the maintenance of life on a basal level and for the performance of activities superimposed upon this; secondly, they must furnish material for growth, for perpetual replacement and repair of tissues, and for reproduction. Thirdly, they must contribute the substances that are implicated in the control and regulation of the innumerable bodily processes, physical and chemical, that constitute life."

In other words, minimum wages for African workers would appear to be calculated on the "cost of the existence and reproduction of the worker", as Marx maintained.

However, because of the migrant-labour system prevailing generally in Africa, with the adult male worker quitting the countryside to seek employment with a European enterprise, leaving his wife and children behind, the minimum wage is based on the minimum requirements of the *single* adult male, and is not intended to provide for his family.

The Carpenter Report drew the conclusion that a half of all urban workers in private industry and a quarter of those in public services "are in receipt of wages insufficient to provide for their basic, essential needs".[1] (Figures show that even this critical assessment made by the Carpenter Committee is unduly generous to the employers, both private and government.) The report points out that this "assessment is made in relation to an adult male labour force living *as single men* under urban conditions". It adds that if, in judging the adequacy of the wage, "we take into account not only the worker's own needs but also those of his wife and children, the picture becomes grim indeed".

The Carpenter Report is obliged to state that for the rural worker the wage is equally inadequate:

". . . having regard to what we know of agricultural wages, we must conclude that the total emoluments of nearly three-quarters of the ticket[2] and monthly contract labour employed

---

[1] Carpenter Report: op. cit., p. 32.
[2] It is customary in Africa for workers to be paid on the "ticket" system. Thirty actual days of work (or "tickets") have to be put in before the wage is paid (as against the 26 days of the average calendar month). If account is taken of Sundays off for rest, as well as time off for sickness, it can be seen that some 35–40 days are the usual period for which the so-called "monthly" pay must suffice.

in non-plantation agriculture are inadequate to support a minimum standard of health, decency and working efficiency. This general inadequacy of wages becomes much more pronounced when viewed in relation to the needs of the worker *and* his family. Wage levels are higher in plantation agriculture but, even there, there can be relatively few cases where the adult male worker's own wage is fully adequate to support both himself and his family."[1]

A recent report on Salisbury[2] comes to very similar conclusions regarding wages of Africans in that city:

"Wages generally are low, especially for Africans who have families to support."[3]
". . . it is always the single adult labourer who provides the foundation of the wages structure."[4]

The interesting admission is made that it is "unrealistic, however, to suppose that the single man is, as a rule, 'single' in the marital sense. Many of them are 'single' only in the sense that they are unable, by reason of the housing situation, to occupy married quarters with their families. To that extent they may have domestic obligations no smaller than those Africans who are designated as 'married'. Indeed, in so far as they have to maintain or to assist in maintaining two establishments their obligations may be greater."[5]

In Nyasaland, the 1957 Minimum Wage Order states quite bluntly that it "does not take into account a worker's family responsibilities". In the Belgian Congo, the only legally enforceable minimum wage under Belgian rule has been that of the unskilled worker on a bachelor basis. Information submitted by the Portuguese Government to the Inter-African Labour Conference held at Lusaka in 1957 indicated that "the basis of the minimum wage does not include the worker's family responsibilities".

[1] Carpenter Report: op. cit., p. 39.
[2] Plewman Report: op. cit.
[3] ibid., p. 73.
[4] ibid., p. 77.
[5] ibid., p. 79.

It is thus clear that reference to minimum wages of African workers are "minimum" in the absolute sense of the term—the lowest wage at which a *single* worker can exist.

This is amply borne out by the very methods used in Africa for calculating the minimum wage. In Salisbury, for example, Dr. D. Bettison has worked out a "Poverty Datum Line" for Africans in the municipal area of the town and its surroundings. The very name indicates the cold, inhuman approach to African wages on the part of the authorities. This rate—P.D.L. as it is called—is based on the following assumptions. It is composed of the absolute *minimum* requirements for food, clothing, fuel and light, cleaning materials, transport to and from work, rent, and taxation. It is assumed that "as far as food, clothing, fuel, lighting, and cleaning materials are concerned . . . purchases are made in the cheapest market open to ordinary consumers."[1]

In other words, to quote the Salisbury Report, the P.D.L. "is simply a statistical calculation of what is required in the way of income to enable the basic and elementary needs of individuals to be met. It takes into account only the barest essentials of food, clothing and shelter and includes no items which are not necessary for the maintenance of life, not even of what are sometimes described as conventional necessities."[2]

Professor Batson points out:[3]

"Such a standard is perhaps more remarkable for what it omits than for what it includes. It does not allow a penny for amusement, for sport, for medicine, for education, for saving, for hire purchase, for holidays, for odd bus rides, for newspapers, stationery, tobacco, sweets, hobbies, gifts, pocket money, or comforts or luxuries of any kind. It does not allow a penny for replacements of blankets, furniture, or crockery. It is not a 'human' standard of living. It thus admirably [*sic!*] fulfils its purpose of stating the barest minimum upon which subsistence and health can theoretically be achieved."

This, then, is the basis on which minimum wages are calculated

---

[1] Batson, Professor E.: *The Poverty Line in Salisbury*, commenting on the Bettison P.D.L. Quoted in the Carpenter Report, pp. 50–1.
[2] Plewman Report: op. cit., p. 77.
[3] Batson: op. cit. Quoted in Carpenter Report, p. 52.

in Africa. An "inhuman" standard of living. But this is still not the worst, for the report on Salisbury states:

"We have found that a considerable proportion of urban Africa labour receives wages which are *below or very close to the P.D.L.*"[1]

The report further states that, according to data presented for a budget survey in Salisbury in 1957, it would appear that "those 'single' Africans whose expenditure fell below the P.D.L. were in fact spending less than their earnings and there is a strong presumption that their savings were being remitted to their families living elsewhere".[2] What a striking commentary this is on the utterly deplorable economic plight of the African people! Even many of those whose earnings carry them a little beyond the miserable P.D.L. find it difficult, in fact, to live above the P.D.L. level because of the desperate need for them to assist their families suffering an equally wretched existence in the impoverished Reserves.

In Kenya, according to the Carpenter Report, the urban minimum wage has been based on a modified P.D.L. and an "Effective Minimum Level". This is calculated by assessing a P.D.L. *excluding housing and transport*, adding 33⅓ per cent to cover "human needs", and then adding allowances for housing, water (in some cases only), 2s. a month for tax, and a "cushion" of 1s. a month.

In terms of actual cash, this worked out, at the time of the Carpenter Report, to a monthly contract wage of 54s. 75 cts. (plus 8s. 25 cts. for housing) in Mombasa.[3] This is the highest rate, in other urban areas and townships the total sum of monthly wage and housing allowance combined sometimes being only 55s. 50 cts. Thus 2s. a day is the average minimum which the Kenya government regards as sufficient to maintain an African urban worker. It should be noted, however, that "a Labour Officer has power, in individual cases, to agree in writing to the payment of a lesser rate".[4] Apparently he has no power to *increase* the rate.

[1] Plewman Report: op. cit., p. 81.
[2] ibid., pp. 82-3.
[3] For ticket workers the rate was 9s. more, the assumption being that the pay in the case of this category of workers would extend over a period of thirty-six days.
[4] Carpenter Report: op. cit., p. 49.

The Central Minimum Wage Advisory Board which devised this handsome scale of pay described it as a "social safety net". It regarded its objective as being to devise a wage which, "while covering the cost of living of a single adult male employee working at unskilled labour, would not give him that feeling of complacent satisfaction in which he would make no effort at self improvement."

The Carpenter Report itself is forced to admit that among the minimum-wage earners themselves "we are conscious of a feeling not so much of 'complacent satisfaction' as of growing discontent and frustration".[1]

The Carpenter Committee, after examining the various methods of computing a minimum-wage formula, based on the previous conception of a "bachelor" wage, recommended the following monthly scale of needs as the foundation:[2]

"A. *Food*—

- 36 lb. maize meal.
- 5½ lb. wheat flour.
- 15 lb. potatoes (European).
- 2 lb. sugar.
- 8 lb. beans (dried).
- 4½ lb. meat.
- 7½ lb. vegetables (green leafy).
- 7½ pt. milk.
- 1 lb. cooking fat.
- ½ lb. tea.
- 1 lb. salt.

"B. *Clothing*—

$\frac{1}{6}$ of $\begin{cases} 1 \text{ K.D. shirt [K.D.}=\text{khaki drill—J. W.]} \\ 1 \text{ K.D. shorts.} \\ 1 \text{ cotton vest.} \end{cases}$

$\frac{1}{12}$ of 1 blanket.

$\frac{1}{24}$ of $\begin{cases} 1 \text{ K.D. jacket.} \\ 1 \text{ K.D. trousers.} \end{cases}$

"C. *Fuel and Lighting*—

- 1 70-lb. bag charcoal.
- 3 pts. paraffin.

[1] ibid., p. 55.   [2] ibid., p. 64.

"D. *Cleaning Materials—*
    2 lb. soap."

The above constitutes the new recommended P.D.L. for Kenya. To this it is proposed to add 33⅓ per cent to establish the "Effective Minimum Level", and to make an additional allowance of 2*s.* a month for taxes, but to exclude the previous allowance for water and the previous 1*s.*-a-month "cushion" for contingencies. A housing allowance is considered as a separate item. After this strenuous intellectual effort, including the increase of the monthly meat ration from 4⅓ lb. to 4½ lb., the Carpenter Committee produced its new recommended minimum wage, for a single man—81*s.* a month in place of the previous 59*s.* 50 *cts.* (Nairobi rate). In percentages this increase may seem substantial, but in actual cash it would still leave the African with less than 3*s.* a day; in other words, a colonial or starvation wage.

Following the Carpenter Report, increases in the statutory minimum wage were introduced, but by 1957 the estimated *average* (not minimum) in agriculture[1] in Kenya was still only 69*s.* a month—12*s.* below the recommended urban minimum of the 1954 report. (In Nairobi, it is true, the statutory minimum by 1957 had reached 85*s.* plus housing allowance, but it is in agriculture that the largest proportion of African wage labour in Kenya is to be found.)

The other main recommendation of the Carpenter Committee was the transition from the "single" or "bachelor" wage to a "family wage" covering a man, his wife and two children. It was calculated at the rate of two and a half times the bachelor wage. The Kenya Government, however, while in words admitting that the family wage was its aim, refused to commit itself to doing anything about it, and would only agree to an "adult" wage sufficient to maintain a man and wife (but not his children), and then *only when economic circumstances admit.*

It is as well to bear this in mind when reading official proposals to "stabilise" labour. As long as colonial governments in Africa continue to base their wage regulations on P.D.L. rates for single men, no serious consideration can be given to any talk of "stabilisation". As we have already seen regarding the question of skill, of social security, and of housing, the colonial system is

[1] N.B.—There is no legal minimum for rural areas in Kenya.

incapable of solving these problems. In the same way, it cannot solve the question of African starvation wages since these are an essential element of the colonial system. If colonial governments were to pay African workers a "civilised" rate of pay, and provide them, too, with decent housing for a whole family, with old-age pensions and other social benefits, with training and facilities to become educated and skilled workers, and with full trade-union and political rights, thus making possible the emergence of a permanent, urbanised, skilled and prosperous working class, they would cease to be colonial governments. All official, semi-official or well-meaning liberal suggestions regarding higher wages for African workers are meaningless if African resources remain in the hands of big European monopolies, and if political power is not held by the African people.

As long as the African economy remains colonial, African wages will basically remain colonial wages.

The "African Standard"

So far we have considered only certain general principles governing the wages of African workers, and examined the basis on which colonial governments compute minimum rates. Consideration, however, needs to be given to the specific reasons operating in Africa which have made it possible for employers and governments to pay such scandalously low wages over such a lengthy period. It is one thing for a government or a group of employers to decide to pay workers a wage which is not even sufficient to maintain a single worker; it is quite another thing to be able to impose such a wage on a working class for over half a century.

Wages, or the value of labour power, are determined by two elements—the one merely physical, that is the ability of the worker to maintain himself and multiply; the other which Marx calls "historical or social". Thus there is a standard of life in different countries, says Marx, "springing from the social conditions in which people are placed and reared up"; for example the English standard and the Irish standard.

"This historical or social element, entering into the value of labour, may be expanded, or contracted, or altogether extinguished, so that nothing remains but the *physical limit*. . . .

By comparing the standard wages or values of labour in different countries, and by comparing them in different historical epochs of the same country, you will find that the *value of labour* itself is not a fixed but a variable magnitude, even supposing the values of all other commodities to remain constant."[1]

As an example of how the historical element—"the social conditions in which people are placed and reared up"—influences wages, Marx cites the example of the United States where, owing to the availability of free land, the early tendency was one of "*the continuous conversion of wage labourers into independent, self-sustaining peasants*". Writing in 1865, Marx could say: "The function of a wage labourer is for a very large part of the American people but a probational stage, which they are sure to leave within a longer or shorter term." Hence the relatively high standard of wages in the United States. The market for labour at the time favoured the workers. If capitalists wanted workers then they had to pay for them; they had, as it were, to attract them into the factories and away from the land.

In this, of course, the conditions in which the American working class grew up were very different from those in Britain, where the Enclosure Acts *drove* the workers off the land and into the factories, and thus compelled British workers in the first half of the nineteenth century to live under conditions which, read today, appear to describe present urban conditions in many towns of Asia or Africa.

Thus, if an examination is to be made of the reasons for the low wages in Africa, and for their persistence over such a long period, then clearly the starting-point must be the *historical and social conditions under which wage labour in Africa came into being, and grew up*.

Wage labour in Africa, as we have seen, came into existence under conditions of colonialism. Conquered by foreign powers—sometimes by force of arms, sometimes by deceit—the African people saw their best lands seized, their native agriculture and village life with its local handicrafts ruined, and their manpower subjected to the imposition of various forms, open and disguised, of forced labour. Hut and poll tax, combined with restrictions

[1] Marx, Karl: *Wages, Price and Profit*. (See *Marx and Engels, Selected Books*, vol. i, pp. 400–401, London, 1950.)

and measures of discrimination to limit the African's own independent development of cash crops, completed the process of forcing Africans into work on European farms and plantations, in European mines, docks, railways and other enterprises.

Thus the Africans were compelled, partly by arbitrary direction, partly by dire economic necessity, to take up wage labour under conditions the least favourable to themselves. And the very drain of male labour from the villages has driven African agriculture still farther down the road to ruin and thus left little alternative but to work for starvation wages.

The combination of all these factors to *compel* the African to work for abysmally low wages is stressed by Noon.[1]

After pointing out how forced labour has enabled employers to obtain labour "without the necessity of offering a wage equal to the market price", and that the "indirect pressures applied by taxation" have maintained this situation, so unfavourable to the African worker, Noon then continues:

"Labour cannot be indefinitely withheld from the market in the hope of obtaining a fair price without the existence of alternative means of securing a living. The practice of alienating large sections of the continent to Europeans has, by limiting the land available to farmers, forced large numbers of Natives to offer their labour for wages and to accept work regardless of the pay which can be earned. The resistance displayed by European settlers in Kenya to all attempts of the government to enlarge Native reserves is a pertinent example of the attempts made to force Africans to find employment at prevailing wages by cutting off their opportunity to earn a living as an independent farmer."

Here is the complete antithesis to the early American worker described by Marx. In America, said Marx, the employer could not "prevent the labour market from being continuously emptied by the continuous conversion of wage labourers into independent, self-sustaining peasants".[2]

It was a case of workers becoming farmers, and employers having to offer high wages to keep or attract their workers. *But*

[1] Noon: op. cit., pp. 23-4.
[2] Marx, Karl: op. cit., p. 402.

in Africa it was a case of farmers being forced to become workers, and the employers thus being free to offer as low wages as they deemed fit.

These, basically, were the historical and social conditions in which African labour was "placed and reared up"—the ruin of native agriculture combined with economic and physical compulsion to work for European masters, and the buttressing up of this system by a complete denial to Africans of political and trade-union rights which otherwise would have provided some opportunity to resist the full effects of this terrible exploitation.

These conditions have persisted over a long period, and, in essence, largely exist to this day. The forms may have been modified in some respects; economic pressures may be today a more dominant factor than physical ones though the latter still exist, constituting in certain territories, such as the Portuguese African territories and the Union of South Africa, a major element of the government's labour policy. Certain trade-union and political rights, too, have been won in a number of territories, but these are still limited; moreover, any attempt to use these rights to improve African wage levels invariably has to contend with the utmost resistance by employers and governments alike.

There are other factors, too, which have helped to keep down African wages.

Employers in Africa have been assisted by the extreme mobility of African labour, in the sense that, under conditions in which the possession of skill is not normally required, one worker is easily replaced by another. "Because this condition exists in Africa with few exceptions", points out Noon,[1] "employers have been able to secure workers generally on the terms they offer."

This type of mobility of labour in Africa is reinforced by the geographical mobility, the tendency of African labour to migrate, which was examined in some detail earlier on. "Were it necessary for employers to rely on the local labour market alone, they would undoubtedly be required to offer a fair wage in order to secure the needed labourers," comments Noon.[2] Leaving aside the question of "a fair wage", it is undoubtedly true that if employers were deprived of their ample supplies of migrant labour, they would certainly have to offer higher wages than they do at present.

[1] Noon: op. cit., p. 24.
[2] ibid., p. 24.

In the Union of South Africa, while the import of migrant labour into the country operates more or less as it does in other parts of the continent, once admitted this labour is affected by additional factors—the pass system, Master and Servants Act, and so on—which, by tying labour down and rigidly controlling its movements, compels it to accept, more or less, the low wages laid down by the employer. Somewhat similar circumstances operate in Central Africa and, to a degree, in East Africa.

Thus mobility and restriction are both pressed into service by the employers to keep wages down to an absolute minimum.

Industrial Colour Bar—Wage Discrimination

Social studies on African problems, when they deal with questions of African wages, point out, almost as it if were due to some fault of the Africans themselves, that wages are low because African workers are mainly employed on unskilled jobs and because there is a surplus of such unskilled, migrant labour.

This, of course, is perfectly true, as has been already noticed in earlier chapters; but surely the significant thing is that this is not due to any quirk or deficiency on the part of the African worker, but is the planned-for result of a deliberate policy pursued by governments and employers alike.

The whole aim of the European rulers of African possessions, as has been already demonstrated, is to use these territories as sources of cheap labour and cheap raw materials. For this purpose they do not require a large, highly trained body of skilled labour, and therefore they are not interested in providing education, skill and trade-training for Africans. Furthermore, as has been noticed, in a number of territories it has long been deliberate policy not merely to neglect training for Africans, but actually to debar them from every facility for acquiring skill, the skilled jobs and posts of responsibility being preserved as a monopoly for the European minority.

Denied by lack of facilities, or debarred by law and custom, from gaining skill, the African worker is condemned to remain largely a hewer of wood and drawer of water—and his wages are consequently kept to a minimum.

Another aspect of the industrial colour bar is the fixing of minimum wages for certain trades under the Industrial Conciliation Act in the Union of South Africa, or under the Industrial Conciliation Act of 1945 in Southern Rhodesia, at rates which are regarded as normally European rates. Employers are reluctant to take on Africans at such wages, and thus insistence on the "rate for the job" (which is usually dictated by European unions anxious to preserve a privileged position for their members) becomes a means of excluding Africans from skilled work. Thus when "the rate for the job" was introduced for building artisans in Bulawayo, the employers responded by immediately dismissing all African building artisans in their employ.

Northern Rhodesia, too, provides an example of the various pressures, economic and otherwise, which maintain a system of exceptionally high wages for Europeans alongside low wages for Africans and barriers to their becoming skilled and more highly paid. In fact, for more than twenty years the Copper Belt has been rocked by important struggles around this very question.

From the foregoing it is clear that, through a variety of measures, African workers are, in the main, deprived of the opportunities to acquire skill—and this, of course, tends to keep their wages down.

"The concomitant . . . of high wages for those within the charmed circle is low wages for those outside the circle. Barriers to the entry of workers into skilled trades swell the numbers of those who must offer their services as unskilled workers, and competition for unskilled jobs keeps unskilled wages low. The Native labour flowing into the towns to seek escape from the poverty of the Reserves and farms is flowing into a pool from which there is only a very inadequate outlet at the other end."[1]

The *International Labour Review* states that "to a large extent, racial wage differentials in Africa are skill differentials".[2] This is broadly true in the sense that the overwhelming majority of African workers are unskilled or semi-skilled, and are paid low wages, while Europeans are employed in skilled jobs or in supervisory posts and receive high wages. But this is still only part of the truth, as the *Review* itself has to admit when it points out

[1] Franklin, N.: *Economics in South Africa*, pp. 193–4, revised edition, London 1954.
[2] *International Labour Review*, July 1958, p. 21.

that figures provided in the *I.L.O. Year Book of Labour Statistics* show "*that even where Africans are admitted to more skilled employment, their cash remuneration may not amount to much more than a tenth of that received by Europeans in the same industry*".

That the wage differential is based not merely on skill but also on race is equally indicated in the *Review's* comment that: "Examination of available statistics indicates that the range between low and high wages is *much greater in Africa than in most other parts of the world.*" [Own italics—J. W.]

In Southern Rhodesia, for example, figures for the period 1939–52 showed African earnings as 4·63 per cent of European earnings in 1938 and 6·65 per cent in 1952.[1] Figures for Northern Rhodesia, in 1956,[2] show that African garage mechanics earned 5·07 per cent of the European rate, bricklayers 11·74 per cent, painters 8·75 per cent and electrical fitters (outside lines) 9·09 per cent. In Kenya, figures for 1956[3] show that in private industry Africans earned 5·37 per cent of European earnings, in public services and local government the percentage was 5·89, and in agriculture as low as 2·95 per cent.

A further factor weakening the bargaining power of the African worker and thus depressing his wages is the agreement of European employers, in practice, not to compete with one another for African labour. This is facilitated by the fact that in most African territories the key resources and enterprises are in the possession of one or two large monopolies who are thus able to dictate their terms with no fear of competition from business rivals. This is so, for example, in connection with the labour-recruiting system operating in the South African gold mines.

Desperate Economic Plight

All these factors which we have described above constitute the particular economic and social conditions determining the wretchedly low level of African wages. Many of these circumstances are referred to in other studies on African questions, and yet they are usually described as if they are merely the blind

[1] *Twelfth Report on the Census of Industrial Production (1938–52)*, Central African Statistical Office, Salisbury.

[2] *I.L.O. Year Book of Labour Statistics, 1957*, p. 326, Geneva, 1957.

[3] *Quarterly Economic and Statistical Bulletin*, p. 69, Nairobi, June 1957.

operations of some "iron law" of wages over which employers, governments and workers can have no control. It is indicative of this approach that it hardly, if ever, refers to the basic factor of imperialist exploitation, nor to the consistent resistance of the imperialist monopolies and governments to any wage increases for African workers.

What these low wages mean for African workers can only be very dimly imagined by people living in the West. The conditions described in earlier chapters in this book will give some indication of the appalling consequences of the colonial wage system. A study[1] of the income, expenditure and consumption habits of African labourers living in Nairobi, carried out in October and November 1950, revealed that no less than two-thirds of the workers in the sample were forced to borrow money during the month, that for many of the Africans "it appeared to be accepted policy to give more than half their wages to their creditors immediately after receipt of their wages; thus they had to borrow again by the middle of the month to balance their budgets to the next pay-day. It was very noticeable that any extraordinary expenditure, such as [upon] illness, resulted in increased borrowing owing to lack of money."

This same survey further discovered that the proportion of the income spent on food was half as much again as that provided for in the minimum-wage formula! And further, that *a large proportion of workers had little or nothing to eat for the last two or three days of the month.*

In Cato Manor, in the Union of South Africa, it has been stated that 95 per cent of the inhabitants live permanently below the bread-line.[2] Even on the Reef, regarded as the richest industrial area of the country, it is estimated that 70 per cent have incomes below the essential minimum. Investigations into wages and expenditure among Africans in a number of towns in the Union have shown that between 69 and 78 per cent of African urban families have incomes below the minimum necessary to provide the barest essentials of living.[3] A survey carried out by the National Building Research Institute in a number of South

---

[1] East African Statistical Department Report, February 1951, quoted in Carpenter Report, pp. 31–2.
[2] Segal, Ronald: *The Agony of Apartheid*, p. 4.
[3] *African Poverty*, South African Institute of Race Relations, 1957.

African towns, between 1951 and 1953, showed a considerable number of Africans unable to afford any rent whatsoever. The figures for Durban were 55·3 per cent, for Vereeniging 57·5 per cent, for Germiston 62·8 per cent, and for Port Elizabeth 70 per cent.

Thus it is clear that in the Union a very large proportion of African families, and probably the majority, live below even "poverty datum" standards.

In addition to surveys and statistics there is another demonstration of the utter inadequacy of the wages paid to Africans, and that is the bitterness and determination with which African workers have fought to secure higher wages or to combat further attacks on their already pitifully low standards.

A striking case in point was the great South African bus boycott.

For twelve weeks, in the early months of 1957, nearly a hundred thousand African working people took part in a remarkable struggle against increased fares and in defence of their rights as Africans.

The struggle commenced when the transport company announced an increase of *one penny* in its fares in Johannesburg and Pretoria. It gives one some idea of the miserably low standard of living of the African workers that they immediately declared their opposition to the increase and began a bus boycott. An African labourer in the Union earns only £2 10s. a week. Of this wage, the bus fare takes up 4s. a week, or a full month's income a year. And those in Pretoria are even worse off. In fact, it has been estimated that seventy per cent of that city's Africans earn a maximum of only £9 a month.

The new fare would have meant, for most passengers, at least 1s. a week more. This would have dragged whole families below the breadline. It should be noted that a survey on *The Cost of Living of Africans*, published by the Institute of Race Relations in 1954, shows that in 1950 a family income in the largest wage-earning classes on the Rand was estimated at only 72·4 per cent of the cost of the minimum essentials. By 1954 the figure had dropped to 63·4 per cent.

If it is asked why people with such low incomes do not live nearer to the towns where they work, the answer is that the Africans have no legal rights to choose where they live. Under the racialist Group Areas Act, Africans have been uprooted and pushed well outside the European residential areas.

And so the boycott began. So·determined were the Africans in this great struggle that 20,000 of them at the Alexandria Township walked nearly twenty miles a day to and from work. In fact, during the period of the boycott some of them must have walked a thousand miles.

Every morning and evening, six days a week, they walked. In the year's worst heat-wave, broken only by torrential rains, working eight to nine and a half hours a day, and harried by the police, they walked. Starting at three in the morning and finishing only at nine at night, they walked, while the long green buses, marked "for coloured people only", roared past, empty.

The spirit of these "proud walkers" (as the London *Times* called them) can be seen in this description by an African Congress leader, Tennyson Makiwane:

> "Your feet are sore and you are tired when you get to bed but you have only the fear that you must not let the people down. So you keep going on, with your neighbour from next door, the woman from over the road, the chap from lower down in the township, and all the others."

The government could not easily declare the boycott illegal— for after all, how can it be illegal for a man to walk to work instead of taking a bus. Instead, it took to additional methods of intimidation: 14,000 were arrested on flimsy charges of not having their passes in order, of sleeping overnight in places where they were not registered, and so on. Africans trying to travel by train instead of by bus were forcibly prevented by police from buying train tickets. Police deflated the tyres of boycotters' cycles. Meetings of boycotters were fired on, and people killed—and 20,000 turned up at the funeral of one of the victims.

When all this failed, the government introduced a new Bill to forbid bus transport along the routes affected by the boycott.

Thus the struggle changed from a mere protest against increased fares and took on a political significance, becoming, in fact, a fight by the African working people for the right to protest against their inhuman conditions and against the racial discrimination which they suffer.

As a result of this great movement, one of the mightiest protest movements the Africans have ever organised, a great victory was won, and at the end of three months the Chambers of Commerce agreed to pay the extra penny, and the workers were allowed to travel at the old fare of 4d.

Only a working class whose economic plight was really desperate would have waged such an heroic fight over a penny fare.

From what has been said, certain conclusions can be drawn. The scandalously low wages paid to Africans, though conditioned by economic and social factors to which attention is frequently drawn by liberal commentators, have their basis in something else, and that is *the determination of European monopolies and farmers, backed by their government, to pay a wage even below the subsistence level.*

Of course it could be argued that employers in Britain, for example, would like to do the same to British workers. They cannot, however, due to a number of reasons which do not exist in African colonies. The industrialisation of Britain compelled British employers to accept a certain level of education and skill and therefore a certain standard of life for the working class without which industry, and therefore profits, could not have grown. Further, British workers, by struggle over a long period of time, won for themselves trade-union and political rights which enabled them to resist and even, to a measure, push back the economic pressure exerted against them by the employing class.

Under capitalism the employers, in a purely economic sense, are always stronger than the workers. It is only by struggle and political action that the workers can wrest any economic concessions from the employers; and it was in this way that the British working class forced on to the Statute Book so many laws concerning their class interests.

In Africa, it is the policy of European monopolies and employers to hold back industrialisation, utilising these territories solely as agrarian and minerals appendages to the industries of the metropolis. Copper is produced in Northern Rhodesia in abundance, but goods made of copper and used in that country are *imported* from Britain. Raw cocoa is produced in Ghana, but chocolate has to be *imported*.[1]

African workers have been allocated the role of manual

---

[1] Only now that Ghana is independent have steps been taken for the local manufacture of chocolate.

labourers, or, at best, semi-skilled workers, and that is the status to which the imperialists intend to confine them. All the social, economic and political factors have been deliberately weighted to keep Africans in this subordinate position and so maintain the low-wage system.

This explains why, for so many years, the imperialist governments resisted any attempt on the part of the African workers to set up trade unions or to win any political rights. The fact that, in the last decade, Africans have achieved minimum rights in these fields is not due to any change of heart or act of charity on the part of the imperial authorities, but simply the logic of history. The imperialists have been *forced* to make concessions owing to the strength of the advancing African movement.

Thus a fundamental cause of the low wages paid to African workers has been their lack of trade-union and political rights, and the policy of the European employers to resist by the utmost violence every attempt by the workers to raise their wages.

One has only to make a cursory study of the main strikes in Africa in the past twenty years to see with what tenacity African workers have struggled to push up their miserable wages, and with what ferocity the employers and governments have resisted them.

The dead, wounded and imprisoned are testimony to both of these phenomena. Mombasa, Nairobi, Enugu, Jos, Dar-es-Salaam, Accra, the Rand, Wankie, Salisbury, Bulawayo, Kitwe, Freetown, Dakar, Cotonou, Douala—what a record they tell of bitter strike struggles for a few-pence increase in wages! Police, troops, teargas, prison and banishment—such has been the imperialist reply to the African workers' demand for higher wages.

Yet it is a remarkable thing that almost every commentator on African wages, even though he may admit that wages are terribly low and indicate many of the correct *economic* reasons for this, fails to mention that every attempt on the part of the African workers to win higher wages has had to face the most bitter opposition of the employers and imperial authorities.

Roper,[1] for example, who is apparently afraid that African trade unions may become "very powerful" and "abuse their strength" (insist on higher wages, perhaps?), refers to the Enugu massacre as "a clash with armed police, and some shooting".

[1] Roper: op. cit., p. 88.

The fact that "some shooting" resulted in *the killing of twenty-nine African miners* he does not mention. The trade unions in Nigeria, he tells us, "do not appear to be strong enough, as yet, to establish minimum wage rates for labourers."[1] Yet nowhere does Mr. Roper explain the terrific battles the Nigerian unions have had to conduct to win higher wages.

In the same fashion, the article previously referred to in the *International Labour Review* states that "African trade unions, where they do exist, probably do not exert a very important influence on the level of African wages". Again, this article does not point out that African unions have had to conduct the most bitter struggles for the very right to exist, let alone face bullets and prison for wage increases. That their efforts have not been sufficient to bring about a radical change in the levels of African wages so far is due not so much to organisational and other weaknesses of the unions—and African union leaders and members will readily admit that there are such weaknesses—but rather to the unconcealed hostility of employers and governments alike to the unions' demands for higher wages.

It is indicative that wage advances secured by African workers, modest as they may be in some cases, have nearly always been the result of bitter strike struggles or threats of strikes, or the later indirect result of wage increases won previously by strike action.[2] And secondly, the rate of advance in wage levels in the post-war period has been markedly more rapid than in the pre-war period, that is to say *wages have advanced most in the period when African trade unions have come into existence and in the period when the biggest strike struggles have been waged.*

In Tanganyika, for example, the post-war wages standstill in the sisal industry was broken in 1958 only after the formation of the 30,000 strong National Plantation Workers' Union and following the great strikes of 1957 and 1958 which, on the sisal estates alone, accounted for a loss of more than 350,000 man-days.

It has been the same throughout Africa. Wage advances have

[1] ibid., p. 92.
[2] This was even true of the pre-war period when there were practically no trade unions in Africa. Thus the 1931 wage cuts introduced in Kenya at the time of the world economic crisis reduced the rate for a casual labourer in Mombasa from 2s. a day down to 1s. 50 cents. It was not until the Mombasa strike of 1939 that the cuts were restored. (See *Report of the Commission of Inquiry Appointed to Examine the Labour Conditions in Mombasa*, Nairobi, 1939.)

been won only as a result of trade-union organisation and by dint
of the most bitter struggles.

Strike statistics show overwhelmingly that the number of
working days lost in strikes during the period 1945–58 far exceeds
that of the previous twenty years—and the majority of days lost
were in disputes concerning wages.

No matter which African territory one turns to, the past two
decades illustrate amply the tenacity with which African trade
unions have had to fight for higher wages, and the almost
frenzied resistance offered by the employers and colonial
governments to the workers' just demands.

This is the reality of the wages problem in Africa. Important
economic factors making for low wages admittedly exist—but it
is imperialist policy to prevent the elimination of these very
factors which are referred to, with such seeming impartiality, in
all the official documents. Therefore, every wage demand,
however modest, becomes the occasion of an intense class
struggle between the workers and the employers, a struggle
which, in the context of the colonial system obtaining in Africa,
inevitably becomes transformed into an anti-imperialist struggle,
all the armed forces, legal apparatus, and resources of the
colonial government (sometimes with additional aid from the
mother country) being brought into play to resist the workers'
demands and to maintain the colonial cheap-labour system.

Wages struggles in Africa have therefore played a key part
in the whole development of the African national movement, and
have given rise to a growth in the understanding of the African
people that low wages are synonymous with the colonial system,
and that to end low wages colonialism itself must be ended.

CHAPTER EIGHT

AFRICA—RICH OR POOR?

THE terrible poverty of the people of Africa is a phenomenon that cannot be concealed. Moreover, as recent reports of the United Nations Food and Agriculture Organisation show, while the world production of foodstuffs has increased in recent years, *relative and absolute consumption by people in underdeveloped countries has decreased.* Inevitably, therefore, the question is posed: Why are the African people so impoverished? What are the causes of their desperate, continuing and worsening poverty?

Why is the average annual income per head only 30 dollars in Ethiopia, 48 in Tanganyika, 57 in Uganda, 69 in Nigeria, 70 in Sierra Leone, 56–70 in Gambia, 76 in the Belgian Congo, 78 in Kenya, 126 in French Equatorial Africa, 133 in French West Africa, and 132 in the Central African Federation?[1] This average, ranging from about £10 a year to £45, be it remembered, covers up the discrepancies between the poorest sections and those relatively better off; the income of most Africans is below these miserable averages.

Numerous theories have been advanced at different times to account for the low living standards of the African people—the climate, the tsetse fly, over-population and under-population the soil, and so on. One United Nations report,[2] for example, makes considerable play with the "sparseness of population" as one of the reasons for Africa's economic backwardness and the poverty of its people. One has only to consider Australia and Canada, countries with sparse populations but with an economic development and *per capita* income vastly above that in Africa, to realise that "sparseness of population" cannot, by itself, be seriously reckoned with as a cause of African poverty. Moreover,

[1] ECSA: op. cit., p. 15.
[2] *Review of Economic Conditions in Africa*, U.N. Dept. of Economic Affairs, New York, March, 1951.

the figures for Africa itself, provided in the very U.N. publication which puts forward this argument, make nonsense out of this contention. Figures provided[1] show that "Ruanda-Urundi with a density of 69 persons per square kilometre in 1947 was the *most densely populated territory* in tropical Africa." [Own italics— J. W.] If the above argument were correct, one would have expected to find the economic development and *per capita* income here above the average for Africa. But the facts in this very report show the exact reverse! Ruanda-Urundi, with *per capita* income of 17 dollars, was at the bottom of the list![2]

So little faith has this review in its own theory, in fact, that a few pages farther on it is solemnly arguing that "pressure on the land" is a cause of the poverty. Of course, it ignores completely the fact that the pressure, where it does exist, is in most territories the result of the seizure of the best lands by the imperialists and European settlers. Moreover, as with all its other arguments, it fails to explain how it is that the white population in the Union or in the Rhodesias is not impoverished, while the Africans in these territories are as poverty-stricken as those elsewhere. In fact, this review admits—though it does not explain—that in the Union of South Africa, despite the higher *per capita* income for the whole territory, the plight of the *African* people "is probably nearer to the general average for other parts of Africa" than it is to the Europeans whose higher standard accounts for the higher average *per capita* figure for the whole Union.

Regarding the soil of Africa, the review states that in many areas "phosphates are lacking";[3] yet it admits that Africa produces no less than 35·5 per cent of the world's phosphates. The fact is that these phosphates are not put back into African soil, to make good the destruction and havoc caused through the accumulated effects of land-robberies, overcrowding of Africans into Reserves, and the ruthless exploitation of the soil for cash crops; they are exported, instead, to enrich the soils in other continents.

All these various "theories" as to the cause of African poverty are seen, on examination, to be extremely thin; and indeed their whole effect is to cover up the real causes of African poverty.

[1] ibid., p. 9.
[2] ibid., p. 6.
[3] ibid., p. 8.

It is, perhaps, not entirely out of place to recall that somewhat similar "explanations" were offered, not so long ago, to account for the misery of China. The Prime Minister of the Chinese People's Republic, Mr. Chou En-lai, speaking recently on the great progress made by his country in the past ten years, pointedly said:

> "Old China had the same population and the same geographical conditions, but semi-colonial and semi-feudal as it was it could never bring about any leap forward."[1]

Of tsarist Russia, too, it used to be said that she lacked resources; but no one would seriously make such an assertion today in relation to the rapidly advancing Soviet Union.

The Schizophrenic Theoreticians

In considering the question of African poverty one cannot but note that the attitude taken up by many commentators, as well as by Western governments and businessmen, often appears to border on schizophrenia. Two quite contradictory views are frequently put forward by the same people; and the calm, bland manner in which they do this might lead one to believe either that they really believe it possible to reconcile these opposites or that they are unaware of the dichotomy which their arguments create.

When it is a question of providing explanations as to why, after decades of Western imperialist rule, the peoples of Africa are underpaid, undernourished, illiterate, ill-clad, ill-housed and diseased, it is solemnly stated that Africans are poor because the African territories are poor, that they lack the natural resources essential to a higher standard of living.

Before examining this proposition in more detail it is not out of place to point out, as African people often do, that if Africa is really so poor why is it that the Western powers fight so desperately to retain their hold on the African continent? Why, for example, do the rulers of France spend so many millions of the French taxpayers' money in a doomed attempt to hold on to

[1] Report on the Work of the Government, to the First Session of the Second National People's Congress, Peking, April 18, 1959.

"poor" Algeria? Why has British imperialism taken such drastic steps to curb the national movements in "impoverished" Central Africa? Why is Portugal reinforcing its military forces in "poverty-stricken" Angola? Is it really worth so much effort and expense to retain Western influence over such allegedly poor territories?

But in reality not only is the argument that "Africa is poor" a false one, but its very supporters themselves daily give the lie to it. For while asserting that Africa is poor when it comes to explaining the poverty of her people or justifying the refusal to grant African workers higher wages, when the question of investments or strategic considerations are under discussion, then, in the best travelling-salesman manner, these very same advocates of the "poor Africa" theory display a glowing list of the riches of Africa, sufficient to recall the fabulous treasures of the Arabian Nights.

". . . the *richest iron ore in the world* can be mined in Liberia in vast quantities."[1]   [Own italics—J. W.]

". . . the sisal industry in Tanganyika—the *most important sisal producer in the world*, with £20,000,000 invested in the industry. . . ."[2]   [Own italics—J. W.]

"A *spectacular growth in oil production* since the discovery of the first wells in 1956 makes the Gabon Republic *the franc area's third largest producer* this year with an expected output of more than 700,000 tons. . . . The Mekambo deposits [of iron ore—J. W.] are considered to be *among the richest in the world*. . . . The *manganese deposits* at Moanda in the Gabon are believed to be *second* only to those at Nikopol in the Soviet Union."[3]

[Own italics—J. W.]

Writing on last year's repression by the Belgian authorities in Stanleyville, Belgian Congo, René MacColl says:

"What stakes there are to play for on the banks of this tremendous river!

[1] Duval-Smith, Peter: "A New Look for Liberia?", *Daily Telegraph*, August 12, 1959.
[2] *The Times*, August 12, 1959.
[3] *Manchester Guardian*, July 4, 1959.

"What is going to happen to all that wealth when the Belgians are gone? To the copper, uranium, diamonds, gold, cobalt, manganese, tin, lead, coffee, cotton, tobacco and rubber?

"The capital value of all this is computed in thousands of millions of pounds."[1]

One could continue endlessly with such quotations, for the real truth, of course, is that the continent of Africa is rich and potentially much richer still. It is indeed not the presence or absence of natural wealth which is responsible for the poverty of the African people, but the system under which Africans are compelled to live and the use to which their wealth has been put by the Western powers who have ruled Africa for so long.

Figures provided by the U.N. for 1956[2] show that Africa produces 96 per cent of the world's[3] output of industrial and gem diamonds, 69 per cent of cobalt, 63 per cent of gold, 48 per cent of antimony, 34 per cent of chromite, 37 per cent of manganese, 32 per cent of phosphate rock, 24 per cent of copper, 19 per cent of asbestos, 15 per cent of tin, 4 per cent of iron ore, 4 per cent of bauxite, apart from uranium,[4] nickel, coal and other minerals. Nigeria produces 85 per cent of the world's output of columbite; and Ghana is the second largest manganese producer in the world.

Africa is rich, too, in a whole range of agricultural products. Figures for 1954 show that Africa produces 66 per cent of the world's cocoa, 58 per cent of her sisal (1954–5), 65 per cent of her palm oil, 26 per cent of her ground nuts (1954–5), 14 per cent of her coffee and 11 per cent of her olive oil.[5] She also produces considerable barley, wool, cotton, maize, tea, rubber, tobacco, wheat, pyrethrum, cloves, and rice.

In addition to her actual output, Africa has immense reserves. She has rich timber reserves and accounts for 27 per cent of all the forests in the world. In July 1944 it was reported[6] that a United States Geological Survey had estimated that Africa's total potential water-power resources were 274,000,000 horse-

---

[1] *Daily Express*, November 2, 1959.
[2] ECSA, op. cit., p. 125.
[3] Excluding the U.S.S.R.
[4] Uranium production is a secret, but it is well known that the Belgian Congo alone is one of the world's chief suppliers of this valuable mineral.
[5] *Economic Development in Africa, 1954–5*, U.N., and *F.A.O. Report 1954*.
[6] *The Economist*, July 1944.

power, which is more than three times as great as the European water-power potential. (Yet, at that time only 210,000 h.p.— less than 0·1 per cent of the potential—had been developed.) In 1951[1] it was estimated that Africa's water-power potential was at least 40 per cent of the world's resources.

Speaking of Africa's rich resources, *The Times* has stated:

"It is impossible to set a limit to the productive capacity of the Sahara as regards oil—not to mention its known wealth of natural gas, iron, manganese, and other metals."[2]

It is believed, in fact, that the Sahara's oil reserves are no less important than those of the Arab peninsula; while her coal reserves are estimated at 4,500,000,000 tons.

It is the desire to hold on to this wealth in "poor Africa" which prompted de Gaulle, in his September 1959 proposals for an Algerian "settlement", to include a specific clause insisting on French retention of the Sahara and its riches.

Other French possessions in Africa are equally rich in resources. They "have immense and largely untapped resources of petroleum, iron ore, manganese, timber and other raw materials".[3]

Northern Rhodesia is reported to have the second largest deposits of vanadium in the world, and Ghana estimated bauxite reserves of 200 million tons.[4]

Africa Could Be Industrialised

So immense, in fact, are Africa's mineral and water-power resources that she has everything necessary to become a powerful, modern, industrialised continent.

Yet it is repeatedly argued, in many quarters, that Africa has not the wherewithal to become industrialised and that, perforce, she must remain dependent on the export of her minerals and agricultural products.

The economy of Tropical Africa, asserts Kenneth Bradley, *"must always be based on peasant farming"*.[5] [Own italics—J. W.]

[1] *Review of Economic Conditions in Africa, 1951*, op. cit., p. 57.
[2] *The Times*, July 29, 1959.
[3] Cutler, B. J.: *New York Herald Tribune*, September 11, 1959.
[4] Hailey (Revised): op. cit., p. 1510.
[5] Bradley, Kenneth: *Britain's Purpose in Africa*, H.M.S.O., 1959.

Batten[1] argues that "most parts of Africa are quite unfitted for large-scale industrial production" and that therefore "agriculture must *always* be the principal source of wealth". [Own italics—J. W.]

"*For many years to come*", it has been stated,[2] "*the main industrial activity in Africa will be the exploitation for export of its rich mineral deposits.*" [Own italics—J. W.]

Many other reports argue in this fashion, that Africa is not fitted for industrialisation, yet at the same time many of them, with that same schizophrenic habit which we have already noted, equally talk about an "industrial revolution" which is sweeping Africa. Thus Kenneth Bradley claims that "industrialisation in Africa has now begun".[3] Others write in similar or even more enthusiastic vein.

One recent booklet[4] has even gone so far as to make the exaggerated claim that in Africa today "there is an industrial revolution going on at a speed faster than anything this country experienced even in the nineteenth century". This sweeping assertion ignores the fact that in Britain in the nineteenth century a real industrial revolution was taking place; iron and steel and engineering were being developed, factory production introduced on an even larger scale, and a stable factory proletariat was being created. Britain, in fact, was becoming industrialised.

But can one assert today that Africa is becoming industrialised? On the contrary, all the available facts demonstrate only too clearly that the continent of Africa, even after all the present development plans have been carried out, will remain a raw-materials appendage to the imperialist powers.

The question of industrialisation is the key to an understanding of African poverty. The countries with the highest standards in the world—and this relates both to the socialist sector as well as the capitalist sector—are those that are industrialised. It is the great non-industrialised regions of the world, Africa, Asia, the Middle East, and Latin America where the greatest poverty resides.

The same holds true for such an industrialised region as Europe; it is in the lesser industrialised countries of Europe such

[1] Batten, T. R.: op. cit., part 1, pp. 167–8.
[2] Organisation for European Economic Co-operation, *Second Report*, para. 546, Paris, 1950.
[3] Bradley: op. cit., p. 24.
[4] *What Does Africa Mean to You?*, Africa Bureau, London, 1959.

as Spain, Portugal or Greece, or in areas such as the non-industrialised south of Italy or Sicily that one finds the same abject poverty, disease, and illiteracy as exist in the colonial and under-developed regions of the world.

The term "industrialisation" is often misunderstood or its meaning stretched to mean something very different from industrialisation in its strict, scientific sense. Not every kind of industrial development can be classified as industrialisation. The development of communications, of a mining industry, of the initial processing of raw materials, even of local factories producing textiles, leather goods, foodstuffs, cigarettes and other products of light industry, is still not yet industrialisation in the full sense of the term. Real industrialisation is the capacity to produce engineering goods—machines, machine-tools, heavy engineering products, bridges, ships, motor vehicles, and the like. Above all, the capacity to produce machines which produce machines. This requires its base in an iron and steel industry, as well as electrical power and a modern chemical industry.

Only on such a foundation can a country embark on a relatively rapid and continuous development of all her industries; and only thus can she provide her agriculture with all the tractors, combines and other machines it requires as well as with its chemical fertilisers, weed-killers, and so on.

Those who are opposed to African industrialisation argue that "except in the Union of South Africa and Southern Rhodesia, the resources of Africa as known at the present time do not appear to favour technically a widespread development of an iron and steel industry, even on a limited scale".[1] Yet Japan has little high-grade iron ore or coking coal, but is one of the world's leading engineering countries. Britain has to import iron ore, yet for decades she has been a leading engineering country. Why, then, should it be so difficult for Africa, with far richer natural resources, to become industrialised? Furthermore, United Nations documents themselves reveal that Africa, far from her resources being inadequate, is probably better equipped for such a basic development than almost any other region of the world.

"In many regions of Africa, iron ore reserves are extensive; coking coal is the limiting resource factor in the development of

[1] *Review of Economic Conditions in Africa, 1951*: op. cit., p. 58.

iron and steel production. However, the two-way exchange of iron ore from northern Africa for coking coal from Europe would not involve uneconomic transportation requirements."[1]

This, it should be remembered, is an estimate made on the basis of the then existing knowledge of Africa's mineral resources. A thorough and systematic survey of the African continent— carried out by a liberated Africa—would no doubt reveal as many untapped and unsuspected natural riches (including coking coal)[2] as have been revealed in the Soviet Union since 1917 and in China since 1949.

The extremely rich mineral resources of the Soviet Union only began to be properly studied after the establishment of the Soviet Government in 1917. For example, before the revolution the coal resources of Russia were estimated at 230,000,000,000 tons. At the present time the total geological supplies of coal are estimated at 8,670,000,000,000 tons, that is nearly 38 times as much as was previously assumed. In the old Russia the supplies of iron ore were estimated to amount to 2,000,000,000 tons. At present the known supplies exceed 38,000,000,000 tons. Similar results have been obtained with regard to other types of minerals. In fact, the U.S.S.R. now holds first place in the world for the known supplies of thirteen out of the sixteen most important minerals, including iron and manganese ores, coal, copper, lead, zinc, nickel, bauxite, tungsten, mercury and potassium salts. She also holds a leading place for prospected oil supplies. In tsarist Russia, only 21 out of the 101 elements of Mendeleyev's periodic table were extracted on a commercial scale; at the present time there is not one element among the 101 that is not being mined for the needs of industry.

There is no doubt that the African people, once they are the real masters of their vast lands, will find similar riches to those in the U.S.S.R. and to those now being found in China.

[1] *World Iron Ore Resources and Their Utilisation*, p. 3, U.N. Department of Economic Affairs, 1950.

[2] Since this chapter was written it has been announced that the coal at Enugu, Nigeria, can be converted into coke. Reporting this, the general manager of the Nigerian Coal Corporation has said that the production of suitable coke on a commercial scale in Nigeria would open the door "for the setting up of an iron and steel industry, chemical industry, tar plant, manufacture of fertilisers, benzol and other products." (Reported in *West Africa*, p. 866, October 17, 1959.)

But even on the basis of its present known supplies of minerals Africa could be industrialised. How immeasurably rich Africa is in iron ore is emphasised in United Nations documents:

> "Among the under-developed areas, Latin America and Africa have larger probable *per capita* reserves of the metal than the United States or Europe. . . . In each of these under-developed areas *the reserves of iron are large enough to support an iron and steel industry at least as large as any industrialised country has so far achieved.*"[1] [Own italics—J. W.]

The *World Iron Ore Resources* report actually states that the potential reserves of iron in Africa would last two thousand years![2] The tables provided in this report[3] give the following instructive picture:

TABLE XIX

POTENTIAL RESERVES OF IRON ORE—IRON CONTENT

Region	Millions of Metric Tons	Per Capita Metric Tons
Africa	57,221[4]	295·2
Canada and U.S.A. ..	27,709	173·3
Latin America	17,090	109·7
Asia	12,924	10·3
Europe	9,333	24·1
U.S.S.R.	4,345[5]	22·5

In other words, Africa has far and away the biggest potential iron-ore reserves in the world, and the biggest *per capita* reserves. Yet in 1956, despite this potential wealth, Africa produced only one per cent of the world's crude steel and only one per cent of the world's pig-iron.[6] Japan, however, with only 38,000,000 metric tons of potential iron-ore reserves against Africa's 57,221,000,000, and with only 0·5 metric tons *per capita* potential reserves against Africa's 295·2, was already able, by 1943, to produce 7,800,000 tons of steel.

It should be clear, therefore, from the foregoing, that whatever

[1] *World Iron Ore Resources and Their Utilisation*, op. cit., p. 12.
[2] ibid., p. 14.
[3] ibid., pp. 11 and 13.
[4] These figures are for thirteen African countries only, and do not include Northern Rhodesia, Tanganyika, Uganda, Nigeria, Ghana and other African territories where deposits occur.
[5] The figures for the U.S.S.R. are very much underestimated. In fact, at the end of 1958 her iron-ore resources were calculated at 38,300 million tons.
[6] ECSA, op. cit., p. 125.

may be the real reason for the poverty of the African people it certainly cannot be the poverty of her resources. Africa has immense riches in minerals, water-power and agricultural products. In fact, she has everything essential for development into a powerful, prosperous continent, capable of giving her people a standard of living equal to that of the most advanced regions of the world.

So once again we are driven back to considering the questions: What is the cause of African poverty? What happens to the wealth she already produces? And why are so many of her resources left unused?

The first thing that strikes the enquirer is that practically all the immense mineral resources of Africa, and a good deal of its land and agricultural resources—not to mention its trade, shipping, banking, insurance, building, transport, communications—are in the hands of foreigners, of American, British, French, Belgian, Italian, Spanish, South African, West German, Swiss, Japanese and Portuguese companies.

The second feature is that the overwhelming bulk of African primary products (with the partial exception of those of the Union of South Africa) are produced *for export* either in their raw state or in semi-finished form. Only rarely is the product used in local industry right up to the stage of the final manufactured product.

"Only in South Africa are local manufacturing and a local market yet large enough to modify the predominant dependence of Africa on the export market for its products—mineral and agricultural."[1]

In other words the natural wealth of Africa is pumped out in ever-increasing quantities by non-African firms, who derive immense profits from this activity. Africa, despite the considerable and still-increasing sums of money invested there by Western monopolies, remains colonial in its economy, and basic industrialisation is held back.

Raw Materials Appendages

In the territories of Africa, with the exception of the Union,

[1] "The African Revolution", *The Economist*, December 13, 1958, p. 6.

no real industrialisation of the type described earlier has yet taken place. The economies of these countries are dominated by the production of one or a few minerals or agricultural items; their exports are equally dominated by these products, while for their manufactured goods they rely almost entirely on imports. Over 63 per cent of Kenya's exports (in value) in 1956 were composed of coffee, tea and sisal, coffee itself accounting for 47·1 per cent. A further 15 per cent was made up of wattle, hides and skins, cotton and pyrethrum. Of her imports, some 60 per cent were manufactured goods and machinery and industrial equipment, and a further 18 per cent fuels, lubricants and chemicals. In the Central African Federation, despite exaggerated claims regarding the "industrial revolution" alleged to have taken place in Southern Rhodesia, the principal domestic exports in 1957 were as follows:

				Value in £000
Copper ..	..	..	..	82,549
Tobacco	..	..	..	27,509
Chrome Ore	..	..	..	5,860
Tea	..	..	..	3,480
Zinc	..	..	..	2,201
Lead	..	..	..	1,196

For the same year machinery and metal manufactures made up over sixty per cent of the Federation's imports.

Figures for the Federation of Nigeria for 1957 show that practically the whole of her exports were made up of agricultural products (oil, seeds, nuts and kernels, animal and vegetable oils, foodstuffs, cocoa, rubber and timber) together with mineral ores. Over sixty per cent of her imports were for machinery, transport and manufactured goods. In Ghana, for which cocoa alone accounts for some sixty-six per cent of exports, the other main exports are gold, manganese, diamonds and timber. Over half her imports are manufactured goods, and a further twenty-five per cent comprise mainly machinery, building materials and transport.

Everywhere the colonial pattern is dominant—Uganda relying on her cotton and coffee, Tanganyika on her sisal, groundnuts, tea and coffee, Zanzibar on her cloves, and so on.

How completely the economy of African territories is dominated by the production for export of one or two commodities or a few minerals and agricultural products is shown by the accompanying table.

TABLE XX
1957

Country	Principal Export Commodities	Principal Exports as % of value of Total Exports
Ethiopia	Coffee	67·5
Gambia	Ground nuts	93·0
Ghana	Cocoa	56·0
Liberia	Rubber, iron ore, palm kernels	88·5
French Equatorial Africa	Coffee, cotton, wood, diamonds	76·9
Federation of Rhodesia and Nyasaland	Copper, tobacco	66·8
Sierra Leone	Palm kernels, iron ore, diamonds	68·8
Belgian Congo and Ruanda-Urundi	Coffee, cotton, palm oil, copper, cobalt, tin	69·3
British East Africa	Coffee, tea, hides, skins, furs, oil seeds, oil nuts, oil kernels, cotton, sisal, diamonds	81·3
French West Africa	Miscellaneous agricultural and forestry products	86·6
Mozambique	Ditto	81·4
Nigeria	Ditto, tin	85·0
Angola	Ditto, diamonds	85·2

(Source: *Economic Survey of Africa Since 1950*, op. cit., pp. 167–70.)

It is also important to note the extent to which the output, and therefore the export, of these commodities has soared enormously compared with pre-war, and is still rising.

TABLE XXI
INDICES OF DEVELOPMENT OF OUTPUT OF PRINCIPAL MINERALS
(1948–50 average = 100)

Mineral	Level of Production 1937–8 average	1955–7 average
Copper	91	155
Manganese	68	136
Iron Ore	96	188
Lead Ore	56	213
Zinc Ore	31	224
Tin concentrate	91	112
Bauxite Ore	–	404
Chromite	54	145
Cobalt	55	196
Asbestos	29	164
Calcium Phosphate	72	167
Gold	132	120

(Source: *Economic Survey of Africa Since 1950*, table 2–1, p. 115.)

In the Belgian Congo, Northern Rhodesia, Southern Rhodesia and the Union of South Africa, the volume of mineral production increased by more than 30 per cent between 1950 and 1953, and between 1953 and 1957 by a further 14 per cent in the Belgian Congo, 20 per cent in the Central African Federation, and 24 per cent in the Union of South Africa. In Africa as a whole, the production of copper rose between 1948-50 and 1955-57 by 55 per cent, manganese by 36 per cent, chrome by 45 per cent, and gold by 20 per cent. For cobalt the figure was 96 per cent; for iron ore, 88 per cent; for phosphate rock, 67 per cent; and for asbestos 64 per cent. For bauxite ore the rise was over four-fold in this period, while for lead and zinc ores it was more than double.[1]

The output of agricultural commodities has also risen since the end of the Second World War, although not to the same degree as minerals.

Thus the picture is one of the increasing export of Africa's raw materials to the metropolitan countries. In fact, in 1954 71·2 per cent of all African exports went to the United Kingdom, France, Belgium, the United States and Canada, and Western Germany. Only 11·3 per cent went to African countries. In the same way, again indicating Africa's dependence on the metropolitan countries, 70·6 per cent of her imports in 1954 came from the above group of countries, and only 10·1 per cent from African countries.

Despite the increase in output of Africa's main commodities over the last twenty years, the African people, as we have seen in earlier chapters, remain poverty-stricken whether they remain on the land or enter European employment.

A case in point is provided by raw cotton and wool. Anyone who has visited Africa—or even if one has had to be content with looking at photos—cannot be unaware of the fact that the people of Africa are among the most poorly clad people in the world. Yet Africa produces far more cotton and wool than she consumes. Figures for 1948-9 showed that consumption of cotton in Africa was "*less than nine per cent of its production and less than one half of one per cent of world consumption*".[2] Similarly African consumption of wool was "a relatively small fraction of its

[1] ECSA, op. cit., p. 115.
[2] *Review of Economic Conditions in Africa, 1951*, op. cit., p. 34.

production", and less than three-fourths of one per cent of world consumption in 1949.[1]

Often it is alleged that if the African workers were only to increase production then they could overcome their poverty. The facts show that the African workers have increased output considerably, but it is not they who have benefited from this. The main beneficiaries of this system are the big foreign monopolies. Indeed, even *The Economist* is constrained to admit as much when it describes the agricultural boom in southern Africa in the following terms:

". . . in the Congo, the output of rubber and coffee, to take key examples, doubled between 1953 and 1957, palm produce and cotton seed rose by 15–20 per cent; while in Central Africa the area under cultivation has increased by 25 per cent in a decade. Tobacco output nearly doubled between 1950 and 1956, while maize and tea increased by 50 per cent; such was the vitalising influence of boom prices for copper after Federation gave Salisbury access to Northern Rhodesia's wealth.

"In the Union, increased wheat output since the war has made the country self-sufficient. A 17 per cent increase in the wool clip between 1953 and 1957 has made it the principal export after minerals. Maize production . . . has increased by over 100 per cent in the last six or seven years; exports jumped by nearly 50 per cent between 1953 and 1956, in both the Union and the Rhodesias, and scale of maize production is now sufficient to permit a start being made on large-scale stock farming on the pattern of the American Middle West. . . .

"*All these advantages have been principally reaped by European capital, intensive farming and the large-scale plantations; as yet, only to a limited extent by the rural areas.*"[2]   [Own italics—J. W.]

Africans, with justice and with ample statistics, would challenge the contention that they had gained even "to a limited extent". In fact, the progressive deterioration of rural Africa is a root cause

[1] ibid., p. 34.
[2] "The African Revolution," op. cit., p. 11.

of the present-day African revolt now embracing the entire continent.

Rich Fruit

Those who have benefited, those who have obtained the "rich fruit", as *The Economist* aptly calls it, from the investment of Western capital in Africa, are the European companies and farmers. It is they who own the mines and plantations, the trading concerns and the banks, the transport and the building firms. Even the limited factory production is in their hands.

It is estimated that over £860,000,000 of British capital is now invested in South Africa, and some £300,000,000 in Central Africa. In the whole of Africa some £1,400–1,500 million are estimated to be invested by British capitalists. From 1950 to 1953 alone £600,000,000 of British capital poured into Africa.

The companies that are concerned with this exploitation are not merely the particular colonial firms specialising in African trade or production but also the African subsidiaries of the big companies whose names are household words in Britain. Thus the Imperial Chemical Industries is part-owner of the African Explosives and Chemicals Company, which supplies the whole of the mines in southern Africa with their explosives, as well as industry in general with its chemicals, and agriculture with its fertilisers. The huge trust of Unilevers, apart from owning innumerable trading, vegetable-oil and other concerns throughout the whole of West Africa, owns subsidiaries in other parts of Africa, such as a soap factory in Nyasaland, the East African trading firm of Gailey & Roberts, and so on. The principal banks in British Africa are owned by British interests. The Standard Bank of South Africa, with London headquarters, has a fine selection of the British peerage and of the British financial world on its board of directors. The Bank of West Africa is controlled by a consortium of four other banks, Lloyds, Westminster, National Provincial and the Standard Bank of South Africa. Barclays also has its own bank operating in territories throughout Africa.

In engineering it is the same story, with such well known British firms as Dorman Long, Allied Ironfounders, Metal Box Company, Stewarts & Lloyds, and others with their subsidiaries in Africa. In building it is the familiar names of Richard Costain,

John Laing and Taylor Woodrow which appear on the big construction sites in Africa. Associated Cement, Portland Cement and Tunnel Cement all have connections in many parts of Africa. The oil trusts, B.P. and Shell, have distributing centres all over the African continent and are also engaged in prospecting for oil in many territories. The big bus combine, British Electric Traction, is associated with bus companies all over East and Central Africa. Two of the main British shipping companies, Elder Dempster and Union Castle, call at all the ports of the west and east coast right down to South Africa, taking their toll of profit from all the goods they carry. A dominant feature of the Salisbury landscape today is the Pearl Assurance building. Buildings of the same firm tower skywards in Nairobi, Johannesburg and Cape Town. Glaxo, British Celanese, Crosse & Blackwells, British Match, Dunlop Rubber and many other well known British firms, all have manufacturing subsidiaries in Africa.

Of special significance are the big mine-owning companies, among which the Anglo-American Corporation of South Africa and its associated diamond combine De Beers Consolidated Mines are outstanding. The latter has a practical monopoly of all the diamonds—both the industrial and the gem variety—produced in Africa, and indeed of the whole capitalist world, since African output, as we have seen, accounts for over ninety-eight per cent of the world's output (excluding the U.S.S.R.). The Anglo-American section of this combine, besides owning many gold and coal mines in South Africa, has a big stake in the Northern Rhodesian Copper Belt, which is the third largest copper-producing area in the capitalist world.

The manner in which the big international mining monopolies participated in the great grab of Africa at the end of the nineteenth century and the first decades of the twentieth is so well known that it needs no retelling here. Yet what is not so widely recognised is that similar intrigues to lay their hands on the rich resources of "poor Africa" are still carried on by these companies today. This is well illustrated by recent events in Basutoland in connection with the considerable diamond deposits which are to be found there.

According to the national organisations of Basutoland—the Basutoland Congress Party and the Basotho National Party—

the wishes of the Basotho and the decisions of the Basutoland Council have both been flouted, and a Colonel Jack Scott has obtained a right to mine for diamonds in Basutoland. This right, it is alleged, he has ceded, against the wishes of the Basotho, to the Bermuda Company, which is a subsidiary of the South African monopoly De Beers, and, moreover, De Beers are to be given a monopoly over the sale of diamonds mined in Basutoland. Further, says the Congress Party (in a resolution passed at Maseru on August 5, 1959), the Basotho have been totally excluded from prospecting or mining for diamonds in Basutoland.

Finally, the Congress Party accuses the Resident Commissioner of having "revised the diamond contract in a manner absolutely contrary to the declared wishes of the Basutoland Council".

The action taken by government officials and company agents in Basutoland is, of course, not exceptional in Africa. In fact, Africans in every territory can narrate similar sordid accounts of the manner in which their land and their mineral wealth have been taken from them by Western monopolies.

It is robbery such as this which is one of the causes of the poverty of the African people.

From the £1,400–1,500 million of British capital invested in Africa, British investors annually draw, directly or indirectly, millions of pounds profits. How substantial these profits are it is not easy to say exactly, since neither is the exact scale of British overseas investments known, nor the profits which they yield. But a recent estimate shows that the average rate of profit on the £860,000,000 invested by British capital in South Africa amounts to some fifteen per cent, an equivalent of almost £130,000,000 a year. This £130,000,000 represents the enormous profits which are derived from the system of *apartheid*.

It should be emphasised that not only is Africa a source of considerable profit for Western firms, but it is increasingly becoming more so, and thus the poverty of the African people is perpetuated and even increased.

In the Belgian Congo, the *Union Minière du Haute Katanga's* capital was only 1,000,000,000 francs in 1946, but its profits rose from 600,000,000 francs that year to 1,838,000,000 in 1950; 4,093,000,000 in 1955; and to 4,571,000,000 in 1956.[1]

[1] *The Economist*, April 20, 1957; *East Africa and Rhodesia*, May 16, 1957.

The steep upward curve of dividends paid by the Orange Free State goldmining companies in recent years shows the same trend.

TABLE XXII
DIVIDEND PAYMENTS OF THE ORANGE FREE STATE GOLDMINING COMPANIES

Year					Dividends—£millions
1955	..	..	..	..	1·5
1956	..	..	..	..	5·7
1957	..	..	..	..	9·4
1958	..	..	..	..	13·3
1959	..	..	..	..	16·7

(Source: *South African Progress*, bulletin issued by Director of Information, South Africa House, London, issue of October 1959.)

It is in these goldfields that a more enlightened policy is alleged to be followed by the companies towards African labour, a greater stress being laid, at least in words, on the need for a more permanent, urbanised proletariat. Evidently these pretensions on the part of the mineowners do not in any way interfere with the soaring increase in profits.

There is no doubt that over the years the Western powers have taken out of Africa an incredible wealth of minerals.

"Up to 1955, the imperialist powers drained at least $14,000,000,000 in minerals from South Africa, over, $2,000,000,000 (mainly in copper) from Northern Rhodesia, $1,000,000,000 in minerals from Southern Rhodesia, untold amounts in uranium from the Belgian Congo. From sub-equatorial Africa the West has taken some $20,000,000,000 worth of minerals."[1]

In comparison with other areas of the world, and taking into consideration the dimensions of the African continent, the population figures and the backwardness of Africa's productive forces, capitalist investments in Africa, though increasing, are

[1] Goshal, Kumar, in the *National Guardian*, April 13, 1959. (Presumably based on the estimates given by Dr. Alpheus Hunton in his *Decision in Africa*, pp. 68–70, New York, 1957.) More recently, Colonel the Lord Robbins, President of the British South Africa Company, in announcing the company's net consolidated profit (before tax) for 1959 at £11,439,026, stated that the total value of copper produced in Northern Rhodesia from the commencement of mining operations up to the beginning of 1960 exceeds £1,000 million. (*East Africa and Rhodesia*, February 25, 1960.)

still small. But profits are right out of proportion and far exceed investment, especially in mining. For certain mining companies *annual* profits of 100 per cent over capital and more are not unknown. This no doubt explains why it is that in a number of branches of mining the growth of production in Africa is more rapid than in the rest of the capitalist world, and her share of total world extraction is increasing. For instance, Africa's contribution to the capitalist world's extraction of copper rose from 19 per cent in 1937 to 24 per cent in 1956; for manganese ore this contribution increased over the same period from 24 per cent to 37 per cent, for tin concentrates from 11 per cent to 15 per cent, for antimony from 5 per cent to 48 per cent, and for gold from 47 per cent to 63 per cent.[1]

Alongside the old-established European powers—Britain, France, Belgium, Portugal—the United States has pushed its way into Africa in striking fashion since the Second World War.

As a result, there has been a really tremendous growth in the export of African raw materials to the United States. Figures for exports to the U.S. from a number of African territories for the year 1949 (the year before the Korean war, and a key period of American strategic stock-piling) compared with 1937, demonstrate this in striking fashion.

TABLE XXIII

	Exports to U.S. in 1,000s of U.S. dollars		1949 Figure in Approximate % of 1937
	1937	*1949*	
Tanganyika	1,147	9,436	850
Northern Rhodesia	620	18,028	3,000
Belgian Congo and Ruanda-Urundi	1,471	21,895	1,500
Nigeria	11,589	26,875	230
Gold Coast	17,937	45,290	250
French West Africa..	2,434	5,609	230
Kenya and Uganda	1,523	7,428	500
Angola	191	8,646	4,300
Mozambique	212	3,831	1,900

(Source: *Review of Economic Conditions in Africa*, op. cit., table 57, p. 92. Note: The percentages in the last column have been added by the present writer—J. W.)

Apart from providing the United States with raw materials,

[1] ECSA, op. cit., p. 125.

another result of this trade has been to supply European imperialists with a regular flow of dollars; and, in fact, a major preoccupation of their policy in Africa in the whole post-war period has been to intensify the exploitation of African materials and manpower in order to secure more dollars.

It may be thought—and indeed is sometimes argued—that the money being invested in Africa by Western monopolies (or through various governmental and other agencies) is of assistance to Africa. In fact, it is said, Africa *needs* Western capital in order to overcome her poverty. Africa's experience, however, over the past few decades, completely contradicts this claim and makes abundantly clear that Western capital investments have had a devastating effect on the people's traditional economic organisation, leading to their impoverishment and oppression, to the complete distortion of the economy of the different territories, the concentration on primary production (minerals and cash crops) and the deliberate stifling of secondary industry. The effect and purpose of Western investment, in fact, is not to assist the African people but to suck Africa dry and exploit her people in order to enrich the investors in the big combines of London, Paris, Brussels, New York and other metropolitan centres.

Who Has Benefited from the Belgian Congo?

The Belgian Congo provides a most instructive example of this process. Belgium herself is a small country, with a population of less than ten million. But, through the continuous reinvestment of unremitted profits from the Congo, she has pushed her investments in that region up some threefold in the last seventy years. The value of foreign investments in the Belgian Congo in 1956 was estimated at some £1,000,000,000, of which close on ninety per cent is held by a small group of large Belgian finance houses who monopolise the entire field of production and distribution, including export, in the Congo.

As far as the African inhabitants of the Congo are concerned, the resultant pattern is the complete stifling of their economic development, the destruction of their traditional agriculture and the transformation of their manpower into wage labour in Belgian-owned mines and other enterprises. Some sixty per cent of the total African wage-earning population is employed in little more than three per cent of the undertakings—and these undertakings account for more than eighty-six per cent of the total capital investment in the colony. Predominant among these enterprises is the giant *Société Générale*, one of the largest enterprises in the whole of Africa. This trust, through its control of the *Union Minière du Haute Katanga*, controls the whole of the Katanga copper region, and also monopolises the production of cobalt, zinc, uranium, manganese and tin. It also holds a commanding position in the manufacture of chemicals and textiles, and is dominant in plantations, commerce, banking, insurance and transport.

The big Belgian investments in the Congo are concentrated in minerals and plantations, and in the connected services and activities; and this is understandable since the very aim of these investments is to siphon off from the country as much of the natural wealth as possible, partly to satisfy the needs of Belgian industry and partly to earn dollars and other foreign currencies for the Belgian capitalist class through the sale of these products to other metropolitan countries.[1] Thus it is that the exports from the Belgian Congo continue to absorb about one-third of the total national product, and the exports themselves are confined to a few key items, in the familiar colonial pattern.

While there has been, as in other African territories, a growth of secondary industry, this is still only a minor part of the total economy (1956 figures showed that manufacturing industry accounted for about ten per cent of the aggregate ascertainable money income in the Congo, while mining and agriculture accounted for fifty-five per cent).

Further, even within the restricted scope of industrial development referred to, it is Belgian capital which is dominant. A class of African manufacturers in the Congo, to all intents and purposes, does not exist.

In this connection it is interesting to note that Nelly Xydias,

---

[1] Belgian investors are not the only beneficiaries. The British firm, Tanganyika Concessions ("Tanks"), controls 21 per cent of the shares of *Union Minière*. Other British interests in the Congo include *Sedec*, a Unilever subsidiary, and the *Compagnie Congolaise de Tabac*, a British-American Tobacco subsidiary. U.S. interests—the Morgan group, Rockefeller, the Lazard Bank and others—have shares in "Tanks", while Rockefeller has its own direct shares in *Union Minière*.

in her analysis of the undertakings in Stanleyville,[1] found that 217 of them were Belgian, 170 were other European, 24 Asiatic, and 7 could be classified as Congo. There were a further eight "unknown" as to nationality of ownership. In other words, less than two per cent of the undertakings belonged to the indigenous Africans; and, although the analysis of Xydias did not concern itself further with this problem, it can be said with certainty that these African enterprises were only small undertakings, probably shops.

The extent to which the African people have been excluded from participation in the profits derived from the mounting output of minerals and agricultural products in the Belgian Congo is shown by the fact that the national income of the African wage-earning population only grew from one-sixth of the total to one-fifth between 1950 and 1956, an increase which is largely accounted for by the larger number of Africans drawn into wage-earning activities. Indeed, available statistics tend to show that the *per capita* income of the African people in the Congo has remained more or less stationary during this period, at about £40 a year. The paucity of African savings—and their decline—also testifies to their growing impoverishment. In 1950 the mobilisable savings of the African people amounted to £5,000,000. By 1956, despite the increased integration of Africans in the money economy, *these savings had fallen to £4,000,000.*

In contrast, profits accruing to the Belgian investors in recent years have amounted to about eighty-five million pounds a year.

Although, admittedly, a good deal of the profits are ploughed back into the Congo—and some even finds its way into the field of manufacture there—the investments, and even the limited range of manufactures, are designed to meet the needs of the metropolitan country and to maintain an ever-growing stream of profits into the pockets of the investors. A recent estimate by the central bank of the Congo states that for the period 1950–6 gross profits of Belgian enterprises operating in the Congo amounted to about four hundred and fifty million pounds.

Thus the wealth of the Congo goes to enrich Belgian investors—while the indigenous Congo people remain impoverished and the proper, balanced economic development of their land, which would provide the basis for eliminating their poverty, is prevented.

[1] Unesco, op. cit.

. . . and from the Central African Federation?

The Central African Federation presents a similar picture of the complete subordination of a people and its natural resources to the interests of overseas investors and white settlers. A recent U.N. report[1] explains that 94 per cent of the value of the Federation's exports in 1956 was derived from primary products (76 per cent *mining* and 18 per cent *agricultural* products); and 75 per cent of the total was derived from two commodities—copper and tobacco. The report further points out that "A high proportion of net domestic income is earned by companies. . . . Many of these companies are branches or subsidiaries of companies with head offices abroad. . . . The income paid abroad is a significant part of net domestic income, varying between ten and fifteen per cent. A large part of these payments was due to interest and dividend, as well as royalty payments by the Northern Rhodesian mining companies. The high income payments abroad reflect that the foreign capital invested in the country is important."[2]

The huge increase in the drain of primary products from the Federation is revealed in the growth of the value of exports from the Federal area from £64,400,000 in 1949 to £188,200,000 in 1956—an almost three-fold increase.[3] For copper alone, the increase was from £27,900,000 in 1949 to £113,800,000 in 1956. In 1953, the year the Federation came into being, African money income, at £57,800,000, was 31 per cent of total personal income; European personal income at £127,500,000 constituted 69 per cent. By 1956 the African share had risen by only 1 per cent, and the European share had dropped by 1 per cent. But even this apparent, infinitesimal shift is misleading, for while the African share in 1956 represented an increase of £23,400,000, the European share was up by £44,300,000.[4]

The significance of these figures becomes clearer when one takes into account the population figures—7,140,000 Africans and 259,000 Europeans. Thus the ratio of Africans to Europeans is 27 to 1; but the African income is even less than half that of the European total.

---

[1] *The Structure and Growth of Selected African Economies*, U.N., New York, 1958.
[2] ibid., p. 14.
[3] ibid., table 6, p. 20.
[4] ibid., table 7, p. 21.

The Federation's mining industry, in particular, reflects the increased exploitation of the African workers over the past decade or more.

TABLE XXIV

Year	Value of Mineral Production £	African Wages £	Gross Profits after Royalty Payments £
1945	13,000,000	1,400,000	5,500,000
1950	49,300,000	2,400,000	29,700,000
1956	129,300,000	6,400,000	80,200,000

(Source: *Structure and Growth*, op cit., p. 27, table 13.)

In a short period of eleven years African wages, relatively speaking, have shrunk from just over 25 per cent of the value of gross profits to approximately 8 per cent. In relation to the value produced, they have dropped from just under 11 per cent to less than 5 per cent.[1] The lion's share of the increased value produced by the African miners has clearly been taken by the companies. In 1949 total wages and salaries (including those of European miners) together with operating costs came to 55·4 per cent of the total expenditure of the mining companies, while gross investments, royalties, taxes and dividends and royalties paid abroad accounted for 31·5 per cent. *By 1956 the position was completely reversed, wages, salaries and operating costs accounting for only 27·3 per cent, while gross investments, royalties, taxes and dividends and royalties paid abroad were up to 61·7 per cent.*[2]

The Northern Rhodesian Mineworkers' Union, in making a proposal recently for nationalising the Rhodesian copper industry, states that the mining companies have paid out £150,000,000 in dividends after taxation during the past ten years, while their total investment on the Copper Belt does not exceed £100,000,000.[3]

The "economic benefits of Federation" has been a phrase on the lips of most of its supporters. It has been used even by leaders of the Labour Party, such as Mr. James Callaghan, the Labour Shadow Cabinet's Colonial Minister. The figures above make abundantly clear that it is the big European companies which derive the main economic benefits—and it is therefore

[1] ibid., p. 26.
[2] ibid., p. 27.
[3] *Africa Digest*, November 1959, vol. vii, No. 2, p. 43.

quite understandable that it should be they who were among the strongest advocates of establishing the Federation before 1953, and who today, after seven years' experience of its benefits, remain among its staunchest backers.

Development Priorities

A striking commentary on European economic policies towards Africa is provided by the figures for electrical production.

TABLE XXV

PRODUCTION OF ELECTRICITY IN SELECTED AFRICAN COUNTRIES AND
TERRITORIES

(In millions of kilowatt-hours)

Country	Pre-war year	1948	1955	1956	1957
Belgian Congo ..	272·3 (1939)	497·3	1,445·0	1,743·0	2,489·0
Nigeria	—	—	243·0	285·0	331·0
Sierra Leone ..	0·8 (1937)	5·1	12·0	14·0	14·34
Kenya	13·7 (1938)	47·6	209·0	240·0	268·0
Mauritius	—	15·4	34·0	37·0	43·3
Uganda	0·3 (1938)	6·1	80·0	95·0	148·8
Northern Rhodesia	—	—	1,268·0	1,372·0	1,054·0
Nyasaland ..	—	—	9·0	...	9·5
Southern Rhodesia	79·5 (1938)	330·0	1,179·0	1,320·0	1,363·0
Ethiopia	—	—	39·0	43·0	72·56
French Equatorial Africa	—	—	44·0	33·0	39·0
Madagascar ..	13·3 (1937)	24·9	57·0	58·0	62·4
French West Africa	8·4 (1937)	202·0	117·0	138·0	168·0
Ghana	—	—	241·0	231·0	282·0
Liberia	1·0 (1937)	9·5	31·0	...	30·54
Angola	7·1 (1937)	22·5	52·0	77·0	95·8
Mozambique ..	11·3 (1937)	18·4	53·0	...	81·8
Sudan	—	16·7	45·0	47·0	60·1
Union of S. Africa	5,336·0 (1937)	9,481·0	16,351·0	17,659·0	18,947·0

[Source: *African Labour Survey*, table 16, p. 676, I.L.O., Geneva, 1958. (Compiled from United Nations: *Review of Economic Conditions in Africa, 1951*, p. 56; *Review of Economic Activity in Africa, 1950 to 1954*, p. 40; and *Economic Developments in Africa, 1956–7*, p. 81.) 1957 figures taken from ECSA, op. cit., p. 35.]

The production of electricity is mainly concentrated in those territories which (a) depend mainly on mining activities and/or (b) have a substantial concentration of white settlers—that is, Belgian Congo, Northern Rhodesia, Southern Rhodesia and the

Union of South Africa.[1] In contrast, those territories which are based mainly on agriculture, whether for local consumption or for cash crops, have an extremely limited development of electricity production, even in the case of Kenya, which has a considerable white-settler population.[2]

It is instructive to note that in Ghana and Nigeria, in proportion as the economic development of the countries has moved more directly under African control, a significant development in the production of electricity has taken place. There is no doubt that the same process will be registered in Guinea now that she has shaken off French political control.

China, at the time of her Liberation in 1949, was even more backward than Africa as regards the production of electricity; but once the Chinese people took over the political control of their own country, and were thus able to take possession of their own resources, they outstripped Africa.

TABLE XXVI
PRODUCTION OF ELECTRICITY
(Millions of Kilowatt-Hours)

China			Africa		
1949	..	4,300	1948	..	10,676
1958	..	27,500	1956	..	23,392
1959	..	41,500	1957	..	29,800

(Sources: *New China News Agency*, September 28, 1959; *African Labour Survey*, op. cit., table 16, p. 676, I.L.O.; ECSA, op. cit., p. 35.)

In ten years China's output of electricity has increased nearly tenfold; in nine years, that of Africa has trebled. China formerly produced only two-fifths as much electricity as Africa; now it produces almost two-fifths more.

But it is not only in respect to the *quantity* of electricity that Africa is found wanting. Electrical development in China is directly linked with basic industrialisation on the one hand, and with the electrification of people's homes and farms on the other. In Africa, however, the output of electricity is almost entirely devoted to European interests—to European homes and farms, and to European enterprises. Throughout most of Africa electric

[1] These are also the territories which have received the largest proportion of foreign investment—and it is to the mineral wealth that this investment has been mainly directed.

[2] It should be noted Kenya also obtains electricity supplies from Uganda.

light for Africans is non-existent. Moreover, apart from the Union, and to some extent in the Belgian Congo and Southern Rhodesia, electrical production in Africa is not linked to the development of basic industry, but to mining (e.g. electrolytic copper in Northern Rhodesia) and the expansion of smelters and refineries.

In South and Central Africa it is the mineral wealth which has attracted Western interest and investment in the past; and to this day it remains the main attraction for overseas investments.

"In a typical 'boom' year, say, 1954, export earnings from minerals—excluding uranium—amounted to approximately $621 million out of total exports of $1,228 million in the Union, $287·3 million out of $351 million in the Rhodesias and $238 million out of $370·8 million in the Congo. . . . Minerals have also been the major magnet of foreign investment. Of the $10 billion invested in Africa since 1947, over $2 billion has been directed to the Union of South Africa, nearly $2 billion to the Congo and $1 billion to the Rhodesias. Three territories with a total population of some 33 million have thus absorbed *half* the capital invested in a continent of nearly 200 million people."[1]

An examination of the recent and current development plans for the different regions of Africa shows that the funds are largely earmarked to develop transport, primarily to speed up the process of robbing Africa of her mineral wealth.

As *The Economist* has pointed out, this is nothing new for Africa.

"Minerals and transport development have almost invariably coincided. Apart from some strategic railways, like the Sierra Leone or Kenya-Uganda lines, the creation of a road and rail network in Africa has been prompted by the need to drain exports to the coast; and minerals provide long hauls which make railways pay.

"Diamonds and gold lay at the basis of South Africa's railway system. Gold prospecting, the discovery of coal at Wankie and the opening up of the Copperbelt fixed the

[1] *African Revolution*, op. cit., p. 8.

pattern of Rhodesia's first railways. Copper linked the Katanga first with Rhodesia and then with railway development in Angola and Mozambique."[1]

Since the Second World War, in order to cope with the big increase in the output and export of minerals, and partly of other products, a considerable proportion of investment in Africa has gone to develop ports and harbours, extend railways, build new roads and airfields. In the Congo ten-year plan, 1949–59, about forty-four per cent of the total expenditure of $1,000,000,000 was set aside for improvements in road and rail transport and on the Congo's river system.[2] A further $70,000,000 scheme for road development has been introduced, backed by a $40,000,000 loan from the World Bank. Of the Central African Federation's £120,000,000 development plan, about a quarter is being allocated for improving transport. It is the same in the Union, where "the first plan to spend $1,400,000,000 on railway transport proved insufficient and a first loan from the World Bank of $160,000,000 has been followed by another advance of $25,000,000. In the next three years, a further $560,000,000 are to be spent."[3]

In West Africa, too, there has been a similar development of transport, "30 per cent of new capital in British areas and 50 per cent in French going to transportation alone".[4] Of the £339,100,000 envisaged for development programmes in Nigeria over the period 1955 to 1962, no less than £120,000,000, or 36 per cent of the total, is devoted to transport—most of it roads and railways. One of the biggest single capital projects planned is a new 400-mile railway extension which will cost some £20,000,000. It is expected that this rail extension will "encourage the production of export crops".[5]

In Liberia, the Liberian American-Swedish Minerals Company (L.A.M.C.O.) is investing $200,000,000 to exploit the iron ore at Nimba, on the Guinea border. Describing this, Peter Duval-Smith writes that they will level "a 4,000-foot mountain that is practically solid iron. They will build a 200-mile railway and

[1] ibid., p. 8.
[2] ibid., p. 8.
[3] ibid., p. 8.
[4] ibid., p. 19.
[5] *West Africa*, October 10, 1959, p. 832.

harbour installations in order to carry the ore away."[1] Though Liberia will receive fifty per cent of the profits, the other fifty per cent will go to foreign monopolies and all the iron ore will be taken out of Liberia. Despite Liberia's immense reserves of iron ore there are no plans to develop a local iron and steel industry. The Western investments are not for the purpose of building up Liberia's economy but are intended to step up the direct robbery of the country's natural wealth.

As regards African territories under French rule, these, too, have witnessed the same concentration on transport. "Half the money for the first French African Modernisation Plan (1946–53) was spent on transport and a quarter of the second plan (1954–7)."[2]

Between 1948 and 1955 some £48,000,000 was spent in East Africa on railway and port developments.[3]

Transport development in Africa, like increased electrical output, is planned almost entirely to meet the needs of European farms, mines, industrial enterprises and residential areas. For the majority of Africans, who live on the land, roads are few and poor, and railways beyond reach. Few railway lines stretch into the interior of the continent. They run only to the mining regions or to centres where cash crops are assembled to be carried to the ports for export. Most lines are single track, carrying Africa's wealth down to the seaports to be laden on ships. Transport systems devised for such a purpose naturally ignore the interests and needs of the African people themselves, who are probably the worst served for transport of all peoples in the world. In the days before Ghana won its political independence complaints were made by the people in the Gold Coast that there was no bridge across a particular river and that people had to wait, without shelter, all through the night for the ferry to arrive, while the "government goes on its way to construct double manganese railway lines from Takoradi to Tarkwa for nothing but to facilitate taking away huge quantities of our manganese and other minerals to enrich other nations".[4]

[1] *Daily Telegraph*, August 12, 1959.
[2] Williams, Shirley: "How Rich is Africa," *The Twentieth Century*, April 1959, p. 408.
[3] ibid., p. 408.
[4] *Accra Evening News*, November 14, 1950; quoted by W. Alpheus Hunton in *Decision in Africa*, p. 79.

Similarly, a four-nation grouping of companies—Miferma[1] (France, Britain, Italy and Western Germany)—is constructing a 400-mile railway from Mauretania's rich, high-grade iron-ore deposits at Fort Gouraud down to the sea, at Port Étienne, where the harbour will be developed to take ships of up to 60,000 tons. Two trains a day, carrying 10,000 tons each, will carry the valuable ore to the port. The initial target is 4,000,000 tons of ore a year, and the aim is to build this up to 6,000,000 tons.

The ore here—some 215,000,000 tons are estimated—exists in an eighteen-mile-long *massif*, rising to a height of 2,000 feet. To take this ore, "whole sections of the mountain are to be cut away".[2] The manager of the mine, M. Jean Painsard, has declared: "When we have finished, there will be no landscape."

The Mauretanian Government, by agreement, will retain fifty per cent of the profits. But she will retain none of the ore for the development of her own industry. And, if the Miferma grouping has its way, there will, at the end, "be no landscape"— and Mauretania's economy will still be that of a backward, colonial country.

There is another purpose which the considerable expenditure on roads, railways, rivers, ports and airfields is intended to serve— and that is military and strategic. African people rightly emphasise that this, too, is not to defend them and their interests but to safeguard imperialist seizures, intimidate the African national movements and provide bases and jumping-off grounds for aggression against other countries, especially the Soviet Union and the rich, oil-bearing lands in the Middle East.

In general, the plans for economic development in Africa being carried out by the different imperial powers are plans to develop the infra-structure of communications and services which will enable the exploitation of Africa's raw materials to continue and be intensified. Real industrialisation is deliberately neglected.

"In general, the tendency is to develop industries concerned

[1] *Société Anonyme des Mines de Fer de Mauretanie.*
[2] *The Times*, December 12, 1959.
[3] ibid.

with processing local primary products, for example, the extraction of palm oil, the ginning of cotton and the processing of sugar cane; industries producing consumer goods, mostly but not invariably based on local raw materials; and industries providing building materials of which cement is of particular importance. . . ."[1]

In the majority of territories, it is admitted, industrial development, such as it is, "is largely limited to the initial processing of agricultural products".[2] The metropolitan countries "provide only limited public financial assistance for the establishment and development of manufacturing industries in the territories under their administration".[3]

In documentation submitted to the South Pacific Commission in 1956, it was suggested that as far as the underdeveloped territories in the South Pacific area were concerned there was a "tendency to discourage the establishment of industries which would have an adverse effect on the sales . . . of goods manufactured in the parent country".[4] There is no doubt that similar motives are behind the official discouragement of industrialisation in Africa. Imperialist shipping interests, too, are reluctant to see the growth of African manufacturing industries which might lead to a decline in the imports they normally carry to the territories concerned, because such national industry will want to break the monopoly of the "conference" rates by shipping their goods in non-conference lines or in nationally owned ones.

The results of this policy of deliberately neglecting, when not preventing, industrialisation can be seen not only in the lack of industrialisation which exists in most of Africa but in the abysmal shortage of funds allocated for industrial purposes in the various development plans of the imperialist powers in Africa.

Out of the £148,000,000 worth of funds allotted between 1946 and 1956 under the United Kingdom Colonial Development

---

[1] NSG, op. cit., pp. 9–10.
[2] ibid., p. 10.
[3] ibid., p. 87.
[4] *Industrial Activity in Selected Areas of the South Pacific*, Technical Paper No. 90, p. 98, South Pacific Commission, Noumea, 1956.

and Welfare Act, only £545,000—less than ½ per cent—was directly for industrial development.[1] Of the £55,000,000 worth of loans made to British colonial territories under the Colonial Development Corporation, between 1948 and 1955, only 7 per cent went for "factories"; agriculture and forestry took 32 per cent and mining 13 per cent.[2] In French West Africa, French Equatorial Africa and Madagascar far less than 1 per cent of commitments authorised in December 1954 were for the promotion of industry[3] (709,000,000 francs out of 242,000,000,000 francs).

The sums allocated for industrial development under the first F.I.D.E.S. plan for French overseas territories, for the period 1949–53, amounted to less than ½ per cent of the total; nearly 65 per. cent went on infra-structure (transport and communications).[4] In the estimates for the Ten-Year Plan for the Belgian Congo, 1949–59, industry does not even appear as an item![5] The Development Plan for Nigeria for the period 1951–6 allocated 3·5 per cent of the total for industry; the plans for 1955–60 allocate only 1·3 per cent for the same purpose.[6] In Kenya "the main objective of the development policy is to step up the expansion of African agriculture".[7] Hence industry does not appear at all in the Kenya development programme for 1954–7.[8]

This open neglect of industrialisation and of manufacturing industry is usually defended on the grounds that "public funds" bear the burden of providing the essential infra-structure which should enable private capital to develop industry.

"Industrialisation is fundamentally a function of private enterprise. The government's task is to provide private initiative with the necessary basic structure. Public authorities take action only in exceptional cases, when private enterprise is not willing to establish an industry which is in the public interest."[9]

[1] *N.S.G.*, op. cit., table 2, p. 28.
[2] ibid., table 3, p. 29.
[3] *Economic Conditions in Non-Self-Governing Territories, 1953–56*, U.N., March 1957.
[4] *N.S.G.*, op. cit., table 4, p. 30.   [5] ibid., table 8, p. 33.
[6] ibid., table 9, p. 42.   [7] ibid., p. 43.
[8] ibid., table 11, p. 44.   [9] ibid., p. 66.

Private investors find no quick and easy profit in roads, bridges, railways, water supplies, harbours and airfields, nor even in power schemes; while essential social services—hospitals, schools and so forth—provide no profits at all. It is for the private investor that these facilities are developed, so that he may continue to reap his profits from the more reliable and massive riches to be found in African raw materials.

This division of labour between "public" and "private" capital is, in fact, openly admitted in a 1951 report of the O.E.E.C. dealing with development plans in Africa south of the Sahara. "It often happens that no profit can be earned for many years to come", it explains, from laying out capital for basic equipment for productive enterprises. "That is why private capital is sometimes not forthcoming and why public capital has had to take its place." The World Bank, in its report for 1946–53, makes a similar point, stressing that the bank's loans are mainly for basic utilities "which are an essential condition for the growth of private enterprise". Describing this activity as taking "steps to encourage a more favourable climate for private business", the World Bank's report pointedly argues:

"Excessive emphasis on industry for industry's sake, above all, heavy industry, may leave an underdeveloped country with the symbol of development rather than the substance . . . in general capital should be applied where it brings the greatest return."

The bank clearly has in mind the "greatest return" to Western interests, not to the people of the underdeveloped regions of the world; for heavy industry is, in fact, the real substance of economic development, the real index of growth and independence. Western investors, however, as we have seen, are not in favour of industrialisation in Africa but, on the contrary, aim to maintain this vast and rich continent as their raw-materials appendage and dollar earner.

Industrial development, therefore, with the exception of the Union of South Africa and to a considerably lesser degree in the Belgian Congo and Southern Rhodesia, remains very much a marginal affair. Apart from cement works, the usual pattern in territories such as Nigeria, Kenya, Uganda, for instance, is that of canning factories, sawmills, match factories, the manufacture of soap, rubber, bricks, lime, jute bags, soft drinks, biscuits, cardboard, and some clothing and textiles. In most of the territories in Africa manufacturing is of this order, and basic industrialisation is absent.

Not that industrialisation of itself can rescue the African people from their poverty and oppression. The Union of South Africa demonstrates this only too well. There the last fifteen years have witnessed a most rapid growth of manufacturing; the Union is, in many ways, a leading industrial country. Yet for the Africans in the Reserves this development has been accompanied by an unparalleled disaster, as earlier ·chapters have shown. For Africans in the towns, too, it has been demonstrated that industrial expansion has been catastrophic. Little wonder that the average expectation of life of the African in the Union is thirty-six years.[1]

Therefore, along with industrialisation the African people are striving to make other fundamental changes in their economic and social conditions. Whoever rules Africa and owns its wealth, decides its distribution. As long as Africa is ruled by imperialists and white settlers, there is a powerful political barrier standing between the African people and their rightful economic and social inheritance. The ending of the present imperialist tyranny and the gaining of political independence is thus seen as the essential first step to abolishing Africa's poverty.

Many attempts have been made by colonialists and others to conceal the real causes of African poverty. The Fabians, too, have joined in this game, Mr. Creech Jones contending that colonial problems cannot be solved by "clichés about imperialism and colonialism".[2] In writing approvingly of this Fabian claim, *The Times* declares: "It is this acceptance that rapacious capitalism and ruthless exploitation are not the cause of what is wrong in underdeveloped territories that gives the new volume of Fabian essays its value."[3]

It is hoped that the evidence provided in the foregoing pages

[1] Gillman, Professor Theodore, Natal University, in a lecture on "Chronic Malnutrition in Africa", reproduced in the *Star* (Johannesburg), April 4 and 5, 1957.
[2] *New Fabian Colonial Essays*, London, 1959.
[3] *The Times*, August 27, 1959, reviewing the above-mentioned book.

will have demonstrated fully enough that it is indeed "rapacious capitalism and ruthless exploitation" which are the causes of African poverty. This is most decidedly the conclusion to which the people of Africa have come and that is why they are struggling with such tenacity, courage and determination to end colonialism and imperialism in every corner of their vast continent and in whatever form it may find expression.

CHAPTER NINE

AFRICA STANDS UP

ALTHOUGH it is only since the Second World War that the national liberation movements in Africa south of the Sahara have become strong enough to roll back the tyranny of colonialism, it should not be assumed that these movements are entirely a post-1945 phenomenon. The African people were never reconciled to foreign conquest and oppression but fought continually, first to defend themselves against the invaders, and then, after defeat, in protest against the consequences of conquest. In the twentieth century these strivings took on a new importance and scope, and began to acquire quite new characteristics. Strikes and political demonstrations took place; there were revolts and nation-wide upheavals; and political parties began to appear. All these struggles in the period prior to the Second World War undoubtedly helped to pave the way for later developments; although, generally speaking, there were as yet no cohesive, permanent, nation-wide African political organisations with clearly defined aims and programmes directed towards gaining complete national independence. The most common demands were for reforms, not for the abolition of colonial rule. The epoch of national political parties, with a broad mass basis and the unequivocal demand for national independence "in our time"—and established in every single African territory—only really opened after 1945.

The Second World War acted as a watershed in African history; and the victory of 1945 ushered in a new stage in the struggle of the African people.

It is precisely since the Second World War that most African national organisations have been formed: the National Council of Nigeria and the Cameroons (1944), the Ghana Convention People's Party (1949), the Kenya African Union (1946), the Uganda National Congress (1952), the Tanganyika African

National Union (1953), the Northern Rhodesian African National Congress (1947),[1] the Southern Rhodesian African National Congress (1957),[2] the Nyasaland African National Congress (1944),[3] Rassemblement Democratique Africain (1946),[4] and, in the more recent period, the Abako Party, the Congolese National Movement, the African Solidarity Party and other parties in the Belgian Congo, and, of late, the national organisations in Angola and Mozambique.[5]

All these parties belong to the post-war era, some even being formed within the last decade. Even the African National Congress in the Union of South Africa, which has existed for nearly fifty years, has reached its highest point of development only in the past ten years.

The post-war period has seen the African people very much on the offensive against colonialism. In particular has the demand for early or immediate independence been more and more loudly voiced. Thus the imperialist powers, while still striving to repress the growing national movement even to the extent of military action in some cases, have, in the main, been thrown on to the defensive. They have had to manoeuvre and try to find new bases from which to maintain their hold and their privileges.

[1] After the establishment of the Central African Federation in 1953, divisions arose within the Northern Rhodesian African National Congress, leading eventually in 1958 to mass resignations and the setting-up of a new, more consistently anti-colonialist organisation, the Zambia National Congress. After the banning of the latter body in 1958, following the crisis in Central Africa, a new body was set up, the United National Independence Party; its president is Kenneth Kaunda, who was president of the Zambia National Congress.

[2] In Southern Rhodesia the African National Congress was originally formed as early as the 1920s, but it went out of existence quite early, and was re-established only in 1957. It was banned in 1959, after which the National Democratic Party was set up.

[3] After the Nyasaland African National Congress was banned, following the 1958 crisis in Central Africa, the Malawi Congress Party was set up in its place.

[4] The R.D.A. was not confined to one territory, but was a federation of the various organisations which had developed throughout the French colonies in West and Equatorial Africa. Serious divisions arose within the R.D.A. in 1955, and a number of organisations were excluded. Since then other parties have come into existence in the French territories, the R.D.A. remaining, in the main, as a more conservative organisation.

[5] In 1953 the Uniao dos Populacaos de Angola and the Movemento Popular de Libertacao de Angola were formed. Eventually, in 1959, together with other groupings, they merged to form the African Revolutionary Front Against Portuguese Colonialism. This latter organisation includes organisations in Mozambique as well as the Patido Africano de Indepencia de Guiné, covering the small Portuguese enclave on the Guinea coast.

But these very manoeuvres have been made from positions of weakness, not of strength. Colonialism, in fact, is now an army in retreat.

On the eve of the Second World War only Liberia and Egypt had even nominal forms of independence. By the end of 1959 there were nine independent African states—Egypt,[1] Sudan, Morocco, Tunisia, Libya, Liberia, Ethiopia, Ghana and Guinea. And 1960 is witnessing the formation of independent states in Nigeria, the Belgian Congo, French Togoland, the French Cameroons and Somalia, together with important progress in the direction of political independence by Tanganyika and Sierra Leone. Many other African territories, too, are pressing for independence in 1960 or at an early date—such as Kenya, Uganda, Nyasaland, Northern Rhodesia and Zanzibar; while the example of Guinea, in conjunction with the general advance of the movements throughout Africa, has pushed forward the African states in the French Community to demand major concessions towards independence in 1960. Only in Angola and Mozambique is there still comparative silence. But who can doubt that Salazar's rule will end there no less decisively and not much later than that of Brussels, Paris, or Westminster in the rest of Africa?

Thus the two post-war decades will go down in history as the period in which colonialism was buried in Africa and the African peoples won their political independence and formed their own, sovereign African states.

This fundamental change in the African situation stems from two main sources; the changes in the world situation, and the maturing crisis inside Africa itself.

The Second World War hastened these developments in both spheres, and thus acted as a prologue to the new stage.

The war weighed very heavily on the African people. Many parts of Africa—the Maghreb countries in the north, Egypt, Libya, Ethiopia and the Somali coast, were, to one degree or another, the arena of military operations. In other parts of the continent, Africans were called to the colours. Not always, and notably not in the Union, did the authorities trust the Africans with arms, but nevertheless the very needs of the war resulted in large numbers of them, possibly as many as a million, being armed.

[1] Egypt, which lies in the African continent, carried through a fusion with non-African Syria, to form the United Arab Republic in 1957.

The African people suffered casualties in the fighting; and in the north and in the Horn of Africa villages were destroyed, wheatlands ruined, and family life frequently shattered.

But the people did not merely suffer; they learnt, too. They were swept up into the orbit of world events, into the world-wide struggle against fascism and for democracy and national freedom. They played a part in this historic struggle and could not but be fundamentally changed by their participation. Even in the most backward areas the people's horizon was widened.

Africa emerged from the war transformed. The defeat of imperialism in Germany, Italy and Japan; the revelation that British imperialism had been totally incapable or undesirous of defending "its own" colonial people in Malaya and Burma, as French imperialism had been in Indo-China, the Dutch in Indonesia, and the Americans in the Philippines; and the key role played by the Soviet Union in defeating fascism—all this had a profound effect on the African people. No longer the same as they had been before the war, they were determined not to live any longer " in the same old way".

In the immediate post-war period, too, events outside Africa played a most important role in accelerating the growth of the African national liberation movements and hastening the death of the colonial system. The colonial system in Asia, already undermined in the course of the war, reeled under the heavy blows of the awakened Asian peoples in the post-war years. Of decisive importance was the liberation of the 600,000,000[1] people of China, whose struggle for independence, unlike that in most other Asian countries, was firmly led by its own working class. India, Burma, Indonesia, Vietnam, Laos, Cambodia, Malaya, Korea—all were scenes of great national upheavals and even of the most bitter fighting against the former imperialist rulers. To one degree or another, all these countries made big advances in the direction of complete liberation, and direct colonial rule was swept aside. Ceylon, too, won new advances in this period.

The destruction of the colonial system in Asia, while it still left the roots of imperialism untouched in a number of countries, had a most profound effect on the African people. It showed how fragile was the colonial system—a "paper tiger" in fact—and demonstrated the invincible power of the oppressed people once

[1] In 1949: today the population is 650 million.

they are inspired to fight in unison for their own national freedom. Thus the determination to end colonialism, the demand for national independence "in our time", swept from Asia across to Africa.

Inspiration and emulation has been followed by an awareness of a common interest. The independent nations of Asia and Africa came together at Bandung in April 1955 to affirm their solidarity in the fight to end colonialism. This concerted action itself has stimulated the African people's struggle still further, for the knowledge that the majority of the people in the world are in the Afro-Asian bloc, and that they stand united against colonialism, has given to each and every nation in Asia and Africa an immense confidence in the strength of the anti-colonialist forces and in the certainty of victory in the struggle for national independence.

Of outstanding importance has been the strengthening of socialism as a world force. It is probably true that most African people do not yet fully realise the extent to which the advances of the Soviet Union, and of China and the other peoples' democracies, have decisively aided the peoples fighting against colonialism. But the growing strength of the socialist camp is the strongest anti-imperialist and anti-colonial factor in the world situation. Without the existence and aid of this camp, the people of North Korea and North Vietnam would be under the heel of imperialism today, and the imperialist aggression against Egypt in 1956 would not have been halted, nor could direct intervention by the Western powers in Iraq after the July 1958 revolution have been averted. Indirectly, too, the existence of this world force compels the imperialist powers to act with more circumspection towards the colonial peoples or those emerging from colonialism.

The winning of independence by Ghana, Guinea and other African states in the post-war period has had a further catalytic effect on the African people's struggle. Nine African states, covering one-third of the African continent, and accounting for 90,000,000 people, nearly half of the total, represents a powerful force which has acted as a constant inspiration and stimulus to the remainder. Moreover, the close working co-operation of these states, as exemplified in the Accra Conference which ended in January 1959, and the other steps that have been taken to develop solidarity and concerted action in Africa, at the United

Nations and in the world arena, makes possible the united aid of independent African states towards those still striving for their freedom. In addition to this all-African unity to be found at State and governmental level, the people's organisations, too, have drawn closer together. The African people's national political parties, as well as their trade unions, are increasingly finding forms of co-operation in their common interests, the interests of destroying colonialism in Africa.

Alongside these global and continental changes, which have influenced so much the growth of the national movements in Africa, class changes inside the different African territories have also played their part.

The speed with which the national movements in Africa have surged forward—and this is a phenomenon which daily becomes more apparent—is partly due to the very rapidity with which African society itself has been changed in this period. The destruction of African traditional agriculture, the drawing of millions into migrant wage labour, the growth of an African capitalist class—all constituting a process which is by no means complete—have undergone acceleration, particularly since the end of the Second World War. Old forms of society are collapsing and new class forces are being thrown up, forcibly and ruthlessly. And as they emerge from the crucible of colonialism they press ever more persistently against the barriers which would hold them back.

The interests of colonialism have hindered and delayed the economic development of the African territories, prevented their industrialisation, ruined their agriculture, and left them with a distorted economy. Thus all national development has been throttled and the whole people, including often the chiefs, have been hurled into the struggle for national liberation as the essential pre-condition for the advancement of their own class and sectional interests.

African Workers—the Pace Setters

The working class, as we have seen, is still a relatively small minority of the African population. Moreover, it is a young class, most workers being of the first generation. But it is a growing force—it has grown particularly during the last two decades—

and already numbers some ten millions. Most of it, it is true, is migrant labour, but labour migration has a two-fold effect. While, on the one hand, it has prevented the emergence of a permanent, stabilised, modern proletariat—and this has meant a weakening of the working-class movement—on the other hand it has resulted in the majority of African males, in large parts of Africa, having experience of wage labour at some stage or other in their lives. In the mines, on plantations, in railways, in factories and on construction sites, they have met migrants from other African territories. They have exchanged experiences, found that they suffer the same common exploitation at the hands of the same masters, and that they have the same aspirations. This has helped to develop a feeling of all-African solidarity which is a powerful force in present-day African politics.

In many cases the workers have joined trade unions, taken part in strikes, become members of political parties, taken part in political processions and demonstrations. Thus, in the busy market-of-ideas of the urban centres they have become new men, with enlarged horizons and an awareness of class interests and class solidarity, and a new national consciousness. On return to the villages they have taken with them their new-found knowledge and experience. The migrant worker is also a migrant peasant, and the African worker-peasant, with knowledge of both worlds, is able to bring to the countryside the spirit and political consciousness that has grown in the towns.

One is inevitably reminded here of Lenin's observations regarding the influence of the Russian workers on the peasants in the period leading up to the Russian revolution of 1905:

". . . a 'striker' was of the people; he belonged to the exploited class; when deported from St. Petersburg, he often returned to the village where he told his fellow-villagers of the conflagration which had broken out in the cities and which was to destroy the capitalists and nobility. A new type appeared in the Russian village—the class-conscious, young peasant. He associated with 'strikers', he read newspapers, he told the peasants about events in the cities, explained to his fellow-villagers the meaning of political demands, and called upon them to fight against the big landlords, the priests and the government officials.

"The peasants would gather in groups to discuss their conditions, and gradually they were drawn into the struggle."[1]

A similar process of returned workers revolutionising the outlook of those left behind in the rural areas has taken place in Africa. While there are obvious differences between Russia in 1905 and Africa in 1960 (both as regards the type of revolutionary development and in relation to the stage reached in each case), yet fundamentally Lenin's observations have a significance for Africa, too.

In a sense, they are even more true of Africa, for labour migration exists on such a large scale that millions are involved in this cycle of movement which brings with it a heightening of political consciousness. Thus the very migrant-labour system, the curse of Africa, becomes the basis for an alliance between workers and peasants, the essential foundation for a powerful national liberation movement.

To maintain their rule over the African workers and to continue their system of exploitation, the imperialists have established autocratic rule, introduced pass laws, enacted anti-strike legislation, clamped down a system of racial discrimination which eats into every political, social and economic aspect of the people's lives, and, even when compelled to make some small concessions in the franchise, have hedged them around with so many educational and property qualifications as to exclude practically the whole of the working class. The restrictions on the normal functioning of trade unions which exist in almost all territories in Africa (Guinea being the only real exception) and the lack of political rights have only served to make the African workers understand more clearly the connection between politics and their own miserable conditions of life and labour. Twentieth-century Africa, especially in the 1950s and 1960s, is very much a political Africa.

The very conditions under which they live act as a most rapid educator of the African workers. Every day of their lives they come up against the realities of European exploitation. Ironically enough, the very absence of large African companies —a natural consequence of colonial oppression—turns the

[1] Lenin, V. I.: "Lecture on the 1905 Revolution", *Selected Works*, vol. iii, p. 8, London, 1936.

African workers in an anti-imperialist direction. It is the European monopolies who pay them starvation wages and resist their demands for a better life. It is the European rulers who daily insult and humiliate them in a thousand and one different ways. It is the European government officials and advisers who back up the employers against the workers and their unions. When the workers go on strike against their shameful conditions, it is European-run newspapers which distort their case and European-led police and troops who fire on the strikers, and arrest their leaders. European warders control the prisons, and if the arrested worker is lucky enough to come up for trial, it is a European judge who passes sentence. Thus the politics of national independence are driven into the heads of the African workers by their everyday experiences. They cannot avoid it. Starvation wages, national humiliation, batons, bullets, prison—this is commonplace experience for so many workers that inevitably they soon come to realise that no fundamental change in their lives, no social and economic advance, is possible without *political* change, and that the essence of this political change must be national freedom and the ending of the rule of the white overlords.

In Africa, where so many have gone to work at some time or other, and where frontiers are crossed so often by workers seeking employment, the migrant-labour system has become a yeast fermenting not only dissatisfaction but an ever wider and deepening understanding. The knowledge, the experience, the bitterness and the determination spreads. Unity grows apace, and out of this growing anger, this shared bitter discontent, arises a solidarity of a new kind—a class solidarity intertwined with a strong feeling of common national bonds: "We are all Africans, with common interests. We suffer the same exploitation and the same misery. We are oppressed by the same enemy, imperialism, and strive for the same goals—freedom, national independence, a decent standard of living, and respect for ourselves, for our personality as Africans who demand the same rights as those enjoyed by other peoples."

The experience of the African working class, the growth of their understanding and of their organisations, and the great struggles they have waged have, in a very real sense, been the forerunners of the present national movements which are sweeping the continent. It is above all the workers who, by their great strikes and demonstrations, have revealed to all Africans the system of imperialist exploitation under which they live, have inspired and encouraged the whole people by their determination and self-sacrifice, and have shaken up the whole imperialist edifice by their repeated blows against their oppressors. The workers' struggles have given rich experiences to the whole people. They have revealed the real character of the colonial system, what it is, what it is prepared to do, its strength and its weakness. Above all, the experiences of the workers' battles have shown what must be done if colonialism is to be eliminated.

African Bourgeoisie

The struggles that have shaken Africa in the past decade—and that will shake her even more in the next ten years—are not purely proletarian struggles, important as may be the participation of the workers in them. They are, as we have noted, *national* movements, movements in which whole peoples are involved and in which the aim is not the particular interests of one class or section but the common aspiration of all to end imperialist rule, destroy the colonial system, and open up the way to the national development of each territory.

An important role in these movements is being played by the African bourgeoisie. It is, of course, true that the national bourgeoisie is still numerically weak in most African territories south of the Sahara, and that economically it is still not a powerful force. Its main spheres are agriculture, trading and commerce, and to some extent transport; but as an industrial and manufacturing bourgeoisie it is naturally in an embryonic stage, for, as we have already seen, industrial development in Africa is everywhere held back by imperialism, and even where it does take place, it is almost completely in the hands of European monopolies.

The small, yet growing, African capitalist class cannot but find itself constantly at loggerheads with the colonial system. As a capitalist class it is naturally concerned with profits. To make profits, it needs control of its own domestic market, and it needs, too, a considerable expansion of that market. No less, it requires to build up its own industry in order to make the goods to supply to that market. But everywhere the African bourgeoisie turns it finds the imperialists holding the controls in their hands, dominating the market, owning the raw materials of which they rob the country and shipping in the manufactured goods with which they flood and monopolise the local market. Even where Africans own the raw materials, such as cash crops (only rarely do they own minerals), they find themselves at a great disadvantage, for the imperialist monopolies, which control the world markets, compel the African growers to sell their crops at a low price but to pay highly for the manufactured goods which they need to purchase.

Recent figures[1] show that 85 per cent of all Ghana's import trade is in the hands of European firms (mainly British), another 10 per cent is in the hands of Asians (Indian, Syrian and Lebanese), leaving at most 5 per cent in Ghanaian hands. Thus, in the field of trade, a main sphere of African capitalist endeavour and a starting-point for its further growth as a class, African enterprise cannot escape the reality of Western monopoly domination. Only recently a delegation of local businessmen in Northern Nigeria called on the Trade Minister of the Northern Nigerian government, demanding that the government prevent foreign firms from taking part in retail trade in the local markets and villages. Such expressions of conflict between imperialism and the African capitalists occur constantly.

But it is not only through their control of trade within the African territories that the imperialists restrict the growth of African capitalism. By their domination of world markets they are able to manipulate prices in a way which reacts most unfavourably on the African territories. Forced to "sell cheap and buy dear", African territories are robbed of millions of pounds a year through this unequal exchange. This open theft—referred to euphemistically as "unfavourable terms of trade"—enables super-profits to be made by Western monopolies, and is a root cause of African poverty. And the very poverty of the African people becomes a further preoccupation of the African bourgeoisie, for the abysmally low purchasing power restricts severely the market which African producers wish to expand.

Just as African producer and trader comes up against the imperialist monopolies and the colonial system within the sphere of trade, so, too, in the sphere of production, especially industrial production, there is the same conflict.

[1] *Report of the United Kingdom Trade and Industrial Mission to Ghana, 1959.*

Explaining how Guinea was exploited by imperialism, Sékou Touré has pointed out that the colonial system was not interested solely in raw materials.

". . . it meant even more to keep for itself the exclusive right in the sale of manufactured products. *Accordingly, it opposed all attempts at industrialisation.* We can draw up an inventory of all the industries of transformation existing in the countries under colonial rule, compare their production in manufactured articles with the needs of the populations, and we shall clearly see that there is no common measure between supply and demand. In this field, the colonial system reserved for itself the privilege, almost the monopoly, of the market of consumer goods in colonised countries."[1]　　　　[Own italics—J. W.]

Even in a territory such as Nigeria, the biggest African state with some thirty-five to forty million people, a relatively strong national bourgeoisie, and shortly to become politically independent, the efforts of African capital to grow are constantly thwarted by the British companies which keep a firm monopoly in most fields of economic activity. These companies are aided by the dominance throughout the government apparatus of British civil servants who, it is constantly alleged in Nigeria, show favour to such companies.

One recent bone of contention has been shipping. Nigeria has established the Nigerian National Shipping Line, but this line has joined the British-controlled West Africa Conference Lines, an action which has aroused considerable indignation in the country. In criticising this situation, the *West African Pilot* said:[2]

"We made a wrong choice of partners for our shipping line . . . for reasons that should be obvious to all. For ten years we have been shouting and groaning about the menace to the economy of our country posed by the Conference Lines. We did say that their monopoly of ocean traffic and of government produce was inimical to our interests."

[1] Touré, Sékou: "Towards Full Re-Africanisation," speech to the Congress of the Guinea Democratic Party, Conakry, September 14, 1959. (*Présence Africaine*, pp. 43–4, Paris, 1959.)
[2] *West African Pilot*, April 27, 1959.

By joining the West Africa Shipping Lines, declared this paper, the Nigerian National Shipping Line was allowing itself "to be led by the nose by British officials".

Another Lagos paper,[1] accusing the British shipping companies who run the Conference Lines of establishing a monopoly over the Nigerian shipping trade, alleged that British shipping companies made use of their influence with British officials in the Federal Government to achieve their objectives. Added point to this latter charge was soon provided by the events which accompanied the resignation of Mr. J. H. D. Singleton, who had been head of the Nigerian Ministry of Transport at the time the agreement was concluded between the National Shipping Line and the British shipping companies. It was alleged by the *West African Pilot*[2] that Mr. Singleton returned to London on May 10, 1959, with a gratuity of £8,000 for his retirement—and then took employment at the London office of the National Shipping Line. How damaging to Nigerian interests is this shipping agreement can be judged from the statement[3] that the Nigerian share of the profits of the Conference Line will be only two per cent. Understandable, therefore, is the *Daily Service* description of the agreement as a "wolf and lamb partnership".

Similar criticisms have been made regarding the Nigerian Government's decision to use diesel oil for the Electricity Corporation of Nigeria and the Railway Corporation instead of locally produced coal. This, too, it is argued, has been done to favour foreign interests at the expense of Nigeria's own economic development. Constant criticisms have been made in Nigeria regarding the tendency of the Government to place contracts with British firms instead of with local ones, as was done, for example, in ordering soldiers' clothing.

The *West African Pilot*[4] has alleged that a department head who awarded a two-million-pound contract to a firm would find himself, upon retirement, a director or executive employee of the beneficiary of the contract. This paper has stated that no less than ten former top civil servants held interests in or were directly connected by way of employment with private concerns

---

[1] *Daily Service*, April 29, 1959.
[2] *West African Pilot*, May 21, 1959.
[3] *Daily Service*, July 31, 1959.
[4] *West African Pilot*, May 21, 1959.

with which their departments had dealings during their period of office.

This is one of the reasons why Africanisation of government departments is such a sharp and insistent demand throughout Africa, even in those countries which have already won their political independence.

Thus the colonial system weighs heavily on the African capitalists who are consequently impelled to raise the banner of national independence in order to further their own class aims and develop the national economy.

However, although cribbed, cabined and confined by the colonial system, the African capitalist class has nevertheless become stronger, especially in the post-war period. In Nigeria, for example, in addition to farming, trade, banking and commerce, a considerable share of road transport is in the hands of African entrepreneurs, albeit small-scale. (This, incidentally, is also true of Ghana.) Foreign transport firms in Nigeria still dominate the freight trade, servicing both import and export needs, but African firms dominate in passenger traffic and in the carriage of internal trade.[1] Despite foreign competition, says Hawkins, the African capitalist "has asserted himself, notably in the field of road transport, but also in retail trade, building and contracting".[2] Hawkins shows how the steps towards independence have given new opportunities to African enterprises, "which have grown in size and number". A number of light industries have begun to develop, including tyre-retreading, woodworking, the supply of building materials, and printing, in which "a number of Africans have become prominent".

The growth of the African bourgeoisie is also particularly marked in Ghana, of course, and in certain regions of French West Africa, notably the Ivory Coast. It is noticeable, too, in Uganda and, to a somewhat lesser degree, in Kenya and Tanganyika, where one should not ignore the effect of land-consolidation schemes in these territories which have made possible the emergence of a stratum of African freehold farmers growing coffee and other cash crops. In the Belgian Congo, the Union of South Africa, and in the Central African Federation, it has been extremely difficult for an African capitalist

[1] Hawkins, E. K.: *Road Transport in Nigeria*, London, 1958.
[2] ibid., p. 93.

class to appear. Yet even here African enterprises have emerged, despite political and legal limitations. "For example, in the Union of South Africa," says Hawkins,[1] "African-owned transport firms have become established to serve the market created by the development of African urban areas."

Generally speaking, however, the African bourgeoisie is a weak force *vis-à-vis* imperialism, especially in east, central and southern Africa.

But, despite its weakness, it is a force which has entered the political arena and which has begun to play an important part in the national movement. In fact, in many territories it is taking a leading role and exercises a political influence far in excess of its numerical or economic strength. Even in those territories where the African bourgeoisie is weakest, and where the movements tend to be led by doctors, teachers or lawyers, these professional and petty-bourgeois sections reflect much more the outlook and class aspirations of a would-be national bourgeoisie than they do of the workers and peasants who constitute the majority and the main force of the national movement.

This influence of the national bourgeoisie over the whole movement, including, to a considerable degree, over the working-class and trade-union movement, arises partly from the fact that the imperialist rulers give a certain encouragement to this class, in the hope that it will be more ready to compromise, and partly owing to the stage reached by the African working-class movement, which has not yet been able to develop its own political party nor to create, on a wide scale, a clear-cut, defined and mature class outlook, as distinct from a purely anti-imperialist one.

African Intelligentsia

The post-war period has also seen an increase in the number of African intellectuals. The African people have made heroic efforts to secure education for themselves, even on occasions setting up their own schools to make up for the appalling deficiencies in official education for Africans. Many an African mother has slaved from morn to night doing domestic work, taking in laundry, making some native brew on the side, all to earn money to give her son an education. Something of the heart-

[1] ibid., p. 92.

breaking sacrifices which this entails have been described with great vividness and poignancy by Ezekiel Mphalele in his *Down Second Avenue*. Kwame Nkrumah worked as a dish-washer in the United States in order to complete his education. Dr. Hastings Banda walked hundreds of miles, as a young man, from his native Nyasaland, to seek education in the Union of South Africa and later to complete it overseas. Many a national leader in Africa can tell similar stories.

Cultural organisations have come into existence and national newspapers been started in the past twenty years. Some institutions for higher education have been set up in a number of African territories, and this too has resulted in an increase in the number of African intellectuals—although as far as the British, or former British possessions are concerned, it is noticeable that it is in Ghana and Nigeria, where more control over such matters has passed to the African people themselves, that the most progress has been recorded.

Of course, the imperialists, in their hope of encouraging a section of educated, "responsible" Africans who would act as political allies, have unavoidably played a certain role in the establishment of higher education. But it has been for a handful only—and its aim has been to turn out an African photograph of a European original, rather than to assist the cultural progress of the African people themselves.

Sékou Touré has well explained the dilemma of the African intellectual, nurtured and taught by imperialism in a manner deliberately designed to separate him from his own culture and his own people.

"Not only did the education that was given us tend to assimilate us, depersonalise us, westernise us, present to us our civilisation, our culture, our own sociological and philosophical conceptions, in a word our humanism, as the expression of a savage, only half-conscious primitiveness in order to create in us the multiple complexes that would lead us to become more French than the French themselves, but even more beside these phenomena, there was, in the concrete field of the position of this intellectual *élite*, a series of advantages and guarantees that were things absolutely foreign to the life of the immense majority of the people and which constituted, compared with the conditions of this people, preferential conditions."[1]

Ezekiel Mphahlele, too, in his thoughtful essay on the African intelligentsia,[2] has pointed out that in the colonies of Africa "the British administration has a quiet way of according such special treatment to the educated African as to cut him off from the masses".

But as against this tendency, Mphahlele has noted its opposite, the gradual identification of the African intellectual (especially in those territories in southern, eastern and central Africa where white settler domination and extreme racial discrimination exists) with the African masses and with the struggle for national independence and advancement:

"The enlightened African looks around him, and according to the degree of his sensitivity perceives the meaning of his position in relation to the masses. He engages in certain intellectual and cultural pursuits in order to adjust himself and to remove whatever obstacles undermine his dignity. At a certain point the bare economic motive to survive merges into the political and cultural motives.

"This is the road the educated African travels in Southern Africa and in Kenya, where the problems of co-existence between black and white are similar in most respects. Here, he is being resisted by the minority group which has entrenched itself economically and politically and which cannot bear the thought of competing against an overwhelming number of black people. He is regarded as a menace. He is victimised, banned, deported or confined to his home town. In many cases he abandons the struggle and leaves it to hardier ones."

Yet, for every one who abandons the struggle, there are others to take his place. For colonialism, in its own way, presses just as heavily on the African intellectual as it does on the worker, the peasant and the African farmer and capitalist. As Mphahlele

---

[1] Touré, Sékou: "Towards Full Re-Africanisation," op. cit., pp. 9–10.
[2] Mphahlele, Ezekiel: "The Dilemma of the African Elite," *Twentieth Century*, April 1959, pp. 319–25.

rightly says, "the white settler fears and resists the educated African and goes out of his way to humiliate him, to deny him the things education gives him the aspirations for, to reduce him economically below the level of the illiterate, and politically to the same level. Thus in a multi-racial community the black man cannot be apprenticed as an artisan or dentist or pharmacist, because neither the law nor the white trade unions will let him. . . . The doctor would not be allowed to examine white patients in a hospital. The clerk who holds a matriculation or some commercial certificate becomes an ordinary messenger. At best, he is given a pencil and note-book to keep an account of the stock in a wholesale warehouse."

The African intellectual or professional worker, under such conditions, is reduced, says Mphahlele, "to the position of a puppet" and forbidden "even to protest against his professional limitations".

The humiliations, insults and indignities suffered daily by African intellectuals cannot but play their part in impelling them towards involvement in the struggles of the whole people. When white doctors from Southern Rhodesia came to work in Nyasaland, following on Federation, they insisted on African doctors no longer being permitted to wear white medical coats, as they had done previously. Frequently the trained African, with many years' experience behind him, sees a raw, white recruit step ahead of him—at several times the rate of pay. The struggle for the Africanisation of government departments in Ghana, Nigeria, Sudan—and soon to open out in other territories—is one long story of stubborn resistance by entrenched interests against ending a situation of white privilege based on no other considerations than those of racial discrimination.

A petition sent to the Nigerian Ministry of Communications in May 1959 by the Telecommunications Technical Officers' Union complaining of the delay in Nigerianising the service, pointed out that in an establishment of twenty-four technical specialists only one was Nigerian; and in an establishment of fifty-eight chief technical officers there were only six Nigerians despite the fact that there was a good number of Nigerians whose training, qualifications and experience both in London and Lagos were in no way inferior to those possessed by the Europeans in these grades. Similarly, complaining of the limited number of supernumerary posts given to Nigerians in the customs department, the Lagos *Daily Service* alleged that the simple reason was that the Customs Authority was making room for all the Europeans to be promoted before promoting Africans.[1] The criticisms voiced in Nigeria against the delay in promoting Africans into various positions of responsibility in the different government departments became so pronounced in 1959 that a special committee was set up to enquire into the whole matter. The committee's report, which declared that "until the indigenous nature of the government itself is truly reflected in public service, independence has very little meaning", proved the contentions of the critics right up to the hilt.

Thus the African intellectual is subject to two opposing influences. On the one hand the imperialists try to suborn and seduce him by offering him small privileges and by smothering his national pride and loyalty through a subtle and deliberate process of de-Africanisation and of Westernisation. On the other hand, because imperialism is anxious to retain all the key strings in its own hands, and because white settlers want all the plums of office and profession, the African intellectual finds his ambitions, both for himself and for his people as a whole, constantly thwarted and frustrated. Thus he comes to realise that neither his own personal or sectional interests nor the total culture of his people can be advanced while colonialism and imperialist rule continues. It is the two-fold nature of the pressures on African intellectuals—to have privileges over the rest of his people, yet be subordinated to the European rulers—that explains the hesitations, indecisions, or sudden shifts of position from one extreme to another which so often characterise their role in the national movement. Yet their influence is a very important one, and there is not a single national political party of the African people, in any of the territories, in which intellectuals will not be found playing a significant and often leading role.

One has only to enumerate some of Africa's most prominent national figures—Dr. Nkrumah, Dr. Banda, Dr. Chirwa, Dr. Kiano, Dr. Moumie, Julius Nyerere, Jomo Kenyatta, Kenneth Kaunda, Leopold Senghor, Gabriel d'Arboussier, and so on—to see how important is this participation.

Thus workers, capitalists, intellectuals—all have been drawn

[1] *Daily Service*, August 7, 1959.

into the African liberation movement in the past few decades, and especially since the end of the Second World War.

Agrarian Crisis

What of the rural African, the destitute land-hungry peasant, and the cash-cropping farmer? For these constitute the majority of the African people. As we have seen, sixty years of imperialism has dealt them devastating blows. Much of the African countryside lies in ruins. The villages and Reserves are largely populated by women, children and old people. Soil erosion spreads like a foul disease, and on his dwindling lands the African peasant sinks deeper and deeper into poverty. His very poverty becomes an additional barrier to economic development, preventing him buying implements or seeds to improve his farming, denying him the possibilities of fertilisers or irrigation projects and periodically compelling him to abandon his poor fields to seek wage labour in European mines, plantations or urban enterprises.

The widespread agrarian crisis in Africa, which is a natural consequence of colonial rule, has been to some extent concealed by the migrant-labour system, just as emigration over the years has successfully masked the agrarian crisis in Eire.

One result of this is that the African peasantry has not yet taken part in the national movement as a separate, conscious and organised political force. No large-scale, sustained peasant revolts have taken place in Africa as they did, for instance, between the two world wars, in China, Burma, the Philippines, Indo-China and Indonesia, although there have been, in the last thirty years, a number of local, sporadic outbursts in Africa, often against taxation or land seizures by European settlers.

The African peasant has, in the main, done his fighting against imperialism in the towns, as a migrant worker.

Thus it is that the names associated with the history of Africa's anti-colonial struggles are mainly those of urban or mining centres—Accra, Lagos, Enugu, Jos, Johannesburg, Mombasa, Nairobi, Dar-es-Salaam, Tanga, Wankie, the Copper Belt, Douala, Dakar, Conakry, Leopoldville, Freetown, and Bathurst. Only more recently, as in Kenya after the 1952 emergency, in the French Cameroons in the past few years, in Sekhukhuneland and Zeerust in the Union of South Africa, and in Central Africa, has the rural African, *as a peasant*, begun to be drawn more directly into the anti-imperialist struggle.

Even the better-off African farmer, growing cash crops for an export market, lives in constant fear and insecurity, his life dominated by the big imperialist monopolies who determine the price they will pay him for his crops and the price he must pay for the manufactured goods he needs to purchase.

"The colonial firms", writes Sékou Touré,[1] "had come to control the market of our goods. They regulated the purchases; they determined the fluctuations in the quotations; they had full charge of the sales. Once the goods had been produced, the Guinean farmer had no alternative than to submit to the masters of the market."

The same difficulty faces African farmers in every territory under imperialist rule. In every direction they turn they come up against the realities of white domination—their best land taken by white settlers, or given as concessions to big European monopolies, the imposition of restrictions regarding what they may grow, how they may market their crop and the price they will get for it, denied the right to move freely throughout the land of their birth—in every way oppressed by conditions from which there is no escape while imperialism continues its rule.

The Chief Becomes a Shuttlecock

There is an assumption among many people that all African chiefs are on the side of reaction, that they represent the forces of feudalism and tribalism and are therefore hostile to the struggle for African independence. Many chiefs do, of course, play such a role, not only relatively powerful ones in West African territories, but even lesser chiefs who are often mere government appointees. But to dismiss all African chiefs as reactionaries would be a distortion of fact.

From the very start of Africa's resistance to European imperialism there have been kings and chiefs who led their people in opposition to foreign rule. Yet it was not merely in the first stage of resistance to imperial conquest that many chiefs played

[1] Touré, Sékou: "Towards Full Re-Africanisation," op. cit., p. 43.

a progressive role. Throughout the twentieth century there have been examples of chiefs siding with their people against particular exactions or acts of repression by the authorities, especially in defence of land or in opposition to taxes. When, for example, in 1905 the Natal Government decided for the first time to impose the poll tax on the Zulus, widespread protests arose despite Chief Dinizulu, who "set an example" by paying the £1 tax and appealing to his impoverished people to do the same. In contrast to Dinizulu, one minor chief, Bambata, took to the bushes with thousands of men, and defied the authorities. The government replied with machine-guns, and in the ensuing massacre four thousand Africans, including Chief Bambata, were killed.

Seven years later the African National Congress was born at Bloemfontein, and among its first supporters were a number of chiefs—Maama, Seise, Molema, Sekukini and others. P.Ka Isaka Seme, who actually summoned the first Congress, regarded the chiefs as being the real initiators of the Congress. This judgment is, perhaps, too sweeping, since the leading forces in the 1912 Congress were, in fact, middle-class intellectuals. But Seme is undoubtedly correct to stress the important role played by the chiefs in establishing the A.N.C.

Notwithstanding these examples, it can be said, broadly speaking, that for the first half of this century imperialism was able to make use of the institution of chiefs for its own ends. The introduction of indirect rule, combined with the deposition of unwilling chiefs, and backed by imperialist arms, proved sufficient in this period to preserve the colonial system.

In the last decade, however, as the movement for national independence has grown stronger, and as the issues around which this struggle is being fought have pressed sharper and sharper, so have the chiefs found themselves, in a number of cases, placed in an acute dilemma.

In many territories the use of chiefs, converted into paid Civil Servants to act as imperial puppets who would hold the African people in check, is no longer possible to the extent that it was in the past. Chief A. Luthuli, President-General of the African National Congress in the Union of South Africa, is only one of a number of chiefs in the Union who have taken a similar stand on the issue of the struggle for national freedom against white domination. For his courageous leadership of the African

National Congress Chief Luthuli has been under constant attack and harassment by the Union Government. The same fate has overtaken Chief Jeremiah Mabe, who was banished to Vryburg in January 1956, for his opposition to the Bantu Education Scheme and to the Bantu Authorities' "betterment and grazing" schemes. Similarly, Twalimfene Joyi, a member of the Tembu Royal House and Chief Bangilizwe Joyi were both deported to remote areas after they had gone with a delegation from Tembu-land to the offices of the Bantu Affairs Department in Pretoria to raise objections to the imposition of Bantu Authorities on the Transkei.

In Tanganyika it is claimed by the Tanganyika Africa National Union that not a single chief now supports the government; all are supporters of TANU. In Kenya the recently deceased Chief Koinange remains as an everlasting symbol of chiefly opposition to British rule.

In Nyasaland many chiefs have repeatedly shown their readi-ness to support their people's struggle for independence, especially in their opposition to Federation. Indicative of their important role was the appointment of Chief Gomani as head of the "supreme council of action", a body set up to co-ordinate the efforts of the trade unions, the Congress and the peasants against Federation. For his leadership in the campaign and for advising his people to take part in civil disobedience, he was arrested, but escaped to Mozambique. There he was apprehended by the Portuguese authorities, sent back to Nyasaland in handcuffs and suspended from his chieftainship, only to die in banishment shortly afterwards.

The dilemma of the chiefs today, and the attitude taken by many of them in Nyasaland towards the national struggle of their people is well expressed in a letter in which Chief M'Mbelwa explained to Kanyama Chiume his opposition to Federation:

"I am a Paramount Chief of 190,000 people, and how foolish I would be to support the Government and be pleased to see my people being terrorised with guns and shot! *Can I be a Paramount Chief of dead bodies?*"[1] [Own italics—J. W.]

Such forceful arguments help to explain why the Nyasaland

[1] Sanger, Clyde: *Central African Emergency*, p. 9, London, 1960.

Chief's Union, at a meeting in 1953, called upon "all Chiefs and people in the Protectorate to support Congress and seek its advice in all matters concerning the development of this country". In the opinion of Clutton-Brock "This alliance between Chiefs and Congress remains as strong although it cannot now always be open."[1]

In Northern Rhodesia many chiefs have adopted a similar position, and have even helped the African copper miners when they were on strike. Only recently the Northern Rhodesian Government took drastic measures against the Bemba people, decentralising its administration and reducing the power and authority of the Paramount Chief, Chitimukulu, because of the "unyielding opposition" of the latter "to the imposition of Federation".[2]

Nor in Southern Rhodesia can the government rely on the total support of the chiefs. When the Royal African Rifles returned to Salisbury from their war-time service during the Second World War and were cheered through the streets, the procession ended with a meeting in the township which was addressed by Chief Nyandero, of the Chieta Reserve. Instead of uttering the pious platitudes which are habitual on such occasions, Chief Nyandero shocked the white rulers of his country by asking the embarrassing question: "You have taken our sons to be killed. What do we get in exchange?"

Six months after posing this pointed but justified question, Chief Nyandero was deposed by the Southern Rhodesian Government from his Chieta chieftaincy.[3] It is, perhaps, not entirely without significance, that his nephew George Nyandero, was later to become the secretary-general of the Southern Rhodesian African National Congress.

In many other territories the same trend is to be noticed of chiefs turning away from the imperialist governments; while those who remain "loyal" to their white rulers become so discredited that their utility and effectiveness is extremely limited.

The dilemma of the chiefs in this new situation is well explained in the fate of Chief Nsokolo, whose conflict with imperialism has been admirably dealt with by Watson in his study[4] of the

[1] Clutton-Brock, Guy: *Dawn in Nyasaland*, p. 52, London, 1959.
[2] *Observer*: August 30, 1959.
[3] Sanger, Clyde: op. cit., p. 28.
[4] Watson, William: *Tribal Cohesion in a Money Economy*, Manchester University Press, 1958.

Mambwe people in Northern Rhodesia. The position of the chief, explains Watson, is not simple. He plays, in fact, a dual role.

"He is an agent of the British administration and the main instrument for the implementation of British policy; at the same time he is the representative of his people to the British, and the guardian and spokesman of what they (his people) consider to be their interests."[1]

When the inevitable conflict between these two sets of loyalties arises, the chief "is compelled either to find a compromise acceptable to both sides, or to identify himself with one of them". But this is where the dilemma and the crisis arises for the chief. "Complete identification with the British will deprive him of the respect of his people and thereby undermine his authority, and consequently his usefulness as an agent to the British; identification with his own people against the British will endanger his tenure of office."

The chief is regarded by the people as their spokesman, especially in relation to the defence of their land. Within the context of the sharpening situation in Northern Rhodesia in the past few years, aggravated by the imposition of Federation, with its further threat to the African people's economic situation, both as migrant workers and as peasants, the chief's position has become more and more acute. He is, rightly, says Watson, "*at the point of contact between two systems which are becoming increasingly hostile*".[2] The conflict which led to Nsokolo's dismissal by the British was expressed in three directions. First, Mambwe people who had been drawn into wage labour joined trade unions, and took part in demonstrations and other activities in urban centres against the colour bar, including strike action against the idea of Federation. Second, many joined the African National Congress which, in addition to supporting the actions of the workers, made political appeals to Britain where it tried to influence public opinion and Parliament. Lastly, the peasants defied the agricultural and fishing regulations of the British authorities, at the call of their chief. Chief Nsokolo identified himself with this

[1] ibid., p. 187.
[2] ibid., p. 188.

whole struggle. He, with other chiefs, openly supported the
Congress and collected funds for their activities. Further, he
supported the strike action taken in the industrial field as a
protest against Federation. And, "encouraged by his people", he
supported, too, the defiance of the agricultural regulations.

"Industrial strikes and agricultural defiance," says Watson,[1]
"were the two final sanctions that Africans could employ
against the Whites, and both were political actions. The people
forced Nsokolo to take action as their representative."

And, as a result, the British authorities deposed Nsokolo.

This conflict between imperialism and the Mambwe people is
indicative of a new stage, in which the strains and stresses of
office are making it more and more difficult for the chiefs in a
number of territories of Africa to fail to identify themselves with
the movement of the people against colonial rule.

Chief Abram Moiloa, of the royal village of Dinokana, in the
Zeerust district of the Transvaal, in the Union of South Africa,
suffered the same fate as Chief Nsokolo. He, too, was deposed by
the authorities; in this case the deposition arose out of the refusal
of the African women in the Reserve to take passes.

Chief Abram's problem, and his attempt to solve it by neither
supporting nor opposing, is well explained by Father Hooper in
his description of Chief Abram's statement to a meeting of his
people on the question of passes for women. Abram produced his
own pass book and said:

" 'I am required to carry a pass. Now the law demands
that you bear them too. This law is not a tribal law. It is the
law of the Government. It is not a law of my promulgating.
I know nothing of this law. I tell you only what I am bidden
to tell you. The matter rests between you and the white
authorities. Consider well how you intend to act. ' "[2]

And, with that said, he left the meeting.

This attempt on the part of Chief Abram to stay "between
two fires" did not, and could not succeed. The authorities
demanded of him more than the mere passing on of their laws.

[1] ibid., p. 219.
[2] Hooper, Charles: *Brief Authority*, p. 152, London, 1960.

They expected him to *enforce* these enactments. And because he refused to do so, he was ruthlessly, and against all traditional custom, deposed by the Chief Regional Commissioner.

The deposition of Chief Abram faced the chiefs of the lesser villages with a severe crisis. They were made fully aware, says Father Hooper, of the strength of their women's opposition to accepting passes; and, at the same time, "they were left in no doubt about the lengths to which the Native Affairs Department was prepared to go" to impose the passes.

Thus the chiefs were placed in an almost impossible position, caught up in the contradiction inherent in the system of indirect rule at a time of sharpened crisis.

> "To whom did they owe their allegiance?" asks Father Hooper. "To their people, whom they were expected to govern peaceably, whose wishes they were by tribal tradition bound to consider and respect, and whom they were supposed to serve as well as rule? To the Native Affairs Department whose minions they were, and in whose name, according to laws passed in a white man's Parliament, they exercised their function?"[1]

Were they to be defenders of their own people's interests, or upholders of Verwoerd and his laws? They could not be both, though for some time a number of them tried to be so. In the final resort, they had to come down on one side or the other. Either they opposed the wishes of the Native Affairs Department and so ran the risk of being deposed, as Chief Abram had been; or they did what the authorities required—which would cost them the support of their own aroused people.

> 'The chiefs had not sought the conflict between the two; but nor could they evade it. *They were the meeting ground of inimical forces. They represented authority derived from two different sources, and the sources themselves were at variance.*"[2]
>
> [Own italics—J. W.]

The Native Affairs Department insisted that the women take passes—but the women refused.

[1] ibid., p. 169.
[2] ibid., p. 170.

"Between these two millstones the chieftainship, in its traditional sense, was ground to powder. . . "[1]   [Own italics—J. W.]

The crisis facing the chiefs in the Union is not confined to Zeerust, nor to the issue of passes for women. It is not even a crisis for South Africa alone. It is a much wider problem, created by the sweep of the African national movement which is washing away the entire edifice of indirect rule all over the continent. As long as the struggle was at a more elementary stage, when the issues were not so sharp and clear nor the whole people yet drawn into battle, the system of indirect rule or native administration as a prop of imperialism was workable. But the strains and stresses have become too great. Now in this territory, now in that, the chiefs face the parting of the ways. To ally themselves with the new upsurge, or to remain with the sinking ship of colonialism? There is no third path.

"The focus of tribal order, the chief, becomes a shuttlecock. The order collapses."[2]   [Own italics—J. W.]

Yes, the order collapses. Not yet entirely or everywhere in the year 1960. But speaking historically, and looking at the whole period of imperialist rule in Africa up to the present great revolt against colonialism, it is clear that the use of chiefs as a mainstay of Western rule in Africa, is dying. Some, of course, will remain with their colonial masters to the bitter end. Some, too, will try and evade the responsibility of choice even at this late hour. Some will resist authority—and be deposed. Others will attempt to hold back progress—and find their powers virtually destroyed by the forces of African independence, as in Guinea and Ghana. But in no territory, no matter what attitude they adopt, can the chiefs any longer be regarded as safe or reliable subalterns of imperialism. For them, too, the old world is dying.

The African People Are Standing Up

Thus Africans, as a whole, have reached the point of no return. The old life has been destroyed—and there can be no going back.

[1] ibid., p. 171
[2] ibid., p. 150.

Africa has been drawn inexorably into the money economy by the forcible actions of imperialism. The destruction of old classes and the formation of new ones is going ahead.

The system of imperialist exploitation and colonialism has brought the African people to the edge of the abyss. It has produced a discontented proletariat, a ruined peasantry, a cramped bourgeoisie and a thwarted intelligentsia.

It has become impossible for the majority of Africans to find a haven and security on the land. Nor can they find security in wage labour in the mines, plantations and urban areas. Like Ishmael, they wander from countryside to town and back. But nowhere is there any hope.

The African intelligentsia and the emergent capitalists, too, find at every turn that their aspirations and advancement are checked. For them, too, colonialism offers little hope.

This shared conviction of all progressive classes in African society, the recognition that only through their joint struggle can they succeed in defeating their common enemy, engenders national feeling and speeds up the national consolidation of the peoples. Tribal loyalties, though still not without influence and utilised very often by imperialism for reactionary ends, are melting in the crucible of the anti-colonial struggle. The concentration of large masses of African people in towns and mining centres, the development of capitalist relations right in the heart of African society, the creation of national and class organisations which group people together independently of any parochial or tribal affiliations—all this is breaking down tribal barriers. National and class interests have now come to the fore, and nations are being formed. Class interests and aspirations have become merged with national interests, and the cry for national independence has been taken up by the whole people.

The people of Africa can no longer bear to go on living in the same old way. Colonialism has squeezed them dry and life has become impossible. The daily humiliations to individual and nation alike can no longer be tolerated. Held back economically, culturally, socially and politically, each class and section is driven to the inescapable conclusion that if they are to live and grow, then colonialism must go.

But equally, the imperialist rulers can no longer rule in the old way. They twist and turn to seek a solution, the rifle in one hand and the restricted ballot paper in the other. They offer a political post under white domination or tutelage, coupled with the threat of prison. While they talk of advancing the people to independence, they lock up the people's independence fighters and strive to uncover a handful of African puppets who will help them to adorn themselves with the fig-leaf of democratic respectability.

But all this cannot stop colonialism hurtling down the road to ruin and disaster. Each fresh attack on the African people, each new wave of repression, only serves to increase the anger, the bitterness, the determination and resolve of the African people to win their freedom, now, "in our time", in 1960. As it feels the ground slip beneath its feet, imperialism attempts to keep its grip by making a concession here and a concession there. But each paltry concession is taken by the African people and used as a platform for further demands, as a stepping-stone to further concessions. The imperialists hesitatingly open the door an inch, hoping to keep it that way. But once ajar, the door can no longer be shut. The African stands with his powerful, calloused foot firmly planted in the doorway, and at his back stands all the misery and horror of the hundred million who died or were taken in slavery, the centuries of massacres and robbery, the whip-lash, the death camps, the finger-printed passes, the ruthless exploitation in field and mine, the starvation, disease and illiteracy, the cultural degradation and national humiliation, the attempt to crush the African personality and maintain Africa in perpetual helotage.

But twentieth-century barbarism, with all its Western refinements, cannot determine the course of history. Africa is not going back. It is going relentlessly forward. Africa, in fact, has reached the stage of revolution—of the overthrow of colonialism.

It is now clear, on looking back, that Accra was the beginning of the end. What had been burgeoning slowly and increasingly beneath the hot soil of Africa suddenly burst forth in all its strength and majesty. *Afrika! Mayiube! Africa! Come back!*— comes the cry from the Union. *Kwacha! The Dawn!*—echo the voices in Rhodesia. *Uhuru! Freedom!*—shout Kenya, Tanganyika and Uganda. *Ablode! Liberty!*—cries Togo.

And the Welenskys and Verwoerds, the Kenya settlers and Algerian *colons*, the Belgian Baudouins and Portuguese slave-owners, the Macmillans and Macleods, turn and twist as they may in their desperate panic to hold on to their African Eldorado, cannot succeed.

They, and their would-be successors in Washington, are too late. The sands are running out. The African people are standing up. And the colonial system in Africa is doomed.

INDEX

INDEX

Aaronovitch, S. and K. 9, 20
Accra Conference, 250, 268
African Explosives and Chemicals Company, 225
Allied Ironfounders, 225
Anglo-American Corporation of South Africa, 226
Angola, education, 154; electricity, production of, 235; exports, 222, 229; forced labour, 70–73; labour migration, 86; political organisations, African, 247; population, 113; railways, 238; taxation, 51; wage workers, number of, 114; wage workers, distribution of, 118; wages, 185
Apthorpe Report, 133
Argyle, W. J., 92
Asia, colonial system undermined, 249; land, 44, 46; migration, 81
Associated Cement, 226
Australia, population of, 210
Agriculture, African traditional, 16–20; African traditional, break-up of, 10–13, 16–24, 24–29, 46–47; cash crops, 37–43, 213–214, 221–225; European, in competition with African, 8–12

Banda, Dr. Hastings, 261, 264
Bandung Conference, 250
Bank of West Africa, 36 225
Barclays Bank, 225
Basutoland,Basotho National Party, 226; cash crops, 37; Congress Party, 226, 227; diamond mining, 227; labour migration, 81, 83, 104; land, 34; malnutrition, 167; population, 112
Batson, Professor E., 192
Batten, T. R., 31, 32, 33, 34, 35, 37, 38, 39, 40, 41, 42, 180, 216
echuanaland, cash crops, 37; education and literacy, 154; labour

migration, 83, 84, 85, 86, 90, 96, 97, 98, 104, 106, 116; population, 112; taxation, 49, 53, 57, 59; traditional economy, 10–11
Beira, Bishop of, 75
Belgian Congo, Abake Party, 247; African Solidarity Party, 247; agriculture, 224; bourgeoise, growth of, 259; children, condition of, 137; Congolese National Movement, 247; disease, 174; electricity, production of, 235, 236; exports, 222; forced labour, 65, 67; income, average annual, 210; independence of, 248; Katanga, 135, 136; labour, efficiency of, 151, 163; migration, 86, 88, 89, 90, 107; labour, stabilisation of, 106, 132, 133, 135, 136; labour, turnover of, 100; land, 2, 18; education and literacy, 154, 156, 158; minerals, production, 223; mineral wealth, 214; nutrition, 166; population, 113; profits, 228, 230–232, 237; railways, 238; taxation, 51; Ten-Year-Plan, 242; *Union Minière du Haute Katanga*, 227, 231; urbanisation, 123, 125; wage workers, distribution of, 118, 119, 120, 121; wage workers, number of, 114. 117; wages, 185, 191
Bermuda Company, 227
Bettison, Dr. D., 192
Bigwood and Trolli, 171
Biney, Pobee, 170
Blundell, Michael, 35
BP Oil Company, 226
Bourgeoisie, African, 255–260
Bradley, Kenneth, 215, 216
Briey, P. de, 53, 146, 149
British Aluminium Company, 174
British Celanese, 226
British East Africa, exports, 222; Statistics Department, 170
British Electric Traction, 226
British Empire Society for the Blind, 176

277